PHILIPPINES

Manila

PA C ...

O C E A N

Sulu
Sea

...akan

...u

...elebes
Sea

0   250   500

Approximate   Miles

■ Malaysia
□ Indonesia
▨ Philippines

E q u a t o r

BIAK

...ULAWESI
(...elebes)

W E S T
I R I A N

Makassar

... N E S I A ...

TIMOR

Dorothy deFontaine

Also by Willard A. Hanna

DESTINY HAS EIGHT EYES
A novel

BUNG KARNO'S INDONESIA

THE FORMATION OF MALAYSIA
New Factor in World Politics

EIGHT NATION MAKERS
Southeast Asia's Charismatic Statesmen

Sequel to Colonialism

The 1957–1960 Foundations for Malaysia

By WILLARD A. HANNA

AN ON-THE-SPOT EXAMINATION OF THE

GEOGRAPHIC, ECONOMIC, AND POLITICAL SEEDBED

WHERE THE IDEA OF A FEDERATION OF MALAYSIA

WAS GERMINATED

AMERICAN UNIVERSITIES FIELD STAFF, INC.

366 Madison Avenue,   New York, N.Y. 10017

Contents

5

PART FOUR   International Involvement

PART FIVE   Malaysia Scene

Preface

In *Sequel to Colonialism,* Willard A. Hanna again demonstrates an ability to write about the contemporary history of Southeast Asia with the kind of perception and acumen usually displayed only by those who look backward in time.

Reporting and commenting on the years from 1957 to 1960, Mr. Hanna shows how and why events, policies, and personalities interacted to bring about the idea of a Federation of Malaysia. His chronicle of a period that might otherwise go insufficiently noticed is a useful companion to Mr. Hanna's earlier book on *The Formation of Malaysia.*

By giving each chapter its date of writing, he conveys a sense of immediacy that will be as important to future historians as it is engrossing to present readers. They will find themselves alongside Mr. Hanna as he moves through Southeast Asia, watching events, getting acquainted with the people who shape history, and identifying trends that few other writers recognized as important in the years just after the British relinquished their colonial claims in Southeast Asia.

Mr. Hanna has identified his prime sources for this book as the local press, local government publicity releases, local citizens, and personal observations. Since the writer of a preface need not be modest about the subject of his essay, let it be added that Mr. Hanna has been immersed in the affairs of Southeast Asia since 1947, and that he has delved into the major library and archival resources on the area to be found in Asia, America, and Europe. His assured touch in analyzing the significance of personalities and the events in which they are involved is no miracle of guessmanship but comes out of imaginative and painstaking scholarship.

Sequel to Colonialism is the fourth of Mr. Hanna's books to be centered on Southeast Asia. It was preceded by *Bung Karno's Indonesia*, first issued in 1960 and in a revised edition in 1961, *Formation of Malaysia*, 1964, and *Eight Nation Makers: Southeast Asia's Charismatic Statesmen*, 1964. As this is written, Mr. Hanna has just returned to a base in Southeast Asia to continue research and writing as an Associate of the American Universities Field Staff. His readers and publishers can be confident that more of his pungent observations from a critical area in world affairs will soon be forthcoming in Reports for the American Universities Field Staff and in the volumes he plans to add to the Hanna bookshelf on Southeast Asia.

Teg C. Grondahl
Executive Director
American Universities Field Staff

New York

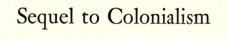

Sequel to Colonialism

1

Introduction -
From Malaya to Malaysia

August 1, 1964

FROM THE time that it became independent on August 31, 1957, the former Federation of Malaya under Prime Minister Tengku Abdul Rahman devoted itself systematically to the business of nation building. By combining democratic self-government and free enterprise with self-financed development programs, all in close cooperation with the Western world, Malaya achieved a truly remarkable degree of stability, prosperity, and integration of its diverse races—a record so unmarred by crisis that it attracted very little international attention. In neighboring Indonesia, however, where the President Sukarno regime has exhibited a predilection for perpetuating the political, economic, and social chaos of the "Unfinished Revolution," the performance of the Tengku Abdul Rahman government was viewed with suspicion, resentment, and growing animosity. As Malaya progressed and prospered, so too did its closely interrelated neighbors, Singapore, North Borneo, and Sarawak. Indonesia, meanwhile, squandering two billion dollars of American and Russian aid on ostentation and armaments, deteriorated more and more dangerously toward total anarchy.

On May 27, 1961, Tengku Abdul Rahman made a surprise proposal for federation of Malaya, Singapore, North Borneo, Sarawak, and also Brunei; on September 16, 1963, after two years and four months in which free debate and free choice prevailed, the federation (without Brunei—a long, complicated story) was triumphantly promulgated. Indonesia's Sukarno, however, once he had relieved himself in mid-1962 of his preoccupation with "liberation" of Irian Barat, had done everything within his power to obstruct the project of the Tengku, whom he branded a

11

"puppet" of the British in their "neocolonialist plot" to "encircle Indonesia." Both before and after the new Malaysia emerged, Sukarno kept cranking up a policy which he christened "*Konfrontasi,*" designed, according to his new revolutionary slogan, to "Smash Malaysia." The most conspicuous manifestations of Sukarno's confrontation have been guerrilla operations in the jungles of Borneo and acts of piracy in the Straits of Malacca. The new Malaysia, which had promised to be as successful and hence as inconspicuous as had been the former Malaya, suddenly became the floodlighted focus of a highly incendiary new Southeast Asian crisis.

The real Malaysia story antedates both the Tengku's proposal and Bung Karno's *Konfrontasi.* The foundations of the nation were laid back in the 1957–1960 period, starting at the time that Malaya itself was just about to receive its independence, extending up to the time that the new Malaysia was just about to be conceived. The story concerns four separate political entities (five, if one includes Brunei, a special case), each working out an admirable solution to its domestic problems only to discover that the problems of relationships with each other and with huge, troubled, expansionist Indonesia next door demanded almost equal attention.

In the chapters which follow, I attempt to give an account of Malaya and Malaysia developments and of the Malaysia-Indonesia conflict during the formative years 1957 to 1960. Originally written as reports for serial publication by the American Universities Field Staff, these chapters are now collected, rearranged, and republished in a close approximation of the original form. Certain pages and paragraphs have been deleted in order to avoid either repetition or exhaustive detail; other sections have been subjected to stylistic revision; one brief chapter on the "Borneo Periphery" has been added in order to introduce the Borneo states in immediate juxtaposition to Malaya and Singapore; but there has been no significant alteration in any respect of the original content.

These reports were written over a four-year period about current history while it was still very much in the making. They do not, therefore, have the advantage of uniform focal length and time exposure, but they may have the more than compensating virtue of immediacy. They are not meant to add up to a complete textbook coverage. They provide, rather, a general introduction to the Malaysian states, plus a record of critical episodes in their political development, a survey of key economic activities, an analysis of significant factors in international relations, and a series of firsthand accounts of representative places with accompanying introduction of representative people. My prime sources are the local press, local government publicity releases, local citizens of all varieties and degrees, and personal observations, none of which requires footnotes to ornament the text.

The explicit and the implicit judgments in these 1957–1960 reports on what is now Malaysia do not seem to me today to require any great amount of revision. Although I was alarmed in 1959, for instance, about Singapore's extremist political manifestations, I allowed, nevertheless, that the People's Action Party, on accepting responsibility for government under Prime Minister Lee Kuan Yew's moderate leadership, might very possibly succeed in providing a good administration, as in fact it has. I was bullish in 1959 with regard to prospects for Malaya's natural rubber industry; prices have declined sharply since then, but all the same, rubber remains a very good gamble. With regard to peaceful development in the Sultanate of Brunei I was basically optimistic—but in 1957 and with reservations which I would prefer at this point boldly to underscore. The collection would be better balanced had I found time during the 1957–1960 period to write at least one report on the retarded East Coast area of Malaya and another on the rapidly advancing colony of North Borneo, but time was limited. There are other errors of omission and commission such as I fear are inevitable in a pioneering effort at representation of an area and of an era which has been deplorably neglected by Western observers. As the frightening Malaysia crisis now succeeds the happy pre-Malaysia interlude with which these reports are concerned, I find that, for myself at least, they constitute what a French compiler might prudently describe as preliminary documents to serve in the preparation of a history.

W. A. H.

PART ONE

Components of a Nation

2

Malaya-Singapore Axis

THE FEDERATION OF MALAYA occupies the southern half of the 1,000-mile-long Malay Peninsula which arcs southward from the Asian mainland into the Indonesian archipelago. It is 75 per cent mountain, jungle, and swamp; 25 per cent rubber, copra, or palm oil plantation, tin mine, general agricultural land, and urban area. It is inhabited by approximately 7 million people: 50 per cent of them Malaysian (Malay, Indonesian, and related peoples), 37 per cent Chinese, 11 per cent Indian and Pakistani, 2 per cent other racial or national groups, including 16,000 Europeans and about 200 Americans.

The State of Singapore is 224.5 square miles of tropical island just barely detached from the southern tip of the Malay Peninsula, lying 1° 17″ north of the equator, well within sight of the nearest Indonesian islets. It is 25 per cent port or urban area, 50 per cent developed rural area, and 25 per cent swamp, waste, or undeveloped land. It is populated by approximately 1.5 million people: 76 per cent of them Chinese, 13.5 per cent Malaysian, 8.5 per cent Indian and Pakistani, 2 per cent other racial groups, including 11,000 Europeans and about 500 Americans.

Singapore and the Federation are semi-integrated by tradition and necessity and by a three-quarter-mile-long causeway; they are semi-estranged by racial and political suspicion. Singapore aspires to merge with the Federation. Its advances are not welcomed, however, by the Malays, who fear Chinese racial and hence Chinese political as well as economic domination. The critical factor is that in a Federation inclusive of Singapore the population would be 44 per cent Chinese and 41 per cent Malaysian.

17

The Federation and Singapore are the newest states of Southeast Asia. The Federation became independent on August 31, 1957, and Singapore became locally autonomous on June 3, 1959. Both remain within the British Commonwealth of Nations. The Federation and Singapore have Southeast Asia's youngest, its fastest growing, and one of its most restless populations. More than 50 per cent of their inhabitants are under twenty years of age; an annual 3.4 per cent to 3.5 per cent population increase (as compared with the 1.7 per cent area norm) forecasts a still younger population average over the next decade. About 40 per cent of the Federation and Singapore under-twenty age group is now in school: 88 per cent and 90 per cent respectively in primary school, 25 per cent and 50 per cent respectively in English-language school, a total of 4,000–5,000 in two universities in Singapore and one in the Federation. Between 10 per cent and 20 per cent of the total working-age population is currently under-employed, unemployed, or hunting new jobs.

Despite the high rate of unemployment, both the Federation and Singapore are phenomenally prosperous, largely as a result of postwar booms in rubber and tin. Except for tiny Brunei in British Borneo, they enjoy the highest per capita income in Asia, the common estimate being M$900 [1] for the Federation and M$1,200 for Singapore. They are confronted, nevertheless, with grave problems of diversification, industrialization, and merely keeping pace, as an independent and a semi-independent state, with the spectacular progress and prosperity of the British colonial period. Both enjoy relatively stable and efficient governments. Yet almost overnight the right-wing, Malay-dominated government of the Federation might encounter sudden obstructionism on the part of the economically powerful Chinese population, while the left-wing, Chinese-dominated People's Action Party government of Singapore might suddenly be overthrown by its own extremists or by outside Communist elements. The two states are obviously dependent upon one another, but such is the extent of racial and political antipathy that political or even economic merger seems distant.

The Federation of Malaya and the State of Singapore together constitute a single strategic unit of immense importance to anyone concerned with the military security, political stability, or economic prosperity of Southeast Asia. Since earliest times, the Malay Peninsula has been the crossroads of the land and sea routes between the Asian mainland and

---

[1] M$3.03 equals US$1.00.

the southern archipelago and between East and West. Since 1819, when it was ceded to the British, the small island of Singapore in particular has been in military, political, and commercial matters the key traffic circle. The Japanese realized its importance when they concentrated their World War II Southeast Asian campaign first upon capture of the Singapore British naval base and colonial headquarters. The Chinese Communists realize it today, when they eye the predominantly Chinese-populated island of Singapore as a potential Chinese Communist state in the climatically and politically torrid tropics.

Thanks to British colonial development, the Federation and Singapore possess a well-developed network of roads, railways, telecommunications, ports, and airfields—the best in Southeast Asia, and certainly the most strategically placed for anyone wishing to dominate the area. Malaya's highly and continuously developed West Coast faces the huge and troubled Indonesian island of Sumatra across the narrow Straits of Malacca and is wide open to infiltration, political or otherwise. Isolated by the jungle-covered central mountain mass which bisects the country along its north-south axis, the underdeveloped East Coast lacks sheltered deepwater harbors, but it is still wide open, as the Japanese showed, to swift penetration by determined men.

The bustling city of Singapore, a city of fine modern skyscrapers, landscaped waterfront esplanades, and luxury suburbs, is also a city of Chinese and Indian tenements, Chinese secret societies, Chinese gang warfare, and Malay kampongs. The Federation is a nation of thriving modern cities like Kuala Lumpur, Ipoh, and Penang. It is also a nation of impoverished East Coast Malay fishing villages, squalid Indian workers' quarters, and virtually impenetrable jungle where aboriginal tribesmen have in the past proved formidable allies of Communist terrorists. Both the Federation and Singapore present to the visitor a façade of astounding modernity and progress; behind the façade lie problems disproportionate to the size of the states. By mere reason of its strategic importance on the map, to the economy of rubber- and tin-consuming nations, and in the plans of new-style colonial aggressors, the Malay Peninsula looms much larger in international politics than it does in square miles of area, millions in population, or dollars of national product.

The Federation and Singapore must logically be considered in immediate juxtaposition, just as geography and history have placed them. They are atypical of most of Southeast Asia in certain very important respects.

They are efficiently and honestly administered by well-trained civil servants, among whom there still remain alien and former colonial officials. They are being effectively and profitably developed by prudent use of indigenous resources, by foreign loans, and by generally non-discriminatory acceptance of private capital and skills, both Western and Overseas Chinese. They are achieving swift expansion of educational, health, and other social services which, in colonial times, were already developed far beyond the area norm. They are typical of the area, however, in that nationalist, racial, religious, and Communist forces of agitation and disruption—or just general forces of social change—are powerful enough to make the present happy situation seem chancy and predictions for the future rash. As very small units in the huge Far Eastern complex, they are highly sensitive to influences from nearby countries—Indonesia, China, and the nations of Indochina, to mention only the most perplexing.

HISTORIC BACKGROUND

The history of the Malay Peninsula remains as yet both obscure and controversial. It has been written mostly by European scholars, interested first in prehistoric migrations of peoples, all highly conjectural; or, second, in the proto-historic period, in which Indian, Chinese, Indonesian, Indochinese, and Siamese empires overlapped shapelessly upon each other and upon Malaya; or, third, in the recent centuries of Western penetration and ultimate British colonial domination. Inevitably, the work of these scholars has been more revealing of the European than of the Malayan mind. Area history is just now beginning to be written from the Malayan point of view, at risk for the next few years at least of replacing alien with home-brewed historiographic bias.

During the long prehistory of Malaya, extending up to the beginning of the Christian Era, successive waves of Palaeolithic and Neolithic migratory peoples apparently passed from mainland Asia into the Malay Peninsula. Many of them moved onward into Indonesia, Melanesia, and Australia; some of them presently backtracked again. The unassimilated residue of these migrants, retreating to the denser mountain jungles and the danker swamps, survive in Malaya today as aborigines and proto-Malay tribesmen. There remain about fifty thousand in all, fragmented into obscure and isolated ethno-linguistic groups, some accepting modern acculturation, others dying out. Later waves of more civilized migrants became more or less assimilated with elements of the old and established clan enclaves which were dignified with the name of kingdoms.

From approximately the first century A.D. to the year 1511 when the Portuguese seized Malacca, these small kingdoms of Malaya were subjected to the paramount commercial, cultural, religious, and military influences of the kaleidoscopically shifting empires of nearby China, Indochina, Siam, India, and Indonesia. The Malay kingdoms themselves overlapped and undermined each other, expanded and contracted, rose and fell. Foreign traders, priests, warriors, artists, artisans, pirates, and such ordinary people as sailors, refugees, and brides converged upon them from insular and mainland Asia. The Malay today, therefore, is the result of the blending of many racial strains and vitalizing or devitalizing influences.

During the period of Hindu and Buddhist ascendancy in Southeast Asia (about 1 A.D. to about 1400 A.D.), Malaya's Indianized rajadoms reflected in miniature the glories of Funan, Sriwidjaja, and Madjapahit. One of the most important was Temasek, the more than half legendary, less than half Madjapahit-dominated minor kingdom which evidently centered on Singapore Island in the thirteenth and fourteenth centuries. Temasek was pillaged and razed, most historians agree, about the year 1377; historians disagree, however, whether the destroyers were marauders from Siam or Madjapahit rivals from Java. At any rate, the Prince of Temasek, kingdomless and fugitive, presumably journeyed northward as far as Malacca and there built a new city. In the early fifteenth century Malacca accepted the Muslim faith, introduced by traders and teachers from the Islamic areas of India. It became the center for propagation of Islam throughout the peninsula and by far the most vigorous and significant of all the Malay states in matters of commerce, politics, and warfare. The glory of the Malacca Sultanate came to an abrupt end in 1511 when the Portuguese commander, Albuquerque, with a fleet of nineteen ships and an army of eight hundred Portuguese and six hundred Indian soldiers, captured the city after a few days' battle. The Portuguese promptly rebuilt Malacca into a center of Europeanized military, commercial, political, and religious power—only to lose it in 1641 to the Dutch. The last Sultan of Malacca, who fled as the Portuguese entered the city, established a new but feeble little sultanate in the Riouw Archipelago. He fathered a ubiquitous progeny which in turn founded half the existing royal houses and feudal lines of Malaya. One of his descendants was the Dutch-denounced, British-acclaimed pretender to the Riouw Sultanate who ceded Singapore to the British in 1819 and thus gained compensatory recognition as Sultan of Johore.

From 1511 onward Malay intrigue and warfare were complicated by the superimposition of European power—first Portuguese, then Dutch and British. Ultimately the British gained control of the whole of Malaya, but as much by accident as by design, with much official misgiving and foreboding. Captain Francis Light, who took possession of Penang Island (1786) and thus gave to British marine and commercial power a Malayan base, acted without clear-cut authorization from the East India Company or the British Government. He entered into an ambiguously-worded private agreement with the Sultan of Kedah and was unable later to persuade the company to fulfill the Sultan's expectation of British military defense against his Thai enemies. Sir Stamford Raffles gained cession of Singapore in 1819 and made the cession stick—in the face of Dutch protests and British official vacillation or indifference—only by converting the island almost overnight into a phenomenally prosperous free port and naval base. The British, who finally took possession of Malacca in 1825, accepting it from the Dutch in return for being relieved of Raffles' troublesome claims to a sector of southwest Sumatra, were betrayed by their own ignorance of Malaya into fighting a punitive war against the neighboring state of Naning (1830). In the end they discovered that they had no just pretext, that the campaign had been a comedy of almost bloodless blunders (there was one British casualty—a war correspondent, shot and wounded, it was said, by his competitor), and that once in control of Naning they could find no one to turn it back to. But then, as Singapore grew each year more rich and powerful, and as Penang, and to a much lesser extent Malacca, enjoyed reflected prosperity, it developed that to maintain British political order and British-Chinese commercial affluence in these Straits Settlements it was necessary to extend British control into the adjacent Malay states.

Malay feuds, Malay piracy, Malay intrigue—all resulting in loss of British life and property—but most of all, Malay-Chinese warfare over the immensely valuable tin-mining resources: these were the reasons for British intervention. By degrees, as each commitment led them still further, the British built up a colonial sphere of influence of "protected" but sovereign Malay states. The British practice of colonial government in Malaya was ill-contrived and ill-coordinated, and yet it worked far better, perhaps, for being tentative and flexible than would any deliberately planned scheme of colonial consolidation. British "residents" and "advisers" established themselves on "invitation" of the traditional Malay rulers in each of the Malay states. British administrative assistants arrogated to themselves greater and greater responsibilities and introduced more and more sweeping reforms. But while British Malaya came to loom on the maps as one political unit, it was in actuality a curious montage: three Straits Settlements (Singapore, Penang, and Malacca) in which the land was Crown property and the inhabitants were British subjects; four "Federated Malay States" in which federation was a flickering ideal, not an actuality; and five "Unfederated States" as various as the Sultanate of Johore, whose late Sultan (died 1959 at age eighty-six) was one of the world's last great feudal autocrats, and the tribal composite of Negri Sembilan, whose rival clans—Sumatran Minangkabau in origin—practice a matriarchal social system and elect a patriarchal paramount chieftain.

Malayan tin and Singapore entrepôt trade, plus assorted spices and incidental items like elephants, were the original basis for British Malaya's prosperity. All of these attracted more and more British merchants, also Chinese immigrants, and more Chinese than British became millionaires. Early in this century rubber began to rival, then surpass, tin in importance. In the course of a couple of decades British- and Chinese-owned rubber estates stretched almost continuously along the whole West Coast area, attracting wave after wave of alien laborers, this time from India as well as from China.

The Malay rulers shared the profits from tin and rubber. They retained also the prestige of protected feudal status. The Malay population itself, save for the intellectual minority which acquired British education and entered the civil service, continued to make its living from rice farming and fishing. The Malay feudal courts, accordingly, grew rich and indolent; the Malay civil servants, who were accorded high positions and important responsibilities, grew Anglicized and to a considerable extent Anglophile; the large part of the Malay population, however, remained aloof from modern developments. It became increasingly evident that there was a wide and growing disparity in the economic and educational levels of the various racial groups. The Chinese exhibited unflagging industry and many achieved spectacular success. The Indians, save for a minority who became prosperous professional men and others who became overeducated, underpaid clerks, exhibited more industry than capacity, and many eventually returned to India with their small savings.

The ordinary Malays accepted what was on the whole a relaxed but improvident way of life, one which suggested, nevertheless, that once they acquired political self-consciousness, they would set about catching up with the Chinese and with no little suspicion and acrimony.

Throughout the British colonial period Singapore remained the political, commercial, and intellectual hub of Malaya, a great, modern, cosmopolitan, and complacent city. Then in December 1941 began the sudden Japanese advance through Malaya, climaxed on February 15, 1942, with the capture of Singapore Island, an "impregnable" military base whose guns were turned in the wrong direction and whose ships and planes had never been built. In September 1945, when the British reoccupied Malaya, they found a nation whose economy was shattered by war, whose people were on the whole grateful for British return but indisposed to regard it as permanent. The British found themselves confronted not just with the necessity for quick economic reconstruction of the biggest dollar-earning properties in the Empire but with two major political problems which grew more difficult over the next few years. First, the people of the Federation and of Singapore were demanding a new form of government, with factions in favor of local self-government and independence drawing inspiration from Indonesia and the rest of Southeast Asia. Second, the Malayan (Chinese) Communist Party challenged British control, first by tactics of infiltration, then of terror.

IMMEDIATE POSTWAR DEVELOPMENTS

The British in October 1945 announced, in January 1946 elaborately justified in a White Paper, and in March 1946 inaugurated a new system of government. The intent—soon drastically modified—was to constitute Singapore a separate Crown Colony under permanent British rule, and to constitute the rest of Malaya, including Penang and Malacca, a Malayan Union. According to the original plan, the traditional rulers were to renounce their sovereign rights in favor of the British Crown; the rulers themselves were to be relegated to the status of mere advisers on religious and customary matters; the government was to be completely reorganized and centralized under a powerful British governor and his administrative staff; the various racial groups were to be accorded equal rights; and state and federal legislative bodies were gradually to be set up, then converted from appointive to elective status.

The plan was neat, logical, and orderly, a departure from previous administrative vagary and a prelude to democratic, centralized, constitutional monarchy. But the hitherto mild and quiet Malay nationalists organized and protested. The new system, they declared, was arbitrary, highly prejudicial to indigenous Malay rights, and hence unacceptable. The Malay rulers reneged on their prior commitments, letting it be known that they had been induced to concur by threat of deposition for having collaborated with the Japanese. The Chinese expressed objections to presumed subordination of Chinese to Malay interests, implicit especially in the separation of Singapore from the Union. The Indians found the whole proposal undemocratic. The Communists branded it an imperialist plot to divide and rule. British liberal leaders, including distinguished elder statesmen of the Malayan colonial administration, condemned the scheme as unfair and unworkable. The British authorities quickly backtracked, negotiated, and compromised. They accepted in principle what they themselves regarded as eventual, and local citizens regarded as imminent: the grant of self-government. Malay feudal prerogatives were restored, and by mutual consent relations between Malaya and the Crown Colony of Singapore were left indeterminate.

THE ACHIEVEMENT OF INDEPENDENCE BY THE FEDERATION

On January 21, 1948, the Malayan Union gave way to the Federation of Malaya. The Federation itself, after an interim period of accelerated transition between British and home rule, emerged on August 31, 1957, as an independent nation, well ahead of everyone's target date, including that (1960) of the leading Malay nationalists themselves.

The Federation today consists of eleven states. Eight of them are sultanates, hereditary within their royal lines, in accordance with decision of the royal court councils; one (Negri Sembilan) is a coalition of clans, headed by a paramount chieftain elected by the clan leaders; two are the former Straits Settlements of Penang and Malacca, each under an appointive governor. The Chief of State, or Yang di Pertuan Agong—currently the Sultan of Selangor—is elected for a five-year term by the council of nine traditional rulers from among their own membership, with mandatory rotation of office. The Yang di Pertuan Agong appoints as Prime Minister the outstanding political leader of the nation—at present Tengku Abdul Rahman, a fifty-seven-year-old prince from Kedah, educated in Penang, Bangkok, and London, and head of the Alliance Party. The Prime Minister in turn selects a Council of Ministers who head the administrative departments and are responsible to Parliament. The Parliament consists of two bodies: the popularly-elected 104-member House of Representatives, and the 38-member Senate, 22 of its members being elected (two each from the 11 popularly-elected state legislatures), the remaining 16 appointed by the Yang di Pertuan Agong to represent various racial and other interests.

Malayan politics is dominated by the Alliance Party, actually a co-alition of three communal (racial-based) parties. In it the United Malay Nationalist Organization (U.M.N.O.) is the decisive—or at times in-decisive—senior member; the Malayan Chinese Association (M.C.A.) is a divided and semi-reconciled junior member; and the Malayan Indian Congress (M.I.C.) is not a silent but a politically impotent partner. The Malays demand and are conceded paramount political position and special government favor. The M.C.A. is willing to accede to this ar-rangement just so long as economic and cultural discrimination against the Chinese does not become flagrant. The M.I.C. is unable to assert itself if it would.

In advance of elections the Alliance Party tries to work out interracial, intraparty compromise agreements on all tendentious matters. At election time it presents a fair facsimile of a united front and a joint list of can-didates. It does not succeed in doing so, however, without cracks and crises, as at the critical point just before the federal elections of August 19, 1959, when the M.C.A. threatened to go it alone and an influential "rebel" faction bolted the party. The Alliance still manages to pile up impressive majorities, but neither as impressive or as consistent as in 1955. In the 1959 state elections, for instance, it lost control of two out of eleven state legislatures. In the 1959 federal elections it gained only 51.4 per cent of the total vote, and 74 out of 102 legislative seats, as compared with 79.6 per cent of the vote and 51 out of 52 elective seats in 1955.

Between 1955 and 1959 a significant change took place in the compo-sition and the attitude of the Malayan electorate. In 1955, out of the total body of registered voters, 84 per cent were Malay, 11 per cent were Chinese, and 5 per cent were Indian. After 1955, largely as a result of the efforts of the M.C.A., the great majority of the Chinese population de-cided to take out Malayan citizenship and thus to acquire and exercise the franchise. Whereas in 1955 there were about eight Malay voters to every Chinese, today there are only about three or four to one. Many of the Chinese voters have proved susceptible, however, to the arguments of opposition candidates that the conservative, Westernized, Chinese-dominated M.C.A. did not represent the true interests of the Chinese community, and that in any event it did not pull its proper weight in the Malay-dominated Alliance. While Chinese voters were listening sympa-thetically to these two arguments, Malay voters were being lured from the Alliance with the argument that U.M.N.O. deferred not too little but too much to its M.C.A. partner. The opposition found much to criticize in the Alliance administration, as well as in the U.M.N.O.-M.C.A. rivalry. It became clear in the course of the 1959 campaigns that while the Alliance was in no immediate danger, nevertheless, it was no longer immune to effective challenge.

The opposition is divided into half a dozen small parties which make political capital of anti-Alliance criticism, intra-Alliance rifts, and appeals to separatist if not fanatical class, race, and religious sentiment, also left-wing polemics reminiscent of, if not identical to, the line of the banned Malayan Communist Party. Most important, and probably most dangerous of the opposition parties, one which won 13 federal parliament seats to the Alliance's 74, and 33 state legislature seats to the Alliance's 207 in the 1959 elections, is the Pan-Malayan Islamic Party. The P.M.I.P. bubbles up a strange brew of Islamic conservatism and intolerance, Marxist idealism and dogma, anti-Western, anti-Chinese, anti-Alliance, and pro-Indonesian bias.

FEDERATION GOVERNMENT ECONOMIC AND POLITICAL POLICY

After victory in the 1955 elections for a partially elective legislature, the Alliance Government concentrated upon achievement of national independence. After attaining its goal in 1957, it concentrated upon smooth continuation of administration, including large-scale development programs, and assurance of victory in the 1959 elections. Now it concentrates upon implementation of its long-standing promise of a vast new development scheme to carry modern improvements to the ordinary people.

In actual fact, during the 1955–1960 period (part of that time under British direction, of course) the government had already spent approximately M$1 billion on special development projects which resulted in tremendous improvement of the nation's plantations, industries, communications, schools, hospitals, and other facilities. In accordance with a recently announced M$1 billion scheme for 1960–1965, details of which remain to be worked out although some projects are already getting under way, the government now proposes to continue development at an even faster pace. This time it is placing special emphasis upon schemes which will improve Malay kampong life and resettle surplus population on newly opened lands.

In now spending the equivalent of US$30 per capita per year on special development schemes, plus US$85 for ordinary administrative programs which themselves include development projects, the Federation Government proposes to raise the nation's US$300 per capita national income still higher and to spread the benefits more equitably. The Federation has financed itself to date largely from its own resources. It has had the benefit, to be sure, of massive assistance from the United Kingdom in back-stopping the military campaign against the jungle terrorists. It has also received cash grants totaling several million pounds sterling for Commonwealth Development Fund projects. Its wealthy Borneo neighbor, the Sultanate of Brunei, has made it a M$100 million loan at low rate of interest. From the United States it has received to date US$20 million in loans to finance roads, bridges, and port improvements. At the present time it is shopping for big international loans commensurate with the requirements of its new program. In view of the success of the projects undertaken to date, it seems likely to receive a sympathetic hearing both in London and Washington.

Prime Minister Abdul Rahman has recently announced that the internal situation in Malaya is now so satisfactory, the ability of his administration to handle its domestic problems so evident, that he himself will devote the major part of his time from now on to international affairs. His first big venture in international affairs has been the condemnation of South African *apartheid* and support for legislative measures boycotting import of all South African goods. Not all political observers inside or outside Malaya share the Tengku's confidence that the nation is over the hump and that it has the answers to international, let alone national, problems. Interracial suspicion and animosity, while they have led as yet only to minor and quickly suppressed outbreaks, require the most alert and adroit long-range handling. Measures to check Communist infiltration and to create adequate opportunity for the nation's proliferating youth may quickly become more, not less, urgent. Prevention of racial and political disorders in Malaya is perhaps far more critical and far more susceptible to Malayan initiative and far more conducive to Malayan prestige than is the projection of Malayan influence into the arena of international politics.

ACHIEVEMENT OF LOCAL AUTONOMY IN SINGAPORE

Singapore's post-1945 political development has been both stranger and stormier than the Federation's and still stops well short of the official Singapore aspiration, namely, complete independence followed by swift integration into the Federation. Since 1945 the most significant developments have been as follows:

1) The rapid increase in number of registered and of actual voters, as a result of the extension of the franchise, automatic registration, and finally, in 1959, compulsory voting. In 1948, when Singapore held its first elections, registered voters numbered approximately 35,000 (all of them British subjects, including Indians, Chinese, and others); in 1959 they numbered approximately 690,000, or virtually the total adult population of the island. In 1948, 22,500 persons actually voted; in 1951, 24,000; in 1955, 160,000; and in 1959, 530,000.

2) The rapid increase in the number of popularly elected members of the State Legislative Council, now the Legislative Assembly, and the corresponding increase in their responsibilities. In 1948, six out of twenty-three members were popularly elected, the others being *ex officio* members, appointed members, or Chamber of Commerce elected members. In 1951, nine out of twenty-seven were popularly elected; in 1955, twenty-five out of thirty-two; and in 1959, the entire body of fifty-one. In 1955 the elected members were authorized to form Singapore's first Council of Ministers, subject to the superior authority of the British governor. Following the May 30, 1959, elections, the new and fully elective Legislative Assembly became in effect the State Parliament, exercising autonomy in matters of local administration but subject still to the United Kingdom in matters of foreign relations and external defense, and in matters of internal security subject to a joint United Kingdom-Singapore-Federation of Malaya council (membership: 3:3:1). From the Assembly are chosen the members of the new and more powerful Council of Ministers, headed by Lee Kuan Yew, the leader of the majority party. On December 3, 1959, the British Crown appointed Inche Yusof bin Isak, a Federation-born Malay, nominal Chief of State, or Yang di-Pertuan Negara.

3) The shift in political center of gravity from the European and the Indian community to the Chinese, and from right to center, and now to the left. In the 1948 elections three of the six winning candidates were Indians, and in 1951, three out of nine. The Chinese community was then politically lethargic, not really feeling or showing its strength until 1955 when it elected fifteen out of twenty-five elective Council members. From 1948 to 1955, when appointive outnumbered elective members, the British naturally dominated the Council. During this period also the elected members were predominantly conservative, favoring British or *towkay* (rich Chinese businessman) interests. In the 1955 Legislative Assembly the focus but not the preponderance of power shifted to the

Socialists. In the background, as coalition partners of the Socialists, were the conservative, often complacent, proponents of British and *towkay* interests. The majority of them were Chinese, who soon proved themselves disposed to get on the Socialist band wagon, all Singapore political platforms being couched more and more in terms of the welfare state. Increasingly in the political foreground were the articulate and vehement representatives of the left-wing Chinese People's Action Party, then very actively in the opposition. In 1959 the P.A.P.—which had already demonstrated its swift increase in strength by winning the 1957 municipal elections and had gained Malay as well as Chinese support—captured forty-three out of fifty-one Assembly seats and 54 per cent of the popular vote. Political power in Singapore had swung decidedly to the left.

Of all postwar Singapore political phenomena, the most significant by far is the evolution of the People's Action Party. The P.A.P. is a left-wing party which has fluctuated between positions which might be distinguished as the far left and the extreme left. It was organized in November 1954 by Lee Kuan Yew, a brilliant young Cambridge-educated lawyer and politician, now aged thirty-seven, who has been the prime mover in the party ever since and now, as a result of the 1959 election landslide, holds the position of Prime Minister. But Lee Kuan Yew has several times suffered periods of near or temporary eclipse in party councils, and these periods have corresponded with periods of P.A.P. extremism. Although he himself objects to the appellation, and although P.A.P. policy and action during his tenure have sometimes belied it, Lee Kuan Yew is a political moderate, at least as compared with many of his associates.

The P.A.P. started off in 1954 as a party of the far left, deriving its main support from Communist-oriented labor unions and student groups, but still, if only because of its initial weakness, exercising restraint in policy and action. In 1955 and 1956 the P.A.P. moved to the extreme left and was deeply implicated in strikes and riots. When top P.A.P. leaders went to jail as a result of the 1956 outbreaks, the party shifted back to the far left. In 1957 it shifted to extreme left again, and extremist elements managed for a brief interval (August 1957) to depose Lee as party chairman. The new leaders themselves went to jail shortly afterward when the Singapore Government staged a series of arrests to forestall new strikes and riots. The party, over which Lee Kuan Yew once more acquired control, swung back again from extremism. From the later part of 1957 the P.A.P. held to the far left, albeit with intimations that a new swing might soon be coming. Rabble-rousing elements of the party gained control of the Singapore Municipal Council in the December 1957 elections. Under P.A.P. Mayor Ong Eng Guan they converted Municipal Council meetings into a Chinese carnival of baiting the British and "cuddling the hawkers."

All party elements combined to fight the 1959 state election campaign by smearing the previous administration, threatening reprisals against critics of the P.A.P., promising an abrupt end to all "colonial abuses" and the beginnings of utopia for the workingman. The party's Municipal Council record and its campaign tactics led to widespread fear that a P.A.P. victory would mean swift disaster for Singapore—if not actual handover to the Communists, at any rate intolerable interference with the British-trained civil service which gives Singapore its stable government and with the capitalist interests which control its trade, industry, banking, and hence its prosperity.

Since May 30, 1959, however, despite certain inevitable moves like the release of many of the jailed P.A.P. leaders, the P.A.P. has swung not closer to but farther away from extremism. Its present top leaders continue to declare that the P.A.P. is as far left as one can go without turning Communist. They declare also, however, that it is their firm intent to maintain Singapore as a "free, democratic, and non-Communist state," and that to do so they must practice not the futile devices of mere liberals but the realistic, if at times Communist-like, devices appropriate to the area. By doing so, they insist, they can bring Singapore the progress the Communists promise without at the same time imposing the political and economic strait jacket. If they fail, they say, then the Communists will have the next try.

P.A.P. POLITICAL AND ECONOMIC POLICY

The postelection P.A.P. position, notwithstanding repeated P.A.P. claims to monolithic stability, has been progressively modified in its details. The modifications, it may be presumed, have resulted in the first place from the party's increased experience with the sobering difficulties of administration and the necessity for reasonable compromise, and in the second place from the increased confidence of the party moderates that they can and will stay in control.

The major objectives of P.A.P. policy remain on the whole unchanged, but also, on the whole, no nearer to realization than one year ago. As its prime objective, the P.A.P. proposes to "Malayanize" the Singapore Chinese so that Singapore can merge with Malaya. The Malayanized Singaporean presumably will talk, think, and act not like the traditional Overseas Chinese, whose first loyalty is usually to China, but like the newly evolving "Malayan" who, whether Malay, Chinese, Indian, or of other racial origin, regards Malaya as his permanent home and over-all Malayan welfare as his personal concern. The P.A.P. has managed to stir up considerable interest in the study of the Malay language; it has set itself to the development of a "Malayan" culture and of loyalty to Singapore's Malay Chief of State. Nevertheless, it has failed to stir up reciprocal enthusiasm in the Federation for the newly self-Malayanizing Singapore Chinese. Consequently, by reason of Federation apathy or distrust, it has been forced into the conflicting deviation of promoting a distinctive Singapore loyalty and indeed a sort of Singapore nationalism.

As a corollary to the "Malayanization" plan, the P.A.P. proposes energetically to promote a Federation-Singapore common market and swiftly increasing economic cooperation. In pursuit of this objective, it has as yet made little measurable progress. It has been forced to emphasize a separate Singapore economic development plan which involves unnecessary duplication of and competition with the Federation's own efforts.

Singapore's new development plan—a five-year M$1 billion program announced soon after the Federation's—is certainly the P.A.P.'s biggest venture and, if successful, may be its biggest achievement. The plan is particularly noteworthy to non-P.A.P. observers in four respects. First, it is nothing revolutionary in Singapore's history. Rather, it is a logical next step in a program which has been proceeding steadily on much the same scale for the last ten years, first under the British colonial, then under the semicolonial administrations which the P.A.P. deplores. Second, unlike previous plans, it is dependent to a considerable extent upon direct foreign aid. Specifically, it is dependent upon a new £7.6 million (M$67 million) loan just negotiated with the United Kingdom, an additional £500,000 per year in British assistance in building up the state's armed forces and military facilities, and an anticipated loan from the United States. Third, the plan emphasizes development of Singapore's port and industrial facilities more than welfare state projects as such. This does not detract, to be sure, from the merit of pet P.A.P. projects like new low-cost urban housing, instead of the medium-income-level apartment buildings favored by the previous governments, and big reclamation and development schemes for heretofore neglected rural areas. Fourth, after a brief flap over the possibility of seeking Russian loans if Western world loans were not forthcoming, the P.A.P. is clearly undertaking the plan as a cooperative venture with the West. Coincidentally perhaps, very little is heard these days, except in the most extreme P.A.P. circles, about renouncing the various agreements whereby Singapore achieved a strictly limited autonomy, about nationalizing foreign business concerns, or about throwing the British out of the Singapore military base or out of Singapore altogether.

As time goes by, the P.A.P. has seemed notably less truculent toward factions of the right and of the center, notably more worried about factions of the extremist left. To be sure, the government has repeatedly put the Singapore civil service and the general public on notice that colonial practices must go and all colonialists with them. Shortly after the elections, for instance, it announced a sharp cut in government salaries, partly to put pressure upon British "expatriates" to get out, partly to impress upon local civil servants exactly who was in command and able, therefore, to mete out punishment or reward. It embarked also upon a campaign against the "English-educated" whom it branded as cultural misfits and anachronisms. Of recent months the P.A.P. has begun openly to backtrack. It has undertaken to reassure the English-educated that they really do have an important role in the community and in the government. It has openly deplored the hasty dismissal of foreign personnel whose skills are crucial to the maintenance of Singapore's high standards of public services. It has let up on its efforts to "purge" the civil service, which remains, despite salary cuts, one of the highest paid in Asia and is now being vaguely reassured regarding raises and promotions.

The P.A.P. Government has repeatedly put Singapore business on notice that the P.A.P., not the colonial government, is now in control and that big business can no longer expect special privileges. Nevertheless, it has begun to talk more openly and frequently of late of the necessity for understanding and cooperation between government and private enterprise; it has gone slow about raising taxes, interfering in management, upsetting the entrepôt trade, or applying the familiar types of bureaucratic regulations which could stall commerce and industry.

The P.A.P. has undertaken various programs which smack of totalitarian ideology and methods. For instance, it has waged a campaign against "yellow culture," with much publicity about the banning of "decadent" publications, the outlawing of jukeboxes, the closing of night clubs, the prevention of prostitution—all attributed to evil Western influences. It has more recently acknowledged, however, that certain party factions have mistaken zealotry for zeal. It has gone in for big "voluntary" Sunday labor battalions, big "people's cultural evenings," and quite a good deal of parading with bands, flags, and slogans. In recent months, however, the labor battalions no longer march off, joyously or otherwise, while ministers grin and motion-picture cameras grind, to shovel earth that can be more swiftly and economically moved by the Public Works Department. Other mass movements, while by no means abandoned, are not very vigorously promoted. One mass movement which the P.A.P. evidently expected to serve its purposes, only rather suddenly to discover otherwise, was a mass labor movement. The government attempted to bring all Singapore labor into a single Trades Union Congress, presumably to put it in a better bargaining position vis-à-vis management. It discovered, apparently to the amazement of the Labor Minister among others, that the most leftist of the existing trade unions—those from which the P.A.P. had derived its original strength—resisted being organized and controlled almost as though the P.A.P. were itself a rightist organization, and that Communist organizers openly competed with P.A.P. coordinators.

In all references above to the P.A.P., the reference is to the present top clique of Lee Kuan Yew and his immediate associates, not to two other important factions. One, that of Lim Chin Sing, Singapore's top labor leader, has not yet showed its hand. Lim, who was jailed after the 1955 riots and released after the 1959 P.A.P. election victory, is a young, fiery, dedicated trade unionist whose deliberate role of the moment is to be enigmatic. The other, the faction of Ong Eng Guan, seems resolved now as in the past to be antic. Its recent antics, however, have been directed against the party and its power has been ruthlessly clipped.

When the P.A.P. came into power in June 1959, Ong Eng Guan became Minister for National Development, with broad responsibilities. Very quickly, however, Ong began to experience P.A.P. disapprobation, and his ministry was shorn of most of its original functions. The Ong Eng Guan "voluntary" labor battalions folded, and the government did not mourn their demise. A gigantic Ong Eng Guan public housing scheme collapsed soon after announcement, and the government disclaimed ever having decided to allocate funds. Then, on June 20, 1960, Ong Eng Guan sponsored a set of sixteen resolutions put forward by the party's Hong Lim district branch. The resolutions in effect attacked party policy and leadership, challenged party accomplishments, and implied that the P.A.P. Government had turned soft toward colonialism. Mr. Ong's fellow ministers promptly and publicly accused him of fostering his own personality cult, exhibiting rampant individualism, fomenting conspiracy, breaching party discipline, defying collective leadership, and committing numerous derelictions of duty. The language of the P.A.P. countercharges, like that of Mr. Ong's charges and rebuttals, was the jargon of Communism. Nevertheless, so far as the ruling party clique was concerned, policies of moderation were reaffirmed and those of extremism condemned. Ong Eng Guan was suspended as Minister and as party member, and then, on July 27, 1960, together with two other P.A.P. members of the Legislative Assembly, expelled from the party.

The questions arise, however: how long can Lee Kuan Yew remain in control? How can he adhere, under no doubt vigorous pressure from the extremists, to policies of moderation? And how peacefully will the extremists submit to the dilution of their demands or the dismemberment of their factions? The answers at the moment in Singapore, where money counts at least as much as it does anywhere else in the world, are to be found in economic indicators. In the last few months three big Singapore government bond issues have been quickly and heavily oversubscribed—and not by the P.A.P. pampered hawkers or taxi drivers. After a sharp decline during the last two years property values are again on the rise. New building operations are once again conspicuous. New industrial establishments are once again being opened up and old ones reopened after strikes. Fear of nationalization, confiscation, regimentation, and discrimination, if far from dispelled, is at any rate diminished. Local and foreign capitalists, if not eagerly seeking out Singapore investment possibilities again, are not so precipitate as a year ago in their flight to Kuala Lumpur or points even more distant.

Speculative alarm over Singapore's future—or that of the Federation—should be tempered by recollection that both have successfully surmounted the hazards of the 1948–1960 "Communist Emergency" and that in certain important respects both are the stronger and sounder for the experience.

THE COMMUNIST EMERGENCY

The campaign of the Communist Party of Malaya to drive the British from the Federation and Singapore constituted first a deterrent, later an incentive to the granting of independence and self-government. The British authorities were disposed at first to withhold political concessions until the terrorist menace was past, later to confer them as inducement and reward for joint effort in the anti-Communist struggle. During the Emergency the British and the local people achieved a high degree of cooperation such as remains mutually agreeable and mutually profitable today.

The "Emergency" as such was formally declared on June 18, 1948, shortly after the M.C.P., following the new line laid down in an international Communist Party conference at New Delhi that year, revised its policy of infiltration in favor of violence. The M.C.P., which had received British arms and aid in waging jungle warfare against the Japanese, had remembered its tactics and hoarded its arms and now turned both very effectively against its onetime allies. Beginning in June, it staged a long series of murders and depredations aimed particularly at British rubber planters, tin miners, and government officials, but including anybody else within range.

As of July 31, 1960, the Federation Government declared that the Emergency was over. By January 1, 1960, the campaign against the terrorists, fought over appallingly difficult jungle and mountain terrain, had cost the lives of 2,473 civilians, 1,865 members of the police, home guard, and military services (Commonwealth and Malayan), and 6,698 terrorists, plus other thousands of casualties and disappearances. It had necessitated the direct outlay of £94 million and at least M$1,750 million—M$1.4 million per day even in 1960, when the victory was already won. It had involved interference with tin, rubber, and other production, and disruption of the lives and livelihood of hundreds of thousands of persons. The terror reached its peak in the years 1950 and 1951. It dropped off in the years 1952 to 1955, when the government reintensified its three primary tactics. First, it conducted relentless action against the armed guerrilla bands. Second, it enforced the removal and resettlement in bleak "new villages" of some 500,000 persons (mainly Chinese, but others also, including aborigines) from whom the terrorists were extorting aid and information. Third, it denied food, medicines, and other essential supplies to the guerrillas by rigorous checks on all traffic out of the cities and villages or along the highways. From 1955 onward the terrorist forces disintegrated so completely that on July 31, 1960, there remained only an estimated six hundred. All but about fifty of them concentrated just across the Thai border in an area from which they can launch occasional small-scale infiltration or attack with impunity from effective pursuit.

In Singapore the terror manifested itself primarily in two waves of mass violence, one in May 1955, the other in October 1956. Communist-dominated labor unions and Chinese student organizations—both, as already noted, strongholds of the P.A.P.—staged a series of strikes, demonstrations, riots and murders. These defiances of authority ended only after the Singapore Government, under Chief Minister Lim Yew Hock, in October 1956 requested use of British troops from Malaya to restore order, authorized use of tear gas to rout the rebellious students, and ordered the arrest, imprisonment, or deportation of the agitators. A renewal of disturbances was precluded in August 1957 when Lim Yew Hock ordered the roundup and imprisonment of some thirty-five known subversives, including top leaders of the P.A.P. who had for a brief interval ousted Lee Kuan Yew and his more moderate associates. No major disturbances have occurred in Singapore since then. As a condition of forming the new government last year, the P.A.P. gained the release of eight of the top political prisoners—the P.A.P. extremist element—and it has since released more. It holds others still in jail. Observers find it difficult, therefore, to draw clear-cut conclusions about Singapore's prospects for a riot-free future.

THE ECONOMIC SITUATION

Despite the Emergency, for both the Federation and Singapore the years 1950, 1951, 1955, 1956, 1959, and 1960 to date have been boom times. The intermediate years were merely prosperous. Both government and private enterprise have profited very greatly from high prices for rubber and to a lesser extent tin, good prices for copra, palm oil, tea, and other products, and fluctuating but on the whole satisfactory proceeds from the Singapore and Penang entrepôt trade. Both government and private enterprise have prudently accumulated and prudently reinvested tremendous reserve funds. The two governments have been able to undertake and to carry out on their own resources immense new development schemes costing hundreds of millions of Malayan dollars. The schemes have resulted in tremendous expansion of government office quarters, public housing, public utilities, communications, schools, hospitals, and much else. Private enterprise, utilizing its own funds plus government subsidies, has been able to replant one half the total rubber-tree acreage with new high-yield stock that produces three to four times the amount of latex of the old. It has completely rehabilitated the tin mining industry and has built industrial suburbs in Singapore and Kuala

Lumpur. It has transformed the skyline of Singapore, Kuala Lumpur, and other cities with big new office and apartment buildings. The Federation and Singapore are today by far the most advanced of all Southeast Asian countries in both rural and urban modernization, as indicated—to take only a few superficial examples—by the prevalence of air conditioning, Mercedes-Benz taxis, public telephones, scheduled bus service, potable tap water, cold-storage supplies, and bountifully stocked stores in which ordinary people can and do buy almost any local or imported commodity at prices that are close to world market prices.

Both the Federation and Singapore, like every other area in the world, have serious economic problems, but theirs are the relatively fortunate problems of prosperous states endeavoring to remain prosperous, rather than those of depressed states seeking to achieve economic stability. Each has a standard of living high above the area norm and hence a high wage and salary level and a high demand for luxury imports. The question arises whether the two states can continue to compete advantageously with lower cost producers in nearby countries and whether they can maintain an abundant flow of expensive imports. Both lack raw materials for any industrial development not based on rubber, tin, iron, and various agricultural crops; specifically, they lack coal, oil, and other minerals. They also lack experience and skill. Nevertheless, each is determined to industrialize. Both lack extensive domestic markets, and even a common market, if it can be achieved, offers only a limited outlet to a combined population of only 8.5 million people. Both are exceptionally vulnerable to fluctuation in world prices on a few raw materials and to economic discrimination on political grounds on the part of their neighbors, Indonesia, for instance. Indonesia's purchases and produce are very important to both the Malayan and Singapore economies, but the suspicious Indonesian Government has attempted intermittently, although not as yet successfully, to bypass Singapore and Penang entrepôt markets. Each has a highly dangerous differential in the economic accomplishments and capacities of its various racial groups, a differential which must be diminished if economic or political stability is to continue. Each, furthermore, is dependent upon the other—the Federation upon Singapore's shipping, merchandising, and banking facilities; Singapore upon the Federation's production and trade. Each, if its development is to keep pace with greatly increased population and expectations, needs tremendous new foreign investment. Such investment is likely to be attracted not so much on the basis of divided and competitive, but of coordinated economic systems—the declared Federation-Singapore joint objective toward which joint effort has not yet been directed.

OVER-ALL PROSPECTS

The Federation, at time of writing, seems economically, politically, and socially more stable than Singapore. And yet it is possible to argue the reverse proposition. The right-wing Federation Government may be complacently glossing over its really critical problems. The left-wing, but more dynamic, leadership in Singapore may be courageously defining and attacking its problems, including the critical one of relations with the Federation.

Singapore is tailoring its basic policy to achieve the immensely difficult transformation into "Malayans" of the Singapore Chinese so that Singapore can merge with Malaya. The Federation Government is tailoring its basic policy to emphasize rapid improvement of the distinctively Malay sector of the population. Such a policy is a political necessity in a nation where Malays are the majority, and it is calculated both directly and indirectly to benefit the whole population. It may prove, nevertheless, a serious psychological barrier, fostering the impression that non-Malays, including the Malayan Chinese, whether Federation citizens at present, or Singaporeans aspiring to Federation citizenship, are to be regarded as having second-class status.

Should either Federation or Singapore basic policy break down, the most likely sequel would be serious racial strife. If such strife begins, it would quickly lead to conspiracy on the part of Federation and Singapore Chinese against the Federation's Malay Government. The result would be disastrous to both Chinese and Malays.

Both the Federation and Singapore, however, have established the precedent of moving steadily forward. Both records are so remarkably good, in fact, as to reflect great credit upon the Alliance and the P.A.P. governments. They invite contrast with the unhappy record of maladministration in huge Indonesia next door, whose rapidly increasing troubles constitute an external threat to the continued peace and progress of its neighbors.

3

Borneo Periphery[1]

August 1960

THE STATES of British Borneo—the Crown Colonies of Sarawak and North Borneo and the protected Sultanate of Brunei—occupy the north-western third of Borneo Island, with Indonesia occupying the remainder. The three states together comprise some 82,000 square miles of forbidding jungle, swamp, and mountain, enhanced by a few towns on the coast and a small amount of developed land not far from the coastal areas. The combined population totals 1,280,000—approximately 50 per cent tribal, 30 per cent Chinese, 20 per cent Malay, plus a few thousand Britishers. It is distributed 750,000 in Sarawak, 450,000 in North Borneo, and 80,000 in Brunei. The three states are closely interrelated with nearby Malaya and Singapore. All five share not only racial ties but also the administrative, commercial, and educational traditions of the British colonial period—a common currency, for instance, and an integrated communications system, to mention only two of the more obvious bonds.

What is now British Borneo participated for many centuries as a significant force in the now obscure pageant of early Southeast Asian commerce and conquest. It was one of the first areas of Asia to command the attention of European voyagers—Pigafetta, the chronicler of Magellan's expedition, devoting many pages to the description of the wealth and power of the then paramount Sultanate of Brunei (or Borneo). But Brunei, whose prestige and profit were rather precariously based upon piracy, was then already started into decline. It almost dropped from view again until 1775, when the British embarked upon a badly

---

[1] This chapter, based upon a draft manuscript dated August 1960, reviews the situation in British Borneo for the same pre-1960 period as that covered in the foregoing chapter on Malaya and Singapore.

managed little colonial experiment on the island of Balembang, which they abandoned in 1803 after experiencing the double disasters of invasion and epidemic. Brunei did not really re-emerge in history until the mid-nineteenth century, when Western newcomers eagerly abetted the last stages of its decline.

A British gentleman-adventurer, by name James Brooke, seeking first to emulate, then later to excel Sir Stamford Raffles, managed by devices of intervention and ingratiation to induce the Sultan of Brunei to grant him sovereign rights over the rajadom of Sarawak. For over a century thereafter (1841–1946), except for the period of Japanese occupation, three White Rajahs Brooke ruled Sarawak under British protection as their private domain. An American confidence man, one Claude Lee Moses, seeking to emulate Rajah Brooke, managed later to procure for himself from the Sultan of Brunei the concession (1865) of a vague but extensive tract of Borneo real estate on which he attempted unsuccessfully to establish a colony. The Moses concession, which was presently mortgaged to another American, Torrey by name, but dubbed Sir Maharajah Torrey by the Sultan, an adventurous Austrian Baron von Overbeck, and some shady Hong Kong Chinese bankers, was reinforced, perhaps expanded, by a vaguely overlapping concession (1878) from the Sultan of Sulu. It was then bought up on speculation by some British merchants, the brothers Dent of Hong Kong and Singapore, who founded the British North Borneo (Chartered) Company (1882) which operated the area thereafter as a private and not particularly profitable business enterprise.

Prior to World War II, British Borneo was little known and—in either the bad or the good sense of the word—it was as little exploited. Oil, to be sure, had already been discovered in Brunei, over which the British had extended their protection back in 1888, but Brunei remained, nevertheless, both poor and backward. In Sarawak, where the third Rajah Brooke ruled with a firm but benevolent hand, schools flourished modestly and pepper proved a satisfactory crop much in demand even in years of world depression, but the general pace of life seemed at least half a century behind that of even the slowest times. In North Borneo the Chartered Company was almost as cautious about permitting development of its lands as it was about introducing education or medicine. Save for the generally successful suppression of head-hunting, piracy, and smuggling, life seemed much as it had been before James Brooke and Claude Lee Moses dreamed of Borneo empire.

The sudden and violent advent of the Japanese in 1941 and their almost equally sudden and violent exit in 1945—with the more destructive violence confined to North Borneo and Brunei—worked the end of British Borneo's isolation. Even so, the rate of change did not become truly rapid or dangerous for another decade.

In Brunei, where oil royalties began to flow into the national treasury at such a rate that administrative outlay could not keep up, the British in the mid-fifties planned and implemented a M$100 million program of national development. Meanwhile they advised the Sultan and his court, who listened and occasionally acted, to prepare to confer self-government. Brunei has now been physically transformed with Aladdin's lamplike suddenness so that it has the shiny new façade of a modern state. It also has a new constitution and the promise of elections, and educational and other social programs are being rapidly expanded for a newly privileged citizenry. Bottle-necked oil revenues, however, now back up an unspent M$600 million plus in the bulging state treasury. Whether Brunei's problems are closer to resolution or to resurgence is a moot point, endlessly debated both by Brunei and its neighbors.

In Sarawak, after the war, the third Rajah Brooke turned over the state and several million dollars of state funds to the British Crown (1946). The Crown thereupon inaugurated a new colonial administration which in the mid-fifties began by gradual stages to introduce representative government. After considerable delay and debate it also set about expanding the educational program and implementing a modest economic development plan. Sarawak, however, has had intimations of serious political troubles—the first governor was assassinated by a disaffected Malay; the local Chinese have been subject to influence and pressure from the China mainland; and efforts to establish a safe, government-sponsored political party have somehow misfired. The Sarawak pepper, rubber, and timber industries, furthermore, have failed really to expand, and oil, so near and so abundant in Brunei, has failed to gush, notwithstanding dogged perseverance in prospecting. All the same, by Southeast Asian standards, Sarawak seems both peaceful and prosperous and promises also to become progressive.

North Borneo has turned out to be the real Borneo success story. At the end of World War II, North Borneo's main towns were bombed-out ruins and its population was badly demoralized. The British colonial administration, putting first priority upon economic matters, invested modest sums of pump-priming money to encourage urban reconstruction and industrial development. North Borneo's timber industry, along with various subsidiary industries and trade and commerce in general, is now producing private wealth and government revenue sufficient to make the state almost self-supporting. British grants-in-aid are being directed more and more toward educational, medical, and other programs to enable the population to achieve social development commensurate with its economic prospects. North Borneo, long one of the world's most backward but not one of its more discontented areas, is at last beginning to catch up and to catch up fast. Even yet it is spared the perils of politics, a state of affairs, obviously, which cannot last much longer.

The present or onetime British colonial possessions of the region around Malaya, in Borneo as on the mainland peninsula, are going through a transitional period which is proving, for each individual state, far more orderly and advantageous than is the postcolonial norm. In each case the problems of domestic development are being successfully surmounted. The equally important problems of relationships with each other and with their great Indonesian neighbor, however, have become both urgent and perplexing.

The three states of Borneo have given slight consideration as yet either to the proposition of independence, or to a three-state federation (which the British have tentatively suggested), or to any other new arrangement, such as merger with the nearby Federation of Malaya, although the days of colonial dependence obviously are numbered. The Federation of Malaya, meanwhile, in savoring the happy record of its first three years of independence, seems to be ignoring the importunities of Singapore, which seeks merger and threatens subversion. Of all the new states, Singapore is the one which seems to be most realistically facing up to the total problem—that of achieving long-term security not just through domestic but through regional cooperation, specifically, so far as Singapore itself is concerned, merger with Malaya. Still, whatever the hazards implicit in the existence of these five small, separate states, each of them retains a profound respect for the British-implanted standards of justice and order, each has weathered the immediate postwar period without falling victim to violence, corruption, or maladministration, and each has achieved remarkable prosperity. Of all the areas of Southeast Asia, these five Malaysian states look to the future with greatest hope and confidence.

PART TWO

Political Evolution

4

Ascendancy of the Alliance

June 10, 1959

THE FEDERATION OF MALAYA is now holding its first general elections since the achievement of independence, and most of the local pundits are experiencing the double gratification of seeing their general forecasts come true and their favorite candidates win. In the eleven separate state elections now being run off (May through June), the governing Alliance Party is managing, so far at least, to pile up very comfortable majorities, just as almost everyone except a few opposition leaders said that it would. Barring the unforeseeable, the Alliance will also win the federal elections, now scheduled for late July or early August, thus assuring itself of continuation in power for the next five years. It is doing so by reliance upon free and honest elections, not dictatorial manipulation; upon moderate policies, not ultranationalistic agitation; and also, in the main, upon responsible candidates, not demagogues.

The winning Alliance is made up of the United Malay National Organization (U.M.N.O.), the Malayan Chinese Organization (M.C.A.), and the Malayan Indian Congress (M.I.C.). It is a coalition, thus, of three "communal" (i.e., racial base) parties, or, to be more precise, three subcoalitions, each the paramount political grouping within its own racial community. As a tripartite, triracial, multilingual, multireligious, and multiclass coalition, the Alliance would seem to combine almost all possible elements of political instability. Each of its three member parties is itself a composite of diverse linguistic, religious, and cultural groups which have a hard time getting along together let alone with their Alliance partners. The three are of widely disparate strength and influence, the U.M.N.O. being distinctly the senior, the M.C.A. the junior, and

47

the M.I.C. the subjunior partner. The real political power lies primarily with the U.M.N.O., which claims 600,000 members out of Malaya's 2,172,000 registered voters but admits that collection of membership dues (M$1.00 per annum) is on a much more modest scale. It lies secondarily with the M.C.A., which used to claim 500,000 members but has recently revised its estimate sharply downward to 50,000. Neither the U.M.N.O. nor the M.C.A. is well-organized or well-disciplined. Both derive their strength not from mass following but from adherence to a basic principle to which there is no reasonable alternative, adoption of an accidental tactic that has proved too good to abandon, achievement to date of a record of good government, and association with leaders who command respect.

The principle which unites the U.M.N.O. and the M.C.A. and draws them popular support is the conviction that Malays and Chinese must cooperate in building the new nation and that failure to achieve cooperation will result in interracial conflict that will destroy them both. This guiding principle has given rise to the basic political tactic, one which U.M.N.O. and M.C.A. leaders stumbled onto during the 1952 municipal elections in Kuala Lumpur and thereupon made the basis for organization of the present coalition. It is a device of most striking simplicity and almost unbeatable potency. The Alliance partners meet in Alliance council well in advance of the elections in order to parcel out the constituencies among themselves; they then enter one joint candidate in each constituency and attempt to swing full Alliance voting strength behind that candidate, regardless of the member party to which he belongs. This tactic is not, of course, without its hazards. Agreement on the actual allocation of candidacies is far from easy to achieve or to maintain; selection of individual candidates is a matter for much horse trading; and mustering Chinese voter support for Malay candidates or Malay votes for Chinese, or either Malay or Chinese votes for Indians, is a chancy business.

The Alliance platform, accordingly, places major stress upon the necessity for continued racial cooperation and upon the danger to the nation from those opposition parties which make race, class, or religion the primary basis of their political appeal or tend toward extremism, fanaticism, and communism in leadership. The Alliance candidates defend the party's record of good government in the past and promise that, after winning the current elections, the Alliance will set about even more vigorously than before to eradicate illiteracy, encourage better agricultural methods, open up new lands, establish new industries, provide more low-cost housing, develop more extensive educational and social service programs, and build better roads, power stations, waterworks, and other modern facilities. The Alliance today, however, does not have any appeal as emotionally potent as its 1955 promise of independence. Its campaign oratory, therefore, tends to lack incandescence, concentrating as it does on warnings against an opposition that is not really very strong and promises of new national development programs that are really not much different from the old. The appeal is on the basis of sheer reasonableness, never a very intoxicating political potion; in this case, at least, despite the efforts of some of the opposition leaders to stir up a flaming cause, it is one that is working out amazingly well.

As corollary to the basic principle of interracial cooperation, the Alliance has adopted the concept that there must emerge in Malaya a new nationality and a new citizenship, which will not be just Malay, Chinese, and Indian but composite "Malayan." In the case of the Malays, the great majority of whom have rated in the past as backward and underprivileged in comparison with the Chinese and the Westerners, to become "Malayan" requires, on the one hand, the development of common loyalty to a new democratic nation, as contrasted with loyalty to the state sultan, and on the other hand the achievement of rapid economic, educational, and social development. To enable them to catch up with the other racial groups, the Malays are to be allowed certain special rights and privileges, some formally guaranteed by the new constitution for a period of fifteen years, some merely accepted in practice. Among these rights and privileges are automatic qualification for citizenship and suffrage (as compared with language and residence requirements for the Chinese and others); priority claims on extensive state lands now being opened up for development; preferential treatment in the assignment of licenses for certain business enterprises, notably fisheries and transportation; reservation of four out of five new openings in the civil service; special consideration for rapid advancement in the civil service and appointment to top positions; appointment to the majority of the chief political posts, such as those at cabinet and ambassadorial level; recognition of the sovereignty of traditional Malay rulers and of Islam as the state religion; and designation of Malay, after a ten-year transitional period, as the official language.

From the Malay point of view, these special privileges do not look very impressive in comparison with the obvious fact that the Chinese control the great part of the modern economic enterprise of the nation. From the Chinese point of view, however, they virtually assure the Malays of political control which could be used to eradicate non-Malay economic, cultural, and other interests. Special Malay privilege, furthermore, makes it automatic that the U.M.N.O., not the M.C.A., will be the paramount partner in the Alliance and that the M.C.A., unless it is willing to risk disruption of the Alliance and quite possibly the eruption of violence, must be willing to yield more in compromise than the U.M.N.O., just how much or how little being largely contingent upon how solid a backing the M.C.A. can itself achieve within the Chinese community.

For the Malays, then, transformation to "Malayan" status means advancement and improvement, so Malay and U.M.N.O. enthusiasm for the process is relatively easy to arouse. For the Chinese the transformation means adaptation, compromise, and even immediate sacrifice; the Chinese and M.C.A. attitude toward the process, consequently, is less one of enthusiasm than of qualified acquiescence. The majority of the Chinese in Malaya have remained distinctively Chinese in patterns of life and thought; the minority have become so Westernized that they frequently speak better English than Chinese and know much more about London than about Canton. To become "Malayan," a Chinese must be willing to learn and to use the Malay language and to train himself to live, to think, and to act, not according to the traditional patterns of the Overseas Chinese, but according to the newly emerging and not yet clearly defined "Malayan" pattern.

The ordinary Chinese finds this transformation very difficult to comprehend, let alone to achieve. Even the thoughtful "Malayan-minded" Chinese hopes that he can "Malayanize" and still maintain both his own cultural tradition and his economic advantage reasonably intact. He is constantly beset, however, by the feeling that while he is willing in general to move toward "Malayan" status, he may be pushed a little farther and yet a little farther, until he has lost more than he has gained. The M.C.A. and its leaders, having publicly accepted and endorsed the concept of a "Malayan" nationality and the obligation to become "Malayan-minded" or "Malayanized," are faced with the extremely difficult task of arbitrating in private the differences of opinion which inevitably arise within and between the parties regarding the pace, method, and limits of change. They are faced also with the equally difficult task of gaining active support for the party's policy not only among the more progressive, more Westernized segments of the Chinese community, but among the great majority of Chinese-speaking, Chinese-thinking laboring classes who are not easy either to reach or to convince.

Both the U.M.N.O. and the M.C.A. leaders are confronted by major problems of achieving discipline and cooperation among their members. For the U.M.N.O. the problems are so serious that Tengku Abdul Rahman temporarily resigned the Prime Ministership in order to devote himself to shoring up the party system during the months before the elections. "Constant strife and bickering," he said, went on within the U.M.N.O. organization, particularly on the part of members who sought to deny to the M.C.A. and the M.I.C. an equitable representation on the panel of Alliance candidates. An alarming number of U.M.N.O. incumbents, he said, exhibited "glaring weaknesses" and engaged in "irresponsible acts," some of them *mentris besar* and aspirants to governorship" who sought "to pack the state legislative councils with their personal supporters," pursuing "their own separate policies, ignoring the basic policies of the party." As an aside regarding the U.M.N.O.'s continuing financial difficulties, he mentioned the persistent failure of many U.M.N.O. officials to pay their special assessment—the 5 per cent of their salaries which they are expected to contribute to party funds.

Whereas the U.M.N.O.'s difficulties have arisen primarily from lack of organizational experience on the part of the Malay community, the M.C.A.'s stem in large part from overorganization of the Chinese—but organization for purposes that often run counter to those of the M.C.A. itself. The Chinese Chambers of Commerce, the guilds, the Chinese schools and clans have generally sought to achieve the supremacy of Chinese economic interests, the preservation of Chinese culture, and the conformity of the Chinese community to the wishes of its self-appointed leaders. Most of these leaders have been the *towkays*, or wealthy businessmen, who have viewed Malaya as a pleasant and profitable place in which Overseas Chinese may settle down, but not as a country to which they owe allegiance. The M.C.A. has had the task of establishing a new sort of Chinese organization, one which would in part cut across and in part supersede the old ones. It has been in constant danger, on the one hand, of being manipulated by or of running into sharp conflict with the powerful *towkays*, and on the other of failing altogether in its appeal to the great majority of "little Chinese" who tend to prefer the old ways or, if change must come, the changes of the China mainland.

The M.C.A. leaders must maintain constant vigilance against Chinese elements which could and would deliberately cause serious trouble—the secret societies, for instance, the Communists and their sympathizers, the hoodlum element among Chinese youth, many of them recent secondary school graduates who find jobs difficult to get. The problems of the M.C.A., then, both as they regard internal maneuvering and maintenance of Alliance solidarity, appear to be considerably more serious than those of the U.M.N.O.

The Malayan Indian Congress deserves at least an aside, and that, from the point of view of its leaders and members, is about all they get in the normal course of events, either from the U.M.N.O. or the M.C.A. The M.I.C. is in the extremely difficult position of representing at optimum considerably less than 10 per cent of the population, and that percentage fragmented among various uncoordinated and conflicting linguistic, religious, and occupational groups. The M.I.C., consequently, is anything but a strong party with strong leaders. The more vigorous Indian leaders—together with the Ceylonese and Pakistanis—are attracted to minor parties promoting communal causes. The M.I.C. itself is part of the Alliance more as a measure of expediency than as an expression of conviction. It is allotted by the Alliance a dole of electoral constituencies in which to enter Indian candidates. It receives the allotment, however, more as a favor than as a right, and it is subjected to severe criticism for not pulling even its very limited weight in the election campaigns. In the Selangor state elections, for instance, three of the four M.I.C. candidates were defeated—three out of the total of five Alliance losers. This poor showing at the polls has already resulted in recriminations—on one hand, that the M.I.C. did not do its part in promoting the candidacies, on the other hand, that the other members of the Alliance (specifically, in one instance, the M.C.A.) did not support the M.I.C. but threw a large block of votes to a non-Alliance rival. Despite frequent admonitions from the Alliance and exhortations from their own M.I.C. leaders, a great many among the Indian minority seem to prefer to live, think, talk, act, and worship not as new-style "Malayans" but as old-style Indians; the appeal of the M.I.C. to the Indian community to cooperate and to Malayanize itself is in general much less effective than the appeal of the M.C.A. to the more readily adaptable Chinese.

* * * * * *

The special flavor of politics in Malaya, as elsewhere, is that imparted by the politicians, and the politicians who here deserve special attention, both for historic and for contemporary interest, are the leaders of the

U.M.N.O. and of the M.C.A., most especially Tengku Abdul Rahman, president of the U.M.N.O. and leader of the Alliance.

Tengku Abdul Rahman Putra ibni Almarhum Sultan Abdul Hamid Halim Shah, age fifty-six, is almost invariably described as "genial," "mellow," "relaxed." He is taller, heavier, and gayer than the average Malay, but then his mother was Siamese, he enjoys good living, and he has a most enviable capacity for worrying only about the things he can change. He is a feudal aristocrat—one of the forty-five children of the late Sultan of Kedah—who enjoys both the pomp of court ceremony (witness his recent state wedding for his son) and the easy give-and-take of democracy (witness his apparently complete lack of reticence with the press corps). He can alternate with contentment between the elaborate official residence of the Prime Minister and his own unpretentious home in Alor Star. One of the nation's intellectual elite without being really an intellectual, he was the first Kedah Malay to graduate from an English university (Cambridge). He subsequently managed happily to put in a record-breaking number of years earning an English law degree, devoting at least as much time to the race course, soccer field, theater, and younger social set as he did to the Inner Temple. He now finds relaxation in turning out what must frankly be termed rather trashy literature, suitable for translation onto the Malayan screen in either of its two favorite media—the romantic thriller or the vampire chiller.

A practical politician, Tengku Abdul Rahman, is more interested in political maneuver than in theory. He frequently foregoes polite platitudes for refreshingly forthright statements of views on national and international problems. He has been capable, recently, of such apparent bloopers as offering his own immediate associates to serve as *mentris besar* in the state governments handicapped by lack of qualified men of their own; asserting that Chinese and Indian Legislative Council members do not work as hard as the Malays; and declaring himself fed up with Indonesian press misrepresentation of his policies.

The Tengku is a Muslim who makes no secret of enjoying a brandy, even though conservative Muslims make frequent cause of backsliding officials who serve or accept hard liquor. He is a nationalist who bears no apparent rancor toward the foreigner, even though he encountered racial discrimination during his student days in England. Instead of ranting against British colonialism and imperialism, he praises the British for bequeathing to Malaya a highly efficient civil service which he proposes to maintain in good working order along with enough Englishmen to ensure smooth transfer of duties. Instead of censuring the local Chinese for capitalistic exploitation, he chose as his Minister of Finance one of the more enterprising of them all, Hong Kong-born Sir Henry Hau-shik Lee, a wartime colonel in the Allied forces, a fancier of fine cars, fine horses, and fine living. When local Chinese Communists become obstreperous, he offers at his own expense to send them to China; and when foreign anti-Communists become insistent, he announces that while he has no intention of joining SEATO, he has every intention of wiping out the Communist menace in Malaya and that he is happy to have British troops to help him do so. When his own U.M.N.O. colleagues become overly zealous for Malay rights or overly confident in Malay political power, he refuses to hear of reducing Chinese or other minority equity in government, candidly reminding everyone that the Malays still lack quite a great deal of political and technical know-how and that the Alliance needs the M.C.A.'s financial contributions.

During his first forty-five years Tengku Abdul Rahman gained the reputation of being a rake and a playboy and he entered politics a bit reluctantly, but he has now come genuinely to enjoy national leadership. He does not enjoy it so much, however, as to be willing to sacrifice totally his individuality, independence, and leisure. He left Kuala Lumpur with obvious relief a couple of months ago, to allow himself a holiday before his political fence-mending tour of the pre-election period. He was in and out of town every few days afterward, however, on visits which he made either more or less official according to his whim, and he acknowledged quite frankly that he felt the pinch when his M$4,000 monthly salary as Prime Minister lapsed.

The Tengku is a most unorthodox nationalist leader, but the peaceful development of the nation depends upon whether his sort of heterodoxy can prevail. The Malays suffer from a serious shortage of trained leaders, but so far, fortunately, the men in authority have been endowed both with competence and tolerance. The acting Prime Minister, for instance, the number-two man in the U.M.N.O., is Dato Abdul Razak bin Hussain, a man as rational as the Tengku, more reserved, more intellectual, more systematic, and more uncompromising, but no more in danger, it seems, of becoming a prisoner of rigidly nationalistic concepts such as can only set the Malays at odds with other races. The Minister of External Affairs, Dr. Ismail bin Dato Abdul Rahman, formerly Ambassador to the United States and delegate to the United Nations, is of the same type. He startled the United Nations, a body more accustomed to outrage than to placidity, by declaring, "We covet nothing. We are happy with what we have." On his return from the United States he told his fellow countrymen, "Modern capitalism on the American pattern and not socialism is the suitable political climate for speedy advancement of underdeveloped countries like Malay." American capitalism, he added, "is not akin to colonialism, which was based on exploitation of the subject peoples. . . . It was an eye opener to me to see it in action in the United States, benefiting not only the capitalist circles but also labor." Dr. Ismail, his critics declared, had been "brainwashed." Instead of qualifying or retracting, Dr. Ismail has stood by his assertions, just as Abdul Rahman and other leaders of the government stand by their repeated declarations that British Commonwealth troops are no menace but a safeguard to Malaya, that Chinese must not be driven out but assimilated, that the Communists are not nationalists and patriots but subversives.

Whereas leadership in the U.M.N.O. has been constant and stable and promises to remain so, leadership in the M.C.A. has passed from an older to a younger group. Even within the new group disputes of serious proportions between old-timers and newcomers, between "Alliance-firsters" and "Chinese-firsters," between national and state leaders, still threaten to cause upsets. To put party politics into the personal dimension, it is useful to single out the previous and the current party presidents, Sir Cheng Lock Tan and Dr. Lim Chong Eu.

Dato Sir Cheng Lock Tan, now seventy-six and physically frail, is a member of one of the oldest and richest Chinese families of Malacca. One of the earliest and most successful rubber planters in Malaya, he has a forty-year career of public service behind him and also, he insists, years of equally useful public service yet to come. Before World War II he was confidant and adviser to British administrators and an appointed member of various legislative and executive bodies. After the war he headed a Chinese movement for formation of a new state based on equal rights for all races but accommodation of alien to indigenous Malay interests. After going through many mutations, some of which brought it into much closer contact with the Communist organizations than its top leaders realized or wanted, the movement led to the founding in 1949 of the Malayan Chinese Association. In 1952 and 1953 the M.C.A. entered into close cooperation with the U.M.N.O. in the newly-formed Alliance Party.

Sir Cheng Lock has devoted himself unceasingly to the task of bridging the gap between Chinese and Malays, and for his efforts he has been not only eulogized but also attacked from both sides. In 1949 he was wounded by a grenade thrown by a terrorist; in 1957 he was passed over for the position he clearly wanted as climax to his political career—that of governor of Malacca; in 1958 he was voted out of office as president of the M.C.A. Nevertheless, he remains the Grand Old Man of Malacca, called upon to serve as acting governor during the absences and illnesses of the incumbent, celebrated in dozens of public testimonials by British, Chinese, Malay, and other distinguished leaders. He has been awarded the K.C.B.E. (1952) and has been granted the title of "Dato" (1949) from the Sultan of Johore and that of "Tun" (1958) from the Yang di Pertuan Agong. He is the active patron of dozens of worthy causes.

On the national scene Sir Cheng Lock Tan has now been succeeded by thirty-nine-year-old Lim Chong Eu, a medical doctor by profession, educated at Edinburgh University, a volunteer in the International Red Cross in China during the war. Vigorous and self-assertive, Dr. Lim is a proponent of Sir Cheng Lock's own thesis that the Chinese must learn to live, act, and think like Malayans and that they must in the meantime respect the special political rights and privileges of the Malay population. He is also a proponent of the thesis that the M.C.A. must acquire greater vitality, better discipline, more widespread public support, and more appealing public leadership than the older group, including even Sir Cheng Lock as a single outstanding individual, was able to give it. In his attempt at once to adhere to the old policy and to supply new drive and motivation, Dr. Lim is facing a tough proposition. He must maintain his personal position at the head of the party and the M.C.A.'s position within the Alliance whose president, Tengku Abdul Rahman, quite openly preferred to work with Sir Cheng Lock Tan.

The Alliance and its leaders, now sweeping to victory against an opposition which is proving weaker than almost anyone had expected, will undoubtedly at some point in the future encounter really powerful opposition, perhaps from within the Alliance rather than from without, perhaps even from without the nation rather than from within.

The Alliance government has not really resolved nor can it soon resolve its own position as regards the Communist, the non-Communist, and the neutralist worlds. It is staunchly anti-Communist, for instance, without being pro-SEATO, and it is confronted with very delicate problems in its relationships with nearby countries, most especially the neutralist republic of Indonesia and the leftist government of the new state of Singapore.

Singapore, lying across a short causeway from the Federation state of

Johore, faces the dangers of political extremism and economic stringency. Yet Singapore is of vital concern to Malaya, whether as a potential factor in disrupting Malay's own politics and economy or as a potential partner within the Federation itself. Indonesia, racially, historically, and religiously akin to Malaya, some of its islands lying almost within sight of the Malayan mainland, is torn by troubles which might prove as contagious as they are contiguous. Developments in Indonesia and in Singapore are as important to the Alliance and to the Federation as are developments within Malaya itself.

5

Anti-Alliance Prospects

June 13, 1959

IN THE Federation of Malaya today the Alliance Party is steadily rolling up victories in the election of eleven state legislative councils and is preparing for certain victory in the federal elections that are to follow in late July or early August. It is still too early, of course, to analyze election results and to predict postelection trends, but it is suitable at this point to supplement an account of the winning Alliance with a description of the losing opposition, its components, its tactics, its policies, and its leaders. The specific parties warranting consideration are as follows: (A) the Pan-Malayan Islamic Party (P.M.I.P.), aiming at a theocratic state and allegedly infiltrated by subversive if not outright Communist elements; (B) the Socialist Front, aiming at a "social welfare" state, one member of which, the Party Ra'ayat (People's Party), has seemed in the past from the Alliance point of view the most likely candidate for the role of "healthy opposition"; (C) the People's Progressive Party (P.P.P.), aiming at "exposure" of the Alliance for alleged arrogance, corruption, and incompetence, and nominating itself as the "healthy opposition"; and (D) the Party Negara, aiming at nobody seems to know quite what, save disputatiousness.

The Pan-Malayan Islamic Party is the creation of Dr. Burhanuddin Al-Helmy, forty-eight-year-old leader of leftwing nationalist movements since 1945, who in recent years, to the surprise of his critics, has transformed himself into a religious leader quoting extensively from the Koran in his campaign speeches. Dr. Burhanuddin was the founder, in 1945, of the Malay Nationalist Party which found inspiration in the Indonesian Revolution and was closely associated with Indonesian residents of Malaya. The party seemed to have been directed, rather vaguely, toward achieving Pan-Malayan independence by coordinating Malayan revolutionary sentiments against the British with the Indonesian struggle against the Dutch. The British authorities took the party seriously enough to dissolve it early in the Communist Emergency in 1948 and to detain Dr. Burhanuddin under the Emergency Regulations which permit imprisonment without trial. Shortly after his release in 1955, Dr. Burhanuddin joined and quickly took over control of the Pan-Malayan Islamic Association, now the P.M.I.P., which claimed orthodox Islamic religious tenets rather than revolutionary nationalism as its basis.

Dr. Burhanuddin, a theosophist as well as a Muslim, also a medical practitioner (but not a Western-style doctor), is given to obscure philosophical and religious pronouncements in the course of his frequent campaign appearances. He is rather less obscure but still far from crystal clear in his political message. His party seems at times to aim at the creation of a Pan-Islamic regional organization, stretching from the Philippines to Indonesia. It also advocates a Malayan state based on Islamic law. Tengku Abdul Rahman and other Alliance leaders object that Islamic law is completely impractical in a modern state of mixed religious composition, indeed, that its adoption would be an invitation to bloodshed and chaos. So the P.M.I.P. now qualifies its statement of objectives by appending "in accordance with the state laws"—a clear contradiction, but one which does not greatly trouble P.M.I.P. supporters. It declares that achievement of independence is an empty victory, so long as the nation tolerates the presence of Commonwealth troops under the "pretext" of fighting Communist terrorists and maintains even indirect ties with SEATO. "We have gained *Merdeka*," says Burhanuddin, "but we have lost our birthright and Singapore."

Dr. Burhanuddin, it appears to many of his critics, would restore Malaya's birthright and Singapore by encouraging Malay nationalist and religious agitation against the West, by accepting guidance from the Communists and from Indonesia, and by utilizing the village mosque as a ready-made, nationwide organization for political activity. He would also, incidentally, ban strip-tease shows, obscene publications, rock 'n' roll dancing, and the hula hoop. Although the P.M.I.P. is commonly dismissed as a fanatical fringe group, it scored the one and only victory against the Alliance in the 1955 elections, gaining the original non-Alliance elective seat in the fifty-two-member Federal Legislative Council. It later gained one additional seat in a by-election. Its strength lies among the uneducated, devout Muslims of the kampongs, who, having little knowledge of, or interest in, political overtones, are apt to regard religious embellishments in political oratory as evidence of piety and probity. The party seeks to clinch its hold and its vote among this group by declaring that all good Muslims must subscribe to P.M.I.P. objectives and by inducing villagers to swear upon the Koran that they will support only the P.M.I.P. candidates. For the sake of the more sophisticated, the party has drawn up a campaign manifesto which mentions all of the usual amenities to be afforded the people—more jobs, more land, more schools, more roads, more mosques, etc., always with special privileges for the Malays and special invocation of divine sanction. The Alliance leaders denounce the P.M.I.P. regularly for "communalism," "prejudice," "ignorance," and "Communist infiltration," and have managed so far to forestall the widespread acceptance of P.M.I.P. leadership except by the religiously devout but politically naïve.

The Socialist Front is led primarily by Inche Ahmad Boestamam bin Raja Kechil, age thirty-nine, a prominent associate of Dr. Burhanuddin in the organizing of the Malay Nationalist Party in 1945, a detainee of the British Colonial Government between 1948 and 1955, and a specialist in "youth" organizations. After his release and his return to political life, Boestamam established the Party Ra'ayat and became the prime mover in negotiations to bring the Party Ra'ayat (Malay), the Labour Party, and the People's Progressive Party (both largely Chinese and Indian) into a little alliance called the Socialist Front. So far, only the Party Ra'ayat and the Labour Party have come together, but the inclusion of the P.P.P. in the Socialist Front might still occur.

The Party Ra'ayat, which Tengku Abdul Rahman in condemning other opposition parties has sometimes declared—but not recently—to be a potentially healthy opposition, needs to be considered in the light of its antecedents, especially the Angkatan Pemuda Insaf (Youth Realization Army), one of the more radical of the early independence movements. The A.P.I. was a youth group formed by Boestamam on the model of revolutionary youth movements in nearby Indonesia. Boestamam, a fiery orator and a tireless organizer, exhorted his young Malay followers in the kampongs to maintain themselves in a condition of readiness, with sharpened bamboo poles, *parangs* (machetes), and krises at hand. He urged them to wear semimilitary uniform and to practice a semimilitary drill. His wife, since divorced, was leader of the women's section of the A.P.I. and armed herself, at least for the benefit of publicity photographers, with two Mauser pistols and a couple of hand grenades. As a guide for his followers, Boestamam wrote a revolutionary pamphlet, "Political Testament of A.P.I.," in which he advocated revolution and "independence through blood." His various activities, speeches, and writings landed him in jail in 1948, and when he emerged in 1955 he soon set about organizing first a "socialist" youth movement, then the Party Ra'ayat.

To date at least, the Party Ra'ayat has none of the revolutionary and military overtones of the now defunct A.P.I., and its election platform sounds moderate. But Boestamam personally has gone on record for policies that go considerably beyond his most frequently stated party endorsements of "equal distribution and accumulation of the products of human labor," "to each according to his need, from each according to his ability," and "control by the working classes of land, capital, and labor." He has declared himself unswervingly opposed to "the idea of collaboration with capitalism," demanding an immediate end to the Emergency Regulations which were "started in the interests of the former colonial masters" and have been continued merely as "a pretext for stationing foreign troops and granting military bases." He has called upon the government to "halt foreign investments" which, he adds, "may help temporarily to solve some of our country's financial problems, but in taking away your wealth, they will eventually endanger our national economy." Furthermore, he has insisted upon the legalizing of the Communist Party and the release of persons jailed on suspicion of subversion—including a number of Party Ra'ayat members.

The Party Ra'ayat, primarily Malay in membership, has discovered its closest political ally in the Labour Party, primarily an Indian-led party to which have been attracted a large number of Chinese. The Labour Party is headed by Mr. D. S. Ramanathan, born in India in 1908, Mayor of Penang, and until recently a senior master in the Penang Methodist Boys' School. The party's area of greatest strength is Penang, and its greatest appeal is to white-collar workers, particularly, in recent months, the unemployed white-collar workers. Mr. Ramanathan himself has declared in moderate terms for a Sunday audience on Penang's esplanade that "for lack of a healthy opposition, the Alliance Government has not only become flabby and inconsiderate, but some of its members have shown a tendency toward autocracy as a result of the uncontrolled and unopposed power they have been exercising during the last four years." The Alliance engages, he says, in "quite irresponsible criticism" of the P.P.P. by labeling it Communistic.

When making its appeal to the nonwhite-collar working-class groups from which it now seeks to win large-scale support, the Labour Party tends to be rather more specific regarding the "evils" of the present administration. It points out, for instance, that the government arbitrarily bans such "legitimate" worker privileges as May Day demonstrations, that it prohibits such "desirable" worker-to-worker contacts as visits to Communist China, that it "prejudices" the workers' peace and security by permitting maintenance of British troops and British bases, that it condones "capitalistic exploitation of the nation's economy" and shows a marked predilection for increasing ministerial salaries, privileges, and prerogatives while it "ignores the working classes."

The Labour Party and the Party Ra'ayat, having lately achieved at least a temporary Socialist Front after many earlier efforts had misfired, now declare that the two parties stand jointly for "economic *Merdeka*, equality, and democratic socialism." Like the P.M.I.P. and everyone else, the Socialist Front promises free education, greater job opportunities, rural and urban development projects, and more and better health, welfare, housing, and library programs. It goes even farther and makes specific promises of old-age pensions, orphanages, old people's homes, unemployment insurance, institutions to deal with delinquents, and sanatoria for industrial workers. Socialist Front spokesmen, incidentally, have made rather unguarded remarks about seizing all companies established by foreign capital, since such companies are "prejudicial to the working masses" and derive their profit "from the sweat and toil of our people."

The People's Progressive Party often seems like the image either of its general secretary, Mr. Dharma Raja Seenivasagam, or of one of its leading spokesmen, Mr. Jag-Jit Singh, president of the Penang branch. One important difference however, is that Mr. Seenivasagam (commonly referred to in newspaper headlines as Mr. S.) is Ceylonese, Mr. Singh is Indian, and the P.P.P. is largely Chinese in upper-echelon leadership and in membership. Another is that whereas Mr. S. has constituted himself the relentless gadfly of the Alliance and the Tengku, incessantly claiming the limelight with some new ploy to tease or torment them, the P.P.P. itself officially declares (in state elections at least), and a good many of its members seem genuinely convinced, that its intended role is not to topple the government or to seek power for itself but merely to provide steady, constructive criticism as a bona fide party of the opposition. To date the Tengku and his Alliance partners have not been disposed to believe that the criticism is half as constructive as it is steady, and they have not been slow to ascribe to Mr. S. and his associates dangerous tendencies, indeed subversion. Recent indications that the P.P.P. is seeking and gaining support from Singapore's victorious left-wing People's Action Party do not serve to lessen Alliance suspicions.

Mr. S. is a lawyer from Ipoh, age thirty-eight, London educated, endowed with a gift for oratory and self-dramatization. He gained his seat in the Legislative Council in an Ipoh by-election in which he defeated the Chinese Alliance candidate 5,911 to 1,820, in one of the most startling upsets the Alliance has ever experienced. He immediately proceeded to convert the Legislative Council, until then generally calm if not placid, into a sounding board off which he bounced a continuing flow of eloquent aspersions against the Alliance. He has attacked it for "squandering" huge sums of money, such as M$3 million for the Merdeka Stadium, M$750,000 for the Tengku Abdul Rahman Hall (both in Kuala Lumpur), and unspecified amounts for good will "junkets" abroad; he ridicules it for being too impractical and fearful to accept "all-expense paid" tours of the USSR's Central Asian satellites. As a result of Alliance tastes for luxury and special privileges, he says, taxes have risen to the point that the workingman has nothing left of his wages and the "ship of state is sailing on the tears and sweat of the nation." (A praoh-like "ship of state" is the Alliance campaign symbol.)

Mr. S. opposes both the Emergency Regulations and the recent Elections Offenses Bill which seem to him to be "destroying every vestige of democracy in Malaya." Mr. S. is opposed also to the new "Malayanized" educational system, under which, he declares, the schools are worse off than they were under the British. In waging an unending campaign for "truly equal" citizenship rights, he declares that he himself, for instance, is now no better than a third-class citizen of the nation he has elected and has been elected to serve. He predicts the imminent downfall of the Alliance, which, he says, is built on "suspicion and distrust" and is neglecting such necessary programs as construction of schools and hospitals in order to gratify its members' desire for luxury.

Mr. S. has been sued for libel by the Tengku, and he is frequently being identified by name as one of the most dangerous of the opposition. After provoking local U.M.N.O. organizations into demanding that he be banished, he has dared the government to find legal means to carry out these demands. He has challenged the Tengku to contest the coming elections as his personal opponent in any electoral district with a non-

Malay majority but has been answered that the U.M.N.O. party, not the Tengku himself, will decide in which electoral district the Tengku will run. When oratory and personal feuding with the Tengku fail to seize the headlines, Mr. S. resorts to such devices as reporting—perhaps accurately—that his house has been repeatedly stoned, that he has received through the mail anonymous "death threats," that he has been visited by masked interlopers, and that eggshells bearing strange devices have been left on his doorstep to induce his death through magical spells.

What the P.P.P. actually does stand for is more difficult to determine than what it is against. Its election slogan is "For Freedom and Equality." Mr. Jag-Jit Singh makes the objectives rather more specific than has Mr. S., stating that "freedom and equality" mean that "all citizens, irrespective of race, color, creed, or sex, get equal treatment," and that his party will advocate a "single citizenship . . . without any special privileges for any class of persons." In other words, the P.P.P. demands for the Indians and the Chinese exactly the same privileges as are accorded to the Malays. It is especially interested in gaining acceptance of the principle that "the best man should be given the top post," regardless of racial origin. It is also interested in "multilingualism," in other words, retention of English, Chinese, and Tamil on an equal footing with Malay as languages of the government and of the schools. The party has made the conventional campaign promises regarding hospitals, schools, economic development, and the like, always stressing the necessity for equality rather than special privilege.

Before the 1955 elections the Party Negara looked like a more serious challenge to the Alliance than any of the others. Its failure then to elect even one candidate and its dismal performance ever since have now led most observers to write it off as an insignificant political force. The widely publicized fact that it managed—or rather mismanaged—between March and November 1957 to allow 97 of its previous total of 257 branches to disappear without a trace has led forecasters to conclude, quite rightly, that it did not stand a chance in the 1959 elections. It has just been resoundingly defeated even in its home state of Johore. The party is still extant, however, if not exactly prospering, and it numbers among its adherents some prominent and capable persons, notably its founder, Dato Sir Onn bin Ja'afar, who is of historic if not immediate consequence to the development of the Malayan nationalist movement.

Dato Onn and his party made the psychologically disastrous error of campaigning in 1955 on a platform calling for the postponement of independence until a considerable body of experienced leaders had been trained. They have recently made the equally disastrous error of campaigning to demolish the "personality cult" of "Abdul Rahmanism," to cut the Federation loose altogether from "Great Britain's apron strings," and to strengthen Malaysian influence by opening the doors wide to Indonesian immigration. Neither the party nor the Dato, however, is incapable of quick and strategic change of policy, although recent evidence indicates that change may be less strategic than it is quick.

Dato Onn, now sixty-four, is a member of a leading court family of Johore. English-educated and English-minded to the point where he felt compelled deliberately to set about reorienting himself as a Malay, he served before World War II in important posts in the government of the Sultan of Johore and gained the reputation of being a most eloquent orator. He made himself the first well-known Malay nationalist leader and was the founder and first president of the U.M.N.O. When the U.M.N.O. rejected his proposal that it convert itself from a Malay to an interracial party, he resigned his membership. He set about founding an interracial Independence for Malaya Party which soon dwindled in importance in comparison with the U.M.N.O. and with the tripartite Alliance which presently emerged. Dato Onn then organized the Party Negara which commanded a considerable following among intellectuals and feudal aristocrats but so little popular support that even he himself failed to win a seat in the 1955 elections and failed again in a 1958 by-election.

The various opposition parties have been confronted, both before and during the elections, with obstacles such as would seem dismally disheartening save for the fact that the political sweepstakes are never irrevocably lost even after the race has been run. They can always retain the hope that the Alliance will fall apart, or that Alliance policies of moderation and compromise will prove vulnerable, or that some quite unforseen circumstance will intervene to change the whole political picture. The Alliance, however, has taken steps to ensure that the forseen, at least, will be forestalled. These steps have included not only an effectual shoring-up of the Alliance's own organization but two important measures to prevent the opposition from adopting the obvious tactics of subversion and coercion.

The first of these measures was a new Elections Offenses Bill designed expressly to prevent rabble-rousing campaigns and voting-place intimidation. The other was the arrest and detention in raids of October

6

Intra-Alliance Crisis

September 6, 1959

UP THROUGH June 19, 1959, just two months before federal election day (August 19), the Malayan politicial barometrical readings had been consistently fair for the Alliance Party. It had won decisive victories in seven out of eleven of the state elections and had finished in a draw in one other; it had lost only 29 out of 204 constituencies and only one of these to the Pan-Malayan Islamic Party, the party most openly inimical to Alliance principles of interracial harmony. Then on June 20 the barometer suddenly shifted to change of weather, four days later to foul, and on July 9 to stormy.

What happened was this: (1) On June 20 the Alliance was "shocked" by the loss of 17 out of 24 state legislative assembly seats in the state of Trengganu, 13 of them to the P.M.I.P., 4 to the Party Negara which had adopted much of the P.M.I.P. line. (2) On June 24 it was "stunned" by the loss of 28 out of 30 seats in Kelantan, all 28 to the P.M.I.P. (3) On July 9 it experienced a sensational intra-coalition clash between the United Malay National Organization and the Malayan Chinese Association.

Between June 20, the day the troubles really began, and July 15, the day the various parties filed their candidates for the August 19 federal elections, the Alliance managed fairly well to pull itself together again. On June 27 it won 23 out of 24 seats in a final state election, that in Pahang, and it began immediately to deploy its forces in order to repair its position in the other two East Coast states of Trengganu and Kelantan. On July 12 it "resolved" the U.M.N.O.-M.C.A. crisis, after leaders of each party had threatened to go it alone in the elections. It was able by

July 15 to come up with a joint list of Alliance candidates jointly endorsed by U.M.N.O., M.C.A., and M.I.C. On election day, August 19, although it made less forceful showing than most forecasters had originally predicted, it did manage to win 74 out of the total of 140 seats—hold it, the slip is the Tengku's, made in a press conference immediately after the elections. The Alliance actually won 73 seats. One seat remains to be contested in a by-election in September, but the Alliance is so confident that it is reserving a ministerial post for the Alliance candidate.

It seems now, with the advantage of historical perspective, that each of the unexpected developments that set almost everyone's forecasts to fluctuating might have been at least half anticipated. The East Coast, home of the most tradition-bound segment of the Malayan population ("ignorant," says the Tengku), is the area in which appeal to Malay racial, Muslim religious, anti-Chinese, and antigovernment feeling ("poisonous politics," says the Tengku) might be expected to have greatest effect. The fact that the P.M.I.P. and the Party Negara had made poor showings there in the past distracted the attention of political observers and non-P.M.I.P., non-Party Negara politicians to areas where, on the basis of previous record, opposition to the Alliance seemed likely to be stronger. The inherent conflict between U.M.N.O. and M.C.A., furthermore, has from the very first made the maintenance of cordiality within the Alliance a delicate operation which calls for a flame thrower in one hand and a fire extinguisher in the other. Despite apparent determination on both sides to cooperate during the elections and to settle outstanding differences later, it was only to be expected that pressure would build up to settle differences first, cooperate later. This was especially to be expected on the part of M.C.A. when and if election returns began to show that the U.M.N.O. was vulnerable.

The exposure of serious U.M.N.O. weakness on the East Coast was not the decisive but was, nevertheless, the precipitating factor in the U.M.N.O.-M.C.A. crisis, and the circumstances warrant elaboration. The East Coast is a Malay stronghold, an area in which the Chinese population is relatively small and the M.C.A. participation in the elections relatively unimportant. The Alliance losses on the East Coast, therefore, were U.M.N.O. losses, and U.M.N.O. friends and foes alike were quick to assess the significance of these reversals to their own interests.

Among those who took a quick reading of the East Coast situation were top leaders in the M.C.A.—specifically, the "young, dynamic, ambitious" group who had come into positions of prominence in 1958 along with the new president, Dr. Lim Chong Eu. Within days of the Trengganu U.M.N.O. defeat in the state election, with such dispatch that the drafting may already have been well advanced before either the Trengganu defeat or the developing Kelantan situation was clear, Dr. Lim had sent a "secret" letter (dated June 24) to Tengku Abdul Rahman. The letter elaborated upon M.C.A. fears of Malay racialism and defined the immediate steps which it regarded as urgent for maintenance of the M.C.A. position in the Alliance and Chinese interests in the nation. These steps were: (1) The allocation to the M.C.A. not of 28, as then proposed, but of 40 out of 104 candidacies in the federal elections and the actual selection of M.C.A. candidates by the M.C.A. itself rather than by the Alliance National Council. (2) The inclusion in the Alliance election manifesto of a clause stating Alliance determination to uphold the Federal Constitution as it now stands, thus precluding any amendments prejudicial to Chinese interests. (3) The inclusion in the manifesto also of a pledge to review Federal education policy in the light of the experience of the last two years, with matters on which the Chinese feel very strongly—language, examination standards, and job opportunities —to receive special consideration.

The Tengku delayed in replying to Dr. Lim's letter, pressure built up rapidly within the M.C.A., and the course and chronology of the resulting U.M.N.O.-M.C.A. crisis were as follows:

July 9: Dr. Lim's "secret" letter to the Tengku was mysteriously "leaked" to the press. The M.C.A. working committee met in a "stormy session" from which the top "loyalist" party leaders pointedly absented themselves. After the meeting the M.C.A. "rebel" leader announced: "If we do not succeed in getting what we think is fair, the M.C.A. general committee will . . . decide whether we fight under the Alliance banner or our own." Late in the afternoon Dr. Lim met with Alliance leaders and reported afterward: "Negotiations are tough, but this is the time for us to remain calm." That evening Dato Abdul Razak, Prime Minister and Deputy Chairman of the U.M.N.O., announced: "Tomorrow you will read bad news concerning the Alliance. . . . The existence of the Alliance is being threatened by a section which has doubted the sincerity of U.M.N.O. . . . If this section continues to cast its doubts on our sincerity, we shall be forced not to cooperate with them."

July 10: Tengku Abdul Rahman released his reply to Dr. Lim's letter which he described as "an ultimatum" and a "stab in the back." "I . . .

have even gone to the extent of saying that I would risk losing every seat rather than lose the friendship of the Chinese," he wrote, "because, in my mind, that is the only guarantee for the happiness, peace, and prosperity of our country." Nevertheless, the Tengku and the Alliance rejected the M.C.A. letter and announced that the Alliance was prepared to contest the elections without the support of the Lim Chong Eu group of the M.C.A. Later in the day Dr. Lim paid a personal call on the Tengku and delivered his own written reply. In it he declared, to practically everybody's surprise: "I realize that I have a fight on my hands to sustain the spirit of democracy within the M.C.A. and that there are forces within the M.C.A. who apparently seek to destroy the good relations that hitherto prevailed between the M.C.A. and U.M.N.O. . . . it is my intention to try with every effort that I command to have a showdown with the M.C.A. itself. . . ." To the press Dr. Lim added that he was not personally responsible for the release of his "secret" letter and, further, that the "decision to release the letter was very unwise and untimely and tantamount to a breach of faith with our partners."

July 11: Daylong consultations occupied the leaders of each party.

July 12: At an U.M.N.O. General Assembly, Tengku Abdul Rahman stated his terms for settlement of the crisis: withdrawal of the Lim letter and expulsion of those M.C.A. members responsible for creating the crisis. At midday Dr. Lim had luncheon with the Tengku and they reached an understanding. The Alliance would "probably" allocate 32 seats to M.C.A. The nomination of M.C.A. candidates would be left to the Tengku ("because of the shortness of time"), but the Tengku would consult with Dr. Lim on the Chinese names; no education proviso would be inserted into the party manifesto, but an "administrative directive" would be published on the subject "as soon as possible." That evening the Central General Committee of the M.C.A. decided by vote of 89–60 to accept the Abdul Rahman-Lim understanding.

July 13: The crisis was jointly declared at an end, with the M.C.A. remaining within the Alliance and the Alliance (the Tengku) preparing a joint list of candidates for the elections. (Final allocation: U.M.N.O. 69; M.C.A. 31; M.I.C. 4.) But two top M.C.A. leaders resigned from the party and many others—mainly the young "rebels"—were soon to follow.

July 14 and later: M.C.A. leaders continued to resign and to denounce the party. Dr. Lim declared his personal position "completely untenable" and his political career "finished." "Never in my life have I been misunderstood or abused so much within so short a time. Never, too, have I so quickly lost my faith in so many people." Dr. Lim called neverthe-less for full M.C.A. support for the Alliance but soon presented his own resignation as president and then, on August 1, "for reasons of health," departed for eight months in Great Britain. Tengku Abdul Rahman presently admitted (July 25) that "In U.M.N.O. itself there were certain unhappy and dissatisfied members striving to agitate others. . . . We will now try to expose such elements and either expel or ask them to leave." The U.M.N.O.-M.C.A. crisis, it seemed, was by no means over, and the internal situation in the U.M.N.O. was comparable in kind but not degree to that in the M.C.A.

Despite all inter- and intra-party difficulties, the Alliance, as noted, successfully contested the federal elections. Despite the crisis, it won almost as many seats as it might have been predicted to win once the East Coast state election reverses were known. The nationwide percent-age of Alliance votes, however, dropped from 55.5 per cent to 51.4 per cent (a net decrease of 72,176 votes). The drop seemed to be accounted for largely by shifting of the Chinese vote plus, perhaps, cynical decisions not to vote at all. Nevertheless, in 40 predominantly Chinese electoral districts the Alliance won 24 seats; of 31 M.C.A. candidates, 18 were elected; conversely, of 14 M.C.A. "rebels" running as indepen-dents, only 2 won. The shift of Chinese votes, which was considerably less dramatic than many observers expected, seems to have resulted in gain mainly to the Socialist Front which registered a net increase of 48,136 votes and elected 8 candidates, among them 4 Chinese. It resulted in gain also for the independents who registered a net increase of 18,367 votes and elected 3 candidates, all Chinese. The P.M.I.P. seems to have gained little in the interim between state and federal elections, noteworthy statistical gains in some states being canceled out by losses in others.

The net effect of the P.M.I.P. victories and of the M.C.A. crisis is as yet difficult to assess. The Alliance is undoubtedly weakened internally and it now commands a smaller and less enthusiastic parliamentary majority than it might otherwise have had. Both U.M.N.O. and M.C.A. continue to experience internal difficulties. The Tengku has been called a dictator by Malay as well as Chinese opponents, and full restoration of his personal prestige and restoration of Chinese-Malay cooperation will take time. The M.C.A. has lost significantly in leaders, members, and public appeal. Many prominent Chinese are even less convinced than before that the chronically disrupted M.C.A. organization is either in the right hands or on the right track. The Alliance Government now resumes office with virtually the same cabinet and the same policy as before, but it faces a 22 per cent opposition—a badly divided opposition, to be sure—as compared with a 2 to 4 per cent opposition heretofore. Still, in comparison with other governments in Southeast Asia, the Alliance Government of the next five years promises to be healthy, stable, and progressive.

"I wouldn't have believed it," the Tengku kept exclaiming after the elections, referring not only to U.M.N.O. reverses on the East Coast but to the fact that in his own home state and home constituency 5,542 out of 18,572 people actually voted against him and for his P.M.I.P. rival. He wouldn't have believed either that the M.C.A. crisis could have arisen when or as it did. He has had a shock, and so, have a great many others, and the result may be not, as many people predict, the death of the Alliance, but the regeneration of the Alliance on the basis of more truly reciprocal interracial understanding.

7

P. A. P. Preview

May 11, 1959

"Bedlam" and "pandemonium" are the words which sober citizens of the city of Singapore are likely to use in describing the goings-on in Singapore's first fully elective City Council. The description fits from the time the council did not quite assume office on December 23, 1957, when demonstrators got out of hand and the mayor-to-be was arrested, up to April 18, 1959, when it did not quite dissolve upon the abrupt resignation of the mayor and all other People's Action Party (P.A.P.) councilors to campaign for election to the more prestigious State Legislative Assembly. To be sure, there were intervals of relative calm. Whenever the mayor prolonged the sessions of the Council to twelve hours or more, with unrelenting verbatim translation into four languages of even the most casual comment and aside, the Council tended gradually to become less explosive and more somnolent. There were also moments of efficient, expeditious action; when the mayor was late or absented himself, the opposition occasionally took over to hustle through decisions which the mayor later arbitrarily rescinded. There were times when the Council heard eloquent pleas for more conventional parliamentary procedures, times when it forebore political and personal bickering to attend to the business of municipal housekeeping, and one time at least when the members—many of them mistakenly believing the mayor was about to be defeated for re-election—devoted themselves to mutual felicitation for statesmanlike conduct.

But overall the record of the Council is one of parliamentary procedures flagrantly breached, personal invective indiscriminately employed, municipal business subordinated to political showmanship, even of all business suspended in favor of attack upon personal and political enemies. It was a fifteen-month-long demonstration on the part of one political party, the P.A.P., and of the P.A.P. mayor, of their determination to slug away at "vested interests" and to cozy up to the "working classes." The total record of the P.A.P.-dominated Council and the P.A.P. mayor supports the preliminary judgment of the P.A.P.-excoriated *Straits Times* that the conduct of their administration was going to be a sort of marathon "Guy Fawkes Day Revels." It also bears out a flippant remark of Singapore's ex-Chief Minister David Marshall, that whereas one ordinarily says "My lord the Mayor," in the case of "Baby" Ong, Singapore's thirty-two-year-old *maire térrible*, one says instead, "My God, the Mayor!"

The record of Singapore's first fully elective City Council, not much worse than that of Penang's, say, and perhaps comparable to that of more than one important American municipal body of more mature years, is of real political or historical significance primarily for a single reason: it may afford a preview of what can be expected if the P.A.P., as its leaders predict and its opponents fear, comes into power in the Singapore state elections of May 30, 1959, or, for that matter, if it should by any chance be defeated in 1959 and come into power later. It does not necessarily follow, of course, that a P.A.P.-dominated State Legislative Assembly, intrinsically a far more dignified body than the City Council, would be as irresponsible or as disorderly. Nor does it follow that the P.A.P. cannot either mend its ways or alter its tactics or appear in a new and more favorable light, once it is accepted as inevitable. Nevertheless, as Singapore's 1,445,929 citizens, or at least the more reflective minority of them, look back over the record of the 1957–1959 P.A.P.-dominated City Council and contemplate the very real probability of a 1959–1964 P.A.P.-dominated State Legislative Assembly, many of them tend to find little that is reassuring either in retrospect or in prospect.

The history of the City Council and of the mayor to date can perhaps be capsulized in the account of the scenes of farce and melodrama which distinguished the first two days of P.A.P. control. On December 23, 1957, Ong Eng Guan and his twelve P.A.P. colleagues (all but one of them in their twenties) arrived together at the City Hall at 2:15 P.M. for the 2:30 inaugural ceremony and for the election by the thirty-two councilors of a new mayor. Outside the City Hall were crowded hundreds of youthful P.A.P. supporters, most of them Chinese high school students, almost all of them equipped with long strings of fire-crackers. Clenched-fist salutes, shouts of *"Merdeka,"* and explosions of firecrackers greeted the P.A.P. councilors as they launched themselves upon the city. The disturbance attracted the notice of the police, who ordered the crowd to desist from setting off fireworks unless they could show police permits to do so. The P.A.P. councilors declared that they were in charge there and that they themselves authorized the fireworks. In the scuffle which quickly developed, demonstrators, councilors, and police got pushed around. In a matter of minutes—so efficient is the Singapore police force—the mayor-to-be and three other councilors, along with fourteen of their more boisterous supporters, had been packed off in a police van to the central police station. The other P.A.P. coun-cilors and a considerable number of demonstrators and onlookers sprinted or taxied after them. Meanwhile, in the Council chamber, non-P.A.P. councilors, the top-echelon civil servants, and a gallery packed with 500 P.A.P. supporters waited for the ceremonies to begin.

At 3:00 P.M. the Council secretary informed the members that for lack of a quorum the meeting had lapsed. Minutes later Ong Eng Guan and his fellow P.A.P. councilors, now released from police custody, came racing back to the City Hall and demanded that the session be opened. While city officials went into consultation, Mr. Ong and his followers took up their seats in the council chamber, amid wild cheering from the galleries. "No power on earth," shouted Ong Eng Guan, could halt the meeting. For the next hour and a half they sat there, acknowledging ovations from the galleries, refusing to listen to official explanations that it was both impossible and unconstitutional to reconvene the Council, that another session would be called for 2:30 P.M. the following day. Former Chief Minister David Marshall enlivened one of the duller intervals by strolling in, dressed in his familiar white bush jacket, armed with a huge hammer which he waved to the galleries, and then confer-ring mysteriously with Mr. Ong and his colleagues. At 4:30 P.M. Mr. Ong took the rostrum, gave a double clenched-fist *"Merdeka"* salute, announced that the meeting was adjourned until 2:30 P.M. the next day, and acknowledged the cheers of his followers.

On December 24, long before the scheduled hour, the portico of the City Hall was jammed with P.A.P. supporters. When the new councilors entered the chamber the crowds packed in along with them, overflowing the galleries onto the main floor, creating a scene of "bedlam" such as the "august City Hall" had never known before.[1] The outgoing City Council president, Mr. J. T. Rea, and the Council mace-bearer had to elbow their way in through a back door, then through a densely packed crowd of union members, schoolboys, hawkers, trishaw riders, and street urchins, the last barefooted and dressed only in flimsy cotton drawers. When the City Council president and the mace-bearer finally made themselves visible, the P.A.P. members refused to rise to their feet according to accepted custom but "sat staring stonily ahead," their coatless, open-collared shirts contrasting with the regalia of the city officials and the coat-and-tie propriety of the opposition. As the meeting finally got under way, the spectators packed themselves in around the chairs of the councilors, leaning over their shoulders and breathing down their necks, the little boys all but crawling between their legs. The crowd clapped for the P.A.P. members, booed one of the opposition members when he began speaking in English, and settled in to enjoy the show. Mr. Ong, as had been arranged in advance, was elected mayor and, as had not been prearranged, promptly called for and got a vote for removal of the council's US$5,000 mace, "a relic of colonialism," and then demanded that a public-address system be rigged up so that he could speak to the crowds outside the chamber and lead them in shouts of "*Merdeka.*" The whole performance left others than the staid Singapore colonials a little dazed.

The principal tactics of December 23–24 have been part of the mayor's and the Council's basic repertoire ever since. These tactics are as follows: (1) machinations, such as packing the portico, the gallery, and at times the floor of the chamber with P.A.P. supporters disciplined to turn disorders on or off at signal; (2) stunts, such as the provocation to arrest; (3) personal insult, such as the deliberate affront to the City Council president; (4) crises, such as the refusal to accept the fact that the session had lapsed; (5) vote-jerkers, such as rejection of the mace. (It was later joined in the council storeroom by the gold chain of office, two Union Jacks, and the Queen's portrait.) Machinations, stunts, insults, crisis, and vote-jerkers are interlocking devices, of course, and by no means original with the P.A.P.; but most of the Singapore municipal administration's recent actions and policies can be conveniently classified under

---

[1] The quotes are from the *Straits Times* which ran headlines "Council Chaos Again" and "May God Protect Singapore City." Continuing *Straits Times* reports on the Council, described as "malicious" and "distorted" by the P.A.P., have proved, nevertheless, an extremely valuable source of factual material for this report.

these headings, with the leading role being taken by Mayor Ong Eng Guan as a sort of P.A.P. Huey Long.

Mayor Ong, age thirty-two, is small, scrawny, shock-haired, and boyish looking. He holds a Bachelor of Commerce degree from the University of Melbourne—not, however, as an Australian Government or Colombo Plan scholarship student, the Australians take pains to make clear. He majored in accounting but specialized in politics, being the organizer and prime mover of the Asian Students' Federation of Melbourne and an avid observer of Australian trade-union operations. He returned from Australia to Singapore planning to prepare a thesis for the Master of Commerce degree, but he quickly became much more involved in helping to set up the P.A.P., in directing labor union activities, and in studying Chinese and Malay in order to reach the non-English-speaking "masses." Outside P.A.P. circles he was a virtual unknown until suddenly he appeared as a top P.A.P. winner in the December 1957 municipal elections. Even within the P.A.P., where he had served as party treasurer, he was none too highly regarded, being in the anomalous position then as now of standing for a middle-of-the-road P.A.P.ism. He is more cautious and law-abiding than the extremists such as Lim Chin Siong, the twenty-five-year-old, Chinese-educated, Communist-affiliated labor-union leader who has been jailed since October 1956 for his part in allegedly subversive activities and labor riots. He is less proper and equivocal than thirty-six-year-old Cambridge-educated Lee Kuan Yew, general secretary and spokesman of the party who alternately or simultaneously threatens and soothes the "vested interests."

Mayor Ong has built up the somewhat inconsistent but always colorful characterization of himself in the minds of the Singapore citizenry as a man of simple tastes, violent temper, and prickly ego. He turns himself and his P.A.P. constituency out for Council meetings and other public occasions in the light-trousered, open-collared shirt "party uniform," scorning official regalia, such as velvet, wig, mace, and gold chain ("the chains of colonialism and the mantle of despotism"). He refuses cigarettes, cocktails, race-meet invitations, and golf-club memberships. He short-cuts the niceties by shouting at those who would prolong a discussion he would rather see closed, favoring such succinct phrases as "Shut up," "Sit down," "Get out," or just "Blab, blab, blab!" He storms through the City Hall, loudly and publicly reprimanding any city employee who seems to him not to be devoting himself enthusiastically to the "people's interests." His combustion point is particularly low when it comes to "expatriate"[2] city officials committing such heinous offenses as walking a dog into City Hall, or when it comes to "helpless and indigent" hawkers being rounded up by the hundreds on charges of peddling their wares without licenses and blocking the arcades in Singapore's business and shopping centers. He declines to move into the official mansion, preferring his own "simple cottage"; he avoids the use of official limousines, preferring his battered five-year-old Morris Oxford; but he takes affront when he is assigned a high license-plate number, or is seated far down the table or in the back row of the platform, or is relegated by protocol to a position less conspicuous than that accorded, say, to the visiting Prime Minister of the Federation of Malaya. He takes obvious satisfaction in exchange of red-carpet official visits with the mayor of Djakarta and in turning up beside Prince Philip at the splendid functions which marked the Prince's state visit to Singapore in February of this year—this latter appearance despite a publicly-announced P.A.P. boycott of such imperialist shows.

The P.A.P. municipal councilors' bent toward machination became apparent from the moment the December 21, 1957, municipal vote was counted. The P.A.P. had succeeded in electing thirteen out of its fourteen candidates, as compared with the Liberal Socialists' seven out of thirty-two and the Labor Front's four out of sixteen. It had done so by the elementary political device of entering into a pre-election understanding with the Labor Front, which then controlled Singapore's Legislative Assembly, to cooperate in the defeat of the Liberal Socialists who controlled the City Council, and then playing each party off against the other. It had polled only 29 per cent of the popular vote, as compared with the Liberal Socialists' 32.5 per cent and the Labor Front's 16 per cent. It had managed, however, very adroitly to split the opposition and thus to seat more P.A.P. councilors than both other leading parties combined.

The Labor Front, which had recently exposed and—its leaders believed—purged the P.A.P. of Communist infiltrators, thus converting the party into an acceptable ally, required a little time to recover from the shock of the elections. Then it began to talk of P.A.P. "betrayal" and "subversion" and to propose a strongly anti-Communist, "Anti-

2 An expatriate, or "expat," is a civil servant or government contract employee of the Federation of Malaya or of Singapore who is not a local citizen. He is usually a British carry-over from the previous colonial regime.

P.A.P. Front" with the Liberal Socialists, to ensure that the state elections, first slated for late 1958, now for May 30, 1959, did not go the same way. The Liberal Socialists put the blame on the Labor Front and acted skittish about an anti-P.A.P. coalition. The Singapore branch of U.M.N.O. (United Malay Nationalist Organization, the Federation of Malaya's paramount party), had also entered into a preelection understanding with the P.A.P. but had emerged less scarred, having placed three out of its four candidates. It continued to a considerable extent to cooperate with the P.A.P., even while its leaders were declaring that U.M.N.O. and P.A.P. ideologies were incompatible and were eying rather queasily the open and successful efforts of the P.A.P. to proselytize some U.M.N.O. leaders and members.

Just one year later, after the Labor Front, the Liberal Socialists, U.M.N.O., and others had had many enlightening lessons in P.A.P. tactics and had decided and announced that a "non-Communist" but heavily Communist-influenced P.A.P. was the gravest hazard to the new state of Singapore, they had yet another jolt. The City Council was again to hold its annual election of mayor, and this time it had been rigged in advance by the non-P.A.P. majority that Ong Eng Guan would be thrown out and U.M.N.O. Councilor Seyed Ali Redha Alsagoff put in. When the votes were counted, however, Mayor Ong had won, seventeen to fifteen. It developed that the two decisive votes had been cast by a Liberal Socialist and an U.M.N.O. member, in defiance of party instructions. Each was promptly expelled from his party, but that did not make Seyed mayor.

Meanwhile, of all the P.A.P. machinations in the Council which had proved educational but not quite educational enough to the opposition, the most sensational had centered upon the party's efforts simultaneously to dispense with the highly paid services of expatriate employees and to increase the mayor's own pay to match the total pay and allowances of the former City Council president. The previous City Council, as one of its last acts, had adopted a "Malayanization scheme" whereby remaining expatriate officials would be gradually retired, with liberal compensations for "loss of career," and their places taken by Singapore citizens. The P.A.P. demanded that the plan for compensation be scrapped, that the exodus of expatriates be speeded up, and that local personnel of P.A.P.'s choice be put into the expatriates' jobs. It demanded also that the mayor's salary be raised from the purely nominal monthly "allowance" of M$200 he received as a theoretical one-day-per-month city councilor to a basic monthly salary of M$2,000 plus a monthly M$5,000 which he would use at his own discretion to contribute to party funds and to dispense among "widows, orphans, or distressed members of the families" of civic employees.

The P.A.P. councilors got their way, for the most part, with regard to the expatriates; but they failed to put across the 3500 per cent salary hike, gaining only a modest 1000 per cent raise to M$2,000. Regardless of the justices or the injustices of the case—and it must be taken into consideration that the expatriates are highly-qualified professional men difficult to replace locally, and that the mayor had himself converted his job from one of chairmanning monthly Council meetings to one of full-time political and administrative activity—the P.A.P. tactics were noteworthy. The mayor packed the galleries with P.A.P. supporters who interrupted proceedings to cheer P.A.P. spokesmen and to boo and heckle the opposition. He extended the Council meetings day after day and far into the night. Several sessions which convened at 2:30 P.M. did not adjourn until about 2:00 or 3:00 A.M., the mayor threatening to continue them to 2:30 P.M. the following day if necessary. He instituted a system of multiple interpretation into English, Chinese, Tamil, and Malay, so that what started as a talkathon ended as an interprethon and threatened, according to opposition members, to reduce them to financial ruin for neglect of their businesses or professions and to physical collapse by reason of boredom and lack of sleep.

The mayor's own energies, however, seemed inexhaustible. He attempted to take over the duties of half a dozen full-time city employees in supervising the day-to-day city business. He managed to stage a non-stop series of political stunts that kept him and his party constantly in the limelight as the protectors of "the people's interests." He established a Complaints Bureau at which he listened to and personally investigated charges of corruption lodged against city officials of the previous or the present administration. Every Saturday morning from 10:00 to 1:00, until he was forced to discontinue the practice—because, he said, the Council would not appropriate the funds necessary for a clerical staff— he held a "Meet the People" session. At these he personally met and talked with an average of 140 persons per session, listening sympathetically to still more complaints of corruption and of inefficiency. He appointed an "efficiency officer" charged with widely publicized responsibility to discharge "redundant" workers and speed up paper work and thus to save the citizens "millions of dollars" and "delay, inconvenience, and discourtesy" in transacting business at city offices. He staged a public debate to defend his stand on protecting unlicensed hawkers against police interference. He seized upon Singapore's long-standing difficulties with Indonesia and its worry about the lucrative but dwindling Indonesian trade to stage an exchange of expensive "good will" visits with the mayor of Djakarta. Mayor Sudiro made the helpful suggestion that since Singapore's airport was maintained primarily for the convenience of the rich and the alien, the city could happily and greatly increase its revenue by imposing a stiff landing fee. Mayor Ong gave Mayor Sudiro his assurances that the P.A.P. backed Indonesia in its claims to West New Guinea and would quickly improve Singapore-Indonesian relations once it came to power in the Legislative Assembly.

Such behavior as this would have attracted plenty of attention without any special effort on the mayor's part, but he left little to chance. He set up a City Hall information bureau, headed by a highly paid newspaperman from Hong Kong, staffed by an increasingly large number of employees whose salaries, the opposition protested, might better be charged to the mayor's personal and the P.A.P.'s party publicity accounts than to the Council. The mayor's highly controversial appointments and patronage, not only of his information chief and staff but of a private secretary who had once been detained for months as a "subversive," served to highlight the personal insults and personal feuding which have been a prominent feature of the current municipal administration. A frequent and prominent protagonist on both sides has been Mr. P. C. Marcus, present city administrative officer, once a P.A.P. man and Mayor Ong's choice as "efficiency officer" to whip the civil servants into line. By early 1959, however, Mayor Ong was accusing Mr. Marcus of "betrayal of responsibility" and "dereliction in duty," and Mr. Marcus was entering suit against the mayor on charges of libel.

In brief, what had happened was as follows: The mayor had returned from his January tour of Indonesia to discover that two difficult issues had not been forgotten during his absence, as he had evidently hoped, but had grown to quite embarrassing proportions. First was the matter of recurrent electrical power failures, following the departure—expedited by the mayor—of some twenty-nine expatriate engineers and the failure to fill many of the vacancies with Malayan employees. Second was the arrest and prosecution of hundreds of unlicensed hawkers, the special protégés of the P.A.P. whose policy, indeed, has been unkindly described by an U.M.N.O. opponent as one of "cuddling the hawkers."

The mayor now announced that the power failures would not have occurred if Mr. Marcus had kept him properly informed of the true state of affairs in the electrical power department. The expatriate city electrical engineer, on retiring from his post nine months earlier, had warned that the electrical development program in Singapore had been "hampered" and the work of his department "frustrated" by political interference, and many others had publicly stated that the situation had since become critical. But Mr. Ong had apparently heard none of this. The P.A.P. had first alleged sabotage; now it was Mr. P. C. Marcus, the city administrative officer, who was held accountable. At the same time the mayor publicly denounced the "persecution" of the hawkers and pinned the responsibility on the superintendent of the Markets and Hawkers Department who happened, by coincidence, to be one L. A. Marcus, brother of Mr. P. C. Marcus, the city administrative officer.

Mayor Ong's feuds with his staff and with opposition members in the Council have been matched by his feuds with "colonial" and "vested" interests in Singapore City. One of the adversaries he lit into earliest was the Royal Island Club. Mayor Ong and the P.A.P. councilors decided that the club's golf course should be opened to the Singapore public for picnics. The club was uncooperative. The mayor threatened to cancel the leases on 199 acres of the 224 which the club occupies. The club still declined to hold open lawn to the picnickers. After a heated debate in which Liberal Socialist members pointed out that, after all, the club had a very sizable investment and high overhead, and that there were plenty of other picnic places nearby, the Council decided by vote of 20–11 merely to request the club to open its grounds to Sunday picnickers. The club still refused. The City Council thereupon voted to cancel the leases but quickly discovered that it was not legally empowered to do so but had to appeal to the British governor for authorization. The governor seemed singularly obtuse as to why such cancellation should be necessary. So the Royal Island remains, for the time being at least, a golf club and not a public picnic ground, as does another club which was also put on notice. It was probably the latter club, largely European in membership, that Mayor Ong was gunning for in the first place, people speculate; but Mayor Ong, who is no golfer, apparently got a little mixed up and went after the club to which the P.A.P. general secretary, Lee Kuan Yew, belongs, as also do some nine hundred prominent Asians and relatively few Europeans.

The Mayor and the P.A.P. councilors had managed to contrive so constant a series of artificial crises in city affairs that by late 1958 real crises began to arise. At the October 31 meeting of the Council the mayor found that the non-P.A.P. members could not be steam-rollered into passing a minor measure he proposed. He even found himself subjected to a vote of censure for unparliamentary procedure. He responded by calling upon the Council to resign and then walking out of the chamber, accompanied by his P.A.P. contingent. When he returned fifteen minutes later, he discovered that instead of resigning the opposition had elected a temporary chairman and proceeded with business. The mayor arbitrarily rescinded the decisions taken in his absence, thus provoking strong protest. At the mid-November meeting he once more called for the Council to resign, and in the ten-hour debate which followed he resorted at one point to calling in the police to remove a disputatious opponent. The Council once more declined to dissolve itself but instead began planning how it might get itself a new mayor in the upcoming December annual election. As already noted, the mayor and the P.A.P. very neatly circumvented this plan, and in any event the mayor had already proposed a new and different plan of his own. He proposed to designate five to ten councilors to constitute themselves a sort of city "cabinet," each member working full time in a sort of "ministerial capacity" to supervise the functions of the various departments. The mayor also wanted a "speaker" to preside over the council meetings—the function which had formerly been conceived as the primary responsibility of the mayor himself. This plan to transform the City Council into a little state assembly failed to take hold, but a few months later he had another idea: the Legislative Assembly would itself assume the functions of the municipal council. He and his P.A.P. contingent in the Council would resign to run for election to the Assembly, a plan which they have just put into effect, although not altogether from choice.

By early 1959, as a result of its interminable feuds and crises, the City Council had all but broken down as an operating body. Then, in March, it was stripped by the Minister for Local Government, Lands, and Housing, Dato Abdul Hamid, of most of its controls over staff and finance—its most "essential" powers, said the mayor. The Council had "lost the confidence" of the people, said the minister, and he was exercising his constitutional right and duty to intervene. It was time, the minister decided, and the Legislative Assembly agreed with him, for a full-scale investigation of what had been going on in the City Hall. As one of its last acts before being prorogued in preparation for the May 30 elections, the outgoing assembly passed a motion for appointment of an investigative commission before which evidence is now being heard with regard to alleged instances of maladministration—none of the evidence, as yet, very damaging.

The mayor and the P.A.P. councilors, meanwhile, after having declared they would not fall into Dato Hamid's "trap" to provoke them into resigning, have resigned nevertheless. They have left the city administration to a rump council whose members have just come forward with proposals which, if adopted, would far out-P.A.P. the P.A.P. in reducing various license fees, authorizing leniency in prosecution of hawkers, conferring free or low-cost electricity, water, medical services, and the like upon the "workers." The P.A.P. itself declares that all City Council decisions taken in the absence of Mayor Ong will be revoked when the P.A.P. comes into power in the Legislative Assembly and thereupon "scraps" the municipal council altogther. For reasons of economy and efficiency, they declare, the City Council functions will be centralized under the new Legislative Assembly, with the Council of Ministers reorganized and enlarged to handle city as well as state matters.

It can be argued that a small island-city-state like Singapore does not need both a state and a city administration. It also can be argued that the P.A.P. mayor and his colleagues are honestly more concerned about the efficiency which might result from the merger than the prestige and power which would attend Legislative Assembly membership. What can scarcely be denied, however, is that the mayor and the P.A.P. have used the P.A.P.-dominated city administration primarily as a political weapon for winning the 1959 Legislative Assembly elections. Their city policies have been designed basically as vote-getters, and their present performance in jettisoning the virtually defunct City Council, which their tactics have brought close to total disintegration, is quite obviously a device whereby they themselves can collect the votes they feel they have earned.

This performance, of course, is practical politics. The P.A.P. from the beginning has proved itself master of this art at which its opponents have on the whole shown themselves maladroit. The degree of mastery—also the degree of actual benefit which the P.A.P.-dominated Council has conferred upon this city of almost one million—may be judged from a brief summary of the Council's practical accomplishments. The following itemization may not be completely inclusive or completely up-to-date—some statistics are hard to get under the new city administration—but it gives the general picture.

The December 1957–April 1959 City Council has installed about 150 new public water faucets (as compared with about fifty the year before it came into power) from which the residents of Singapore's crowded kampongs can get free water within easy walking distance of their houses. It has put up between thirty to fifty new bus-stop shelters (previous figures unavailable) where patrons of the public transport system can take cover from sun or rain. It has reduced electricity rates for the small consumer. It has planned, or has actually put into service, five public dispensaries, three mobile clinics, three crèches, two infant and maternity clinics, all of which charge merely nominal fees. It has halved the annual license fees for taxi drivers, bus workers, and trishaw riders. It has gone easy on prosecutions of unlicensed hawkers. It had built two new city markets, started several new swimming pools, and proposed the establishment of new public parks—including one on the site of the Royal Island Club's golf course, and another that would cover the present parking lot in the middle of Raffles Place, Singapore's busiest and most congested shopping and traffic area. It has also streamlined the processes of billing and receiving payment for public utilities, which used at times to be tedious and for that matter still is. It has perhaps improved upon courtesy and service in government offices. It has also conducted a three-antis campaign, first "anti-spitting," then "anti-litter," then "anti-pests," all reminiscent in method and purpose, to many non-P.A.P. observers, of recent campaigns thought up in Peking.

With this record to go on, and with claims of a M$3.8 million budget surplus for 1959 (whereas others declare categorically that the City Council has bankrupted itself and is carrying on only because it floated large loans), Mayor Ong has announced the glorious success of his policy of "Priority for the Poor" and a "New Deal for hawkers, taxi drivers, and trishaw riders."

What Mayor Ong chooses to overlook, and what his critics seem to forget also, is that the P.A.P.-dominated City Council inherited a city which was already by far the most splendid and progressive of Southeast Asia. Singapore was already provided with the area's most adequate and modern public utilities; the most numerous, spacious, and well-kept public parks and playgrounds; relatively well-developed and well-equipped health, police, and educational services; good roads; spectacular business district developments; and vast new housing areas in the suburbs.

Singapore was also, to be sure, a city of congested, badly constructed, unsanitary Chinese and Malay slum areas. There, among the slum dwellers, for the price of a few water faucets, electric lights, bus-stop shelters, reductions of license fees and remissions of fines, the P.A.P. has made its play for the votes of some 50,000 hawkers, taxi drivers, trishaw riders, and their wives and children. The shrewdness of the P.A.P.'s play is as undeniable as the actuality of the limited benefits it has offered—benefits which the previous administration had been extending, too, but without fanfare; benefits which the opposition parties now promise on their election platforms, but with a "me too" overtone.

One does not require a Univac to compute the P.A.P.'s basic election chances: it had 29 per cent of the votes in the 1957 municipal elections; it has gone after a minimal 10 per cent additional votes in the crowded slum areas in which the great majority of new, inexperienced, impressionable voters are living. Even with 29 per cent of the votes, it placed thirteen out of thirty-two municipal councilors, gained control of the Council, and added a fourteenth P.A.P. councilor in a later by-election. Now that the opposition parties are more divided than ever—largely as a result of P.A.P.'s shrewd tactics for preventing the formation of an anti-P.A.P. front—even with a modest 39 per cent of the vote in the next elections, P.A.P. stands to control a majority of the Legislative Assembly seats. The bus riders, hawkers, taxi drivers, and trishaw men, the free-water users, and all their families, including the superannuated twenty-one- to twenty-five-year-old Chinese high school students who remain in school for lack of jobs, give every evidence of intending to vote for the P.A.P.

8

P. A. P. Victory

THE BRITISH Crown Colony of Singapore, founded by Sir Stamford Raffles just 140 years ago, is scheduled on June 1, 1959, to become the state of Singapore, still dependent upon the United Kingdom in matters of foreign policy and defense, but independent in all matters of local self-government except internal security. On May 30, under compulsory voting regulations which attach a M$5.00 (US$1.65) penalty to failure to exercise the franchise, the 600,000 registered voters of this 225-square-mile island will go to the polls to elect the 51 members of Singapore's first fully representative Legislative Assembly. From a total of 194 candidates, 160 of them put forward by a bewildering conglomeration of thirteen political parties, the other 34 running as independents, Singapore's new, inexperienced, and largely Chinese working-class electorate will pick the men who are to rule Singapore, presumably for the next five years, under a constitution which provides for a parliamentary-cabinet system of government.

In Singapore today, among many of the educated, prosperous, thoughtful sector of the population—Chinese, Indian, Malay, and European—there is less jubilation than apprehension as the long-awaited local self-government actually comes in view. The reason, in three letters, is P.A.P. The P.A.P., or People's Action Party, is commonly—but perhaps pessimistically—considered to be the next worst thing to a Communist party under Communist leaders, and the P.A.P. alone among Singapore's thirteen political parties now exhibits really effective leadership, organization, discipline, program, campaign drive, or widespread public appeal. The P.A.P. may not sweep the elections, as its leaders predict and its op-

ponents warn, but if there is any such thing as a foregone political conclusion, then the P.A.P. is going to win more seats than any other party,
more seats than any coalition of opposition parties, and more than a clear
majority.

The prospect of a P.A.P. victory has been clearly apparent for well
over a year, and the reaction to it has seemed more fatalistic than galva-
nizing on the part of large segments of the public. British officials have
long opposed outright grant of independence on the grounds that this
minute but highly strategic island, with its Chinese population of one
million (out of a total of 1,446,000), is highly vulnerable to Communist
subversion or seizure. They now seem to regard the P.A.P. show of
strength alternatively as evidence of the validity of their worst fears or,
more commonly, as evidence that their policy of "calculated risk," "bold
experiment," "abiding confidence," and "refusal to intervene" will somehow generate public response of sufficient stability to offset the apparent
P.A.P. menace. Top officials of the Federation of Malaya next door,
outspoken anti-Communists themselves, make no secret of their dismay
at the prospect of a "non-Communist" (the equivalent, many say, of
pro-Communist) P.A.P. victory in Singapore. They now cite Singapore
extremist political trends as compelling evidence in their arguments
against accepting Singapore into the Federation and thereby creating a
Chinese, perhaps soon a Communist Chinese, instead of a Malay racial
preponderance. In recent months non-P.A.P. political leaders in Singapore have become increasingly alarmist—indeed, at times almost hysteri-
cal—over prospects of a P.A.P. "totalitarian state." They have used the
P.A.P. threat, to date at least, less as an incentive for cooperation in a
long-proposed "Anti-P.A.P. Front" than as a basis for reshuffling and
refurbishing a lot of feuding political factions, all of which aspire to
rival and defeat the P.A.P. but seem much more likely to rival and
defeat each other.

The appraisal seems grim; but it may be quite unrealistic. In any
analysis of Singapore's political prospects it is only prudent to hedge
alarmist speculation by pointing out a few relevant, complicating, and
even ameliorating circumstances. First, Singapore's politics and Singapore's politicians are at least as volatile and as stagy as any other
country's, and election-day surprises have been the rule rather than the
exception in recent years. Second, Singapore has already for a number
of years been practicing a rapidly increasing measure of self-government
with a very great deal of P.A.P. participation, and the results, if far

from uniformly happy, have been reassuring in that, in general, moderate leaders still can and do somehow manage to prevail. Third, the P.A.P. itself, although vulnerable to Communist infiltration, need not necessarily be judged pro-Communist. If it comes to power, it may be compelled for the sake of preserving peace and order to adopt strong measures against extremist and Communist elements. It has already intimated, indeed, that it will do so. Fourth, Singapore, like a great many other areas, has survived crisis after crisis in recent years. Recurrent predictions of disaster, as, for instance, at the time of the bloody riots of May 1955 and October 1956, have presently transformed themselves into predictions of the imminent dawn of a new and more glorious era.

The description of the true nature and dimensions of the P.A.P. threat to Singapore necessitates an analysis of Singapore's tangled political record over the past few years. The account can be simplified by lumping its dozen or more parties into three groups and by viewing the many conflicting forces through the personalities of three men.

The three political groups, all of them professing to be socialist in base, most of them interracial in composition, can best be differentiated as the extremist, the radical, and the moderate. The most extreme of the extremist, in other words the Communists, along with certain Communist-front labor and student unions from which they draw their popular support, have been declared illegal. By application of "Emergency" (1948) or later "Public Security" (1955) regulations which permit arrest and detention without trial of suspected subversives, they have been kept fairly well under control, but not without sporadic resurgence and outbreaks into violence. Many of the Communist leaders and of the more outspoken Communist sympathizers have fled into the Malayan jungles where they have been killed or captured; others have gone to jail, where many of them still remain; still others have gone underground and infiltrated other organizations, the most vulnerable and receptive of which has been the P.A.P.

Of the radical groups, the strongest by far is the People's Action Party. Founded in November 1954, it has drawn many of its present leaders from the more Marxist-minded of the dissatisfied young Chinese intellectuals, much of its popular support from the left-wing labor unions and student organizations which it has sponsored. The P.A.P. has passed through phases of both more and less reliance upon revolutionary violence as a primary tactic. It now seeks to gain control of Singapore by "democratic processes." It describes itself as a "revolutionary" but "non-

Communist" party, dedicated to a policy of "Priority for the Poor." It is being reorganized on the basis of mass membership and strictly selected, highly trained leadership "cadres." It is determined to eliminate "colonial vestiges" and to develop a true "people's government." In answer to accusations that it is Communist or pro-Communist and the enemy of anti-Communists, its leaders now draw the following distinctions: "We differ from the Communists in that we do not believe that a revolution by violence can succeed in Malaya. . . . We differ from the anti-Communists in that we consider the present social and economic order intolerably unjust and that it is the purpose of the democratic social revolution to sweep away these injustices as rapidly and as vigorously as conditions permit. . . . To be anti-Communist is to play into the hands of the reactionaries. It is a sterile, negative policy and disastrous in the end."

In competition with the P.A.P. and with each other there have sprung up various "labor" parties, radical, but on the whole anti-Communist in base. They have drawn their strength from the less extreme labor unions, their leaders from the Chinese professional classes and from the Singapore-born British or Eurasians who profess much the same political point of view as the British Labour Party. Most significant of these parties in the past was the Labor Front, actually a coalition, but an unstable coalition which lost its leaders progressively to the less or the more extreme factions. The Labor Front was the government party from 1955 to late 1958. It stood originally for almost complete independence from Great Britain, swift conversion to a welfare state, and an immediate end to the undemocratic Emergency Regulations. Its leaders found themselves involved in such incessant compromise between what they regarded as ideal and what they knew to be practical that the party gradually lost its sense of cause and of identity, and even its founder left it to establish a new party.

The third group, the moderates, traditionally members of the Progressive, the Socialist, the Liberal Socialist and similar parties, lately including as top leaders former members of the Labor Front, is now being identified more and more commonly as the "right" or even as the "conservatives." Their leaders include many of the younger, better educated, more civic-minded Chinese, frequently well-to-do but determined to depart from the tradition of the Chinese *towkay* who has been interested almost exclusively in commerce. They include also a high proportion of the well-educated, extremely articulate Indian group. They are associating themselves with the better educated, more prosperous members of Singapore's Malay minority, as contrasted with the P.A.P. which makes its biggest play among Malays for the "oppressed" and the "exploited." These "moderate" or "rightist" parties all advocate a welfare state, and they seek to achieve it by gradual and democratic rather than revolutionary processes. They propose to improve the condition of the common man but at the same time to preserve private capital investment and liberal democratic principles. Most significant of this group of parties at present is the newly organized Singapore People's Alliance which has drawn its leaders mainly from the now decimated Labor Front and the much weakened Liberal Socialists. The S.P.A. has attempted, unsuccessfully to date, to set up an "Anti-P.A.P. Front" in order to save Singapore from its present "uncertainty, insecurity, and gloom" and to protect it from the "poverty, adversity, and perdition" which a P.A.P. administration would allegedly induce.

The extremist, the radical, and the moderate parties, whose platforms seem frequently to blend, since all advocate some form of independence and a social welfare system, and whose membership seems fluid and indeed at times interchangeable, are best typified in the personalities of three key Singapore politicians: the moderate radical, Lee Kuan Yew; the radical moderate, Lim Yew Hock; the complete individualist, David Marshall; with some incidental mention of the extreme extremist, Lim Chin Siong.

"Flamboyant," "ebullient," "exotic," "contentious," "theatrical," "eloquent," "impassioned," "unpredictable," and "egocentric" are the adjectives used most often to describe David Marshall. He does his best to live up to the billing. His best, as Chief Minister of Singapore from early 1955 to early 1956, brought him close to political ruin and physical collapse and Singapore to the brink of chaos. Marshall resigned from politics "for keeps," then recuperated in resort spots in Switzerland, vacationed in Japan, recouped his fortunes by return to an extremely lucrative Singapore law practice, re-entered politics, and now acts less and less like a man whose thirst for national and international prominence has been slaked, let alone satiated. He has just recently organized a new party, the Workers' Party, described as "honestly nationalist and honestly socialist," and proposes to campaign vigorously in the coming elections. Characteristically, he has chosen to contest the elections in the same electoral district with the present Chief Minister, Lim Yew Hock, so that with regard to Singapore's two most prominent anti-P.A.P. candidates, in the next government it will be a case not of both-and but of either-or.

David Saul Marshall, age fifty-one, was born in Singapore of Iraqi-

Jewish parents. He was educated in Singapore Catholic, Protestant, and city schools. He distinguished himself as a brilliant student even though twice before the age of twenty-one he suffered physical breakdown and was each time sent off to Switzerland to recuperate. In 1930 he decided to try his luck as a salesman, and in spite of the depression he did so well that by 1934 he had saved enough money to go to England to study law. He completed his law studies in record time, being admitted to the bar after only eighteen months. He returned to Singapore to set himself up in practice and was beginning to prosper when World War II broke out in the Pacific and he was interned by the Japanese—his second internment incidentally, his first having been as a young boy in Baghdad during World War I when he was picked up together with his father by the Germans. After Singapore's liberation in 1945, Marshall resumed his law practice and became the colony's most successful criminal lawyer, specializing in courtroom histrionics that almost inevitably gained the acquittal of his clients. He was earning, according to common report, at least US$4,500 per month as a lawyer when he decided suddenly in 1954 to go into politics and to contest a US$170 per month seat as legislative assemblyman. In order to fight the April 1955 elections the better, David Marshall organized the Labor Front which, to everyone's surprise (including, he has admitted, his own), won ten of the twenty-five elective seats. As head of the party which made the strongest showing in the elections, he became Singapore's first Chief Minister.

In his election campaign Marshall had promised independence, social welfare benefits, and repeal of the "Emergency" Regulations. He had scarcely assumed office before he found himself confronted with widespread and continuing disorders such as made fulfillment of his promises impossible. Wildcat strikes and mob action were instigated by labor agitators and Chinese high school students, themselves inspired by P.A.P. officials—a long series of unhappy and violent episodes which proved that Marshall, despite his rhetorically vigorous stand against subversives, could not maintain order in Singapore or gain concession of independence from Great Britain. After the failure of his 1956 "Mission to London" to negotiate for limited independence, Marshall returned to Singapore to resign from the post of Chief Minister. As his successor he recommended the present Chief Minister and his 1959 election rival, Lim Yew Hock.

Marshall is most famous in Singapore for his brilliant, if often brilliantly purple, speaking style, whether in the Legislative Assembly, in press conferences, or merely among the droves of guests with whom he surrounds himself on Sundays at his bachelor home on a palm-fringed Singapore beach. "It would be foolish," he declared in one of his most famous Legislative Assembly debates, "for Singapore to beguile herself with sophisticated phrases of liberty, democratic rights, and freedom, while we go down the drain." He seems, nevertheless, to many of his opponents still to be so beguiling himself, as, for instance, when he brands Singapore's new constitutional agreement "a shocking document," a "fraudulent" legal device, "nothing but an instrument to retain Singapore as a colony in fact, but with a few trappings of power." Such self-rule as Singapore will achieve on June 1, 1959, is for Marshall a "farce." "The truth," he said, "is that now Singapore will be crushed between the Imperialist millstones from London and Kuala Lumpur." David Marshall, alone among prominent Singapore politicians, still seems to buck the trend toward Malayanization of Singapore, but not quite to the extent of advocating, as he used to, something that might be called the "Singaporeanization" of Malaya. He also bucks the trend toward declaring him an ornamental and diverting has-been in Singapore politics, and if he defeats Lim Yew Hock in the elections, he will establish his point.

If David Marshall is flashy and erratic, his successor as Chief Minister, Lim Yew Hock, age forty-five, is sober, earnest, modest, and patient, but also warmly friendly in private contacts and increasingly fluent and forceful in debate. A third-generation Singapore-born Chinese, Lim is an Overseas Chinese Horatio Alger hero who rose from poverty and obscurity to prominence and relative affluence in twenty-five years of unremitting hard work. He was graduated from Singapore's Raffles Institution (high school) in 1931 as a government scholarship student of superior academic record. His first job was as a clerk in the Singapore offices of the Imperial Chemical Industries at a salary of US$8 per month. His next was as a stenographer in the Singapore Cold Storage Company at somewhat better pay. The Japanese invasion interrupted his climb upward, and he had to work during the occupation as a seller of charcoal, a job which gave him plenty of contact with the laboring classes. After the war he returned briefly to stenography, then became active in labor-union work, and in 1946 became secretary to the Singapore Clerical and Administrative Workers' Union. As one of the most prominent of Singapore's postwar labor-union organizers, Lim was given a British Council grant to visit England in 1947 and a State Department grant to visit the United States in 1951. In 1948 he was named by the governor as a member of the Singapore Legislative Assembly. In 1951, as a candidate of the Labor Party to which he had just switched from the Progressive Party, he won one of the twelve elective seats in the Assembly, polling the highest majority of votes of any candidate. He continued to be active in trade-union activities and he attended various local and international labor conferences, including the I.L.O. regional conferences in New Delhi in 1948 and Tokyo in 1952.

Lim Yew Hock in 1954 at age forty, despite heavy official responsibilities, decided that it was still not too late to further his education and to qualify for the bar. He therefore entered the law office of David Marshall as a part-time clerk and law student. He did not become a lawyer, but he did become a close associate of David Marshall's in organizing the Labor Front. He became one of the Labor Front candidates for the Legislative Assembly in the 1955 elections, and when the Labor Front won the elections he was appointed Minister for Labor and Welfare. When Marshall resigned as Chief Minister, Lim became his successor—reluctantly, at Marshall's behest, and against the advice of many of his associates who thought him neither brainy nor tough enough for the job.

One of Lim's earliest acts after assuming the Chief Ministership was to pose for press photographers as he squatted down to sweep up cigarette butts dropped by his colleagues during a Labor Front meeting. After this one experiment in David Marshall-style publicity, an experiment which provoked more ridicule than acclaim, he gave up the staged stunt and even the synthetically animated camera smile in favor of his more accustomed métier—hard, constructive work.

Whereas Marshall had been inclined, on the whole, to be soft on subversives and had thereby invited disorders, Lim turned tough. When the subversives attempted disorders, he jailed the ringleaders, dissolved the recalcitrant unions, tolerated no nonsense or intransigence on the part of the rebellious Chinese high school students, deported a few pro-Communist Chinese spokesmen to China, and in a surprisingly short time restored confidence at home and abroad in Singapore's political sanity. In London in April 1957 he negotiated successfully with the British Government for limited home rule.

Lim returned to Singapore to be acclaimed by major segments of the public and vigorously to defend his concessions to Great Britain against such accusations as David Marshall's that they constituted political "fakery." Despite, or indeed partly because of, his success in negotiation of local self-government, the Labor Front was beginning to melt away for lack of a program. In any event, since it had been hastily patched together in the first place and run on a strictly *ad hoc* basis—finances, for instance, being completely disorganized—Lim was compelled to set about reorganizing and revitalizing the party. Personal frictions and political differences made the job appear hopeless. Increasing realization of the P.A.P. strength and threat made drastic action imperative. In November 1958, after many preliminary maneuvers, Lim himself, together with his close associates, jettisoned the Labor Front and launched the new Singapore People's Alliance which, by commanding the support of the Liberal Socialists in the Assembly, became the government party. The objective of the S.P.A. has been to unite all moderate political parties and leaders in Singapore to fight the P.A.P. in the coming elections and thus "to save the people of Singapore from fear, slavery, and dictatorship."

Lim Yew Hock, the onetime US$8 per month petty clerk, now the US$1,325 per month Chief Minister, comes increasingly under both political and personal attack by the P.A.P. Some of his closest associates, furthermore, are being shown up in public investigation to have been rather casual in their acceptance and utilization of political gift funds, allegedly American in origin. Lim Yew Hock himself is charged with tolerating this deplorable state of affairs. The public evidence to date suggests that neither the S.P.A. nor Lim Yew Hock may be able either to refute or to top the accusations. Certainly they are dealing with a formidable and a formidably documented adversary—Lee Kuan Yew.

Lee Kuan Yew, age thirty-six, the original organizer of the P.A.P. and its leader in the Legislative Assembly, is young, shrewd, and tireless. He can, if he chooses, be both personally agreeable and publicly appealing. He is also brilliant, as has been apparent at every stage of his still brief career. He was an outstanding government scholarship student in Raffles Institution, Raffles College, and Cambridge University. He took the prized "double first" in law at Cambridge and returned to Singapore to become a notably successful lawyer in partnership with his brother, to become exceedingly active in labor union matters, to enter politics "on the side of the people," and to set about mastering Mandarin and Malay in order to communicate with his chosen constituency. He has also— as his critics point out—married the daughter of an extremely wealthy Chinese merchant, settled into a luxurious modern home, become a fancier of fine cars and a keeper of fine Alsatian dogs. His bills for dog food alone, his S.P.A. opponents declare, run to more than the total income of a day laborer.

Since October 1954, when he and a few of his associates brought the

P.A.P. into existence before an enthusiastic audience of labor-union members and Chinese high school students in Singapore's historic Victoria Hall, Lee Kuan Yew's personal record is almost inextricable from that of the party. Like that of the party itself, it is a strange and far from clear composite of undeviating pursuit of power and of conflict and contradictions as to how power might best be attained. The P.A.P. calls itself a "disciplined" party in which members "place their lives in each other's hands," but its discipline has not prevented sharp disagreement in top party echelons over basic strategy and tactics. Lee Kuan Yew, the P.A.P. founder and—most of the time—its general secretary, has not always been in control; but in the internal struggles for power and decision Lee has now emerged on top as the exponent of the "moderate" as contrasted with the "extremist" party factions. On such crucial party issues as the limit of safe relationships with the Communists, the relative roles of violence vs. vote-getting, and the permissible degree of cooperation with the opposition, Lee's stand becomes clear, or at any rate fairly clear, from a brief recapitulation of the key Singapore events of May 1955, October 1956, and August 1957, after all of which Lee remained at large while a good many of his close associates went to jail.

It was in May 1955 that the P.A.P. first fully disclosed its early tactics and strength. Shortly after the Marshall government took office, some of the P.A.P. leaders, working through certain labor unions and Chinese high school student unions in which Lee and his associates were the most active organizers, staged a succession of disorders that rocked Singapore. First came a series of wildcat strikes that paralyzed the colony, then a series of mob scenes which terrified it and resulted in at least four deaths, then a series of defiances of government authority on the part of the Chinese high school students who had been the most active agitators of mob violence. Chief Minister Marshall took belated, reluctant, and inconclusive action. He denounced the P.A.P.; he pushed through the "Preservation of Public Security Ordinance" which made repressive action possible, and he achieved an uneasy and partial moratorium on disorders. But he exhibited such signs of weakness, as, for instance, in rescinding his order for expulsion and discipline of student ringleaders, that labor and youth agitators felt confident enough, under continued P.A.P. leadership, to prepare for still graver disorders to follow. Lee Kuan Yew, it is to be noted, was absent from the scene during the actual period of the disorders and was not personally implicated in them.

October 1956 brought a repetition of scenes of violence, only on a larger scale and with different prelude and sequel. Lim Yew Hock had replaced David Marshall as Chief Minister and had adopted a policy of getting tough with subversives and suspected subversives. Lim's government took action in September to arrest extremist union leaders, to deport pro-Communist Chinese teachers, and to dissolve Communist-front organizations. There followed in October a series of labor-union strikes, street riots, and Chinese high school sit-down strikes, with students barricading themselves in their schools in defiance of teachers, parents, and police and then, upon being forcibly driven out, joining bus company strikers, secret society members, and others in terrorizing the city. The government called in armed troops to help the police restore order; the death toll rose to at least fourteen, and only by resort to armed patrols and tear gas were the authorities able to clear the streets, the Chinese high schools, and the barricaded union headquarters of agitators armed with rocks, clubs, iron bars, and bottles. The Lim Yew Hock government had acted swiftly, decisively, and effectively to reassert its authority. The labor unions and the students were brought under control. The P.A.P. denounced the government both for "ineffectiveness" in permitting the riots and for "brutality" in putting them down. But the P.A.P. itself had been badly shaken and had a major job of party reorganization to do. Among the hundreds of persons arrested in connection with the riots were many of the leaders of the P.A.P.-dominated unions, including fourteen top P.A.P. members or officials. Most important among them was Lim Chin Siong, P.A.P. member and spokesman in the Legislative Assembly, leader of Singapore's most powerful trade union, and Lee Kuan Yew's chief rival for power in his own party. Lee Kuan Yew himself had recently resigned from the Legislative Assembly; he had not been associated with the disorders; he had retired briefly from the Singapore limelight at precisely the time when it was most discreet not to be there.

Whether as a result of the P.A.P.'s nearly disastrous implication in the October riots, or whether as a result of challenge to his own position within the party from Lim Chin Siong and other late-comers of all but open Communist affiliation, Lee Kuan Yew now led the P.A.P. in a sharp swing to the right and manifested a marked interest in parliamentary as opposed to people's action tactics. "Let those who talk glibly about armed revolution consider carefully the consequences of armed revolution, both to themselves and to their compatriots. If they are still convinced that the only way out is armed revolution, let them leave our party, go across the Johore Causeway, and take up arms in the Malayan jungle." This was the Lee-inspired official policy statement of the P.A.P. as it set about rebuilding its strength.

The party rebuilt itself with astounding speed. It did so, however, with the help of organizers who adopted all the familiar Communist tactics—songs, slogans, dances, plays, study clubs, women's groups, youth organizations—all with high ideological content of recognizably Communist inspiration. It did so against the increasingly open and outspoken disapproval of Lee Kuan Yew himself who, in mid-August 1957, declined to accept re-election as party general secretary. Lee, along with five of his closest associates in the "moderate" faction, accepted the six "member" posts on the party executive council but relinquished the six "officer" posts to the "extremists." Then, coincidentally perhaps, although many people in Singapore are inclined to doubt it, after an interval of exactly ten days, during the night of August 22–23, 1957, the Lim Yew Hock government swooped up thirty-five subversives. The haul included politicians, trade-union leaders, newspapermen—and the six new "officer" members of the P.A.P. executive council, also thirteen other prominent P.A.P. officials of the "extremist" group. Simultaneously the government released a White Paper documenting its charges that the P.A.P. had been infiltrated by Communist and pro-Communist elements, describing recent P.A.P. Communist-type promotional activities, asserting that if no precautionary measures had been adopted the result would have been "more rioting and bloodshed."

Lee Kuan Yew, who had so opportunely dissociated himself in advance from his "subversive" colleagues, quickly resumed office as party general secretary and his activities as party leader in the Legislative Assembly (which he had just re-entered upon winning a June 29 by-election). He revitalized the party to the degree that just four months after its August fiasco it won thirteen out of the fourteen seats it contested in Singapore's municipal elections. Then, by shrewd coalition, the P.A.P. gained control of the thirty-two-member City Council and secured the election by the council of a P.A.P. mayor. Ever since then Lee Kuan Yew has been understandably confident and cocky about his own and his party's chances in the 1959 state elections, never more so than in recent weeks as his election campaign has got rolling and his strategy for assuming control by parliamentary means has proved, at the outset at least, almost as upsetting and unnerving to the opposition as he could have hoped.

The 1959 Lee election strategy, insofar as it has been revealed, has involved two simultaneous phases, one of offense, the other of defense. The offense has involved sensational "revelations" that top members of the S.P.A. are both corrupt and incompetent. The defensive tactic—forced upon him, he says, by S.P.A. efforts to produce a red herring to distract public attention from its own peculations—has been to cry "Shame!" "Political Prejudice," and "Abrogation of Democratic Rights" in response to S.P.A. action and investigation with regard to the P.A.P. mayor and City Council. The two stories are involved and interrelated and are best taken up chronologically along with recurrent references to some of the chief actors, namely, P.A.P. Mayor Ong Eng Guan, S.P.A. ex-Minister of Education Chew Swee Kee, and Singapore U.M.N.O. (United Malay National Organization) Deputy Chief Minister Dato Abdul Hamid bin Haji Jumat.

The record of the P.A.P.-dominated City Council under the P.A.P. mayor, Ong Eng Guan, has given Singapore a preview of what it may have to expect under a P.A.P.-dominated Legislative Assembly. The mayor, a young man of thirty-two, who looks and—according to his critics—acts like a brash schoolboy of nineteen, has gone in for what the great majority of Singapore political observers refer to as "stunts," "antics," and "vendettas." The City Council, under his guidance, has devoted itself to "soaking the privileged and the competent," and staging "circuses" for the needy and inexperienced, giving far less attention to the routine matters of city management than to operating a "People's Court," a "Gestapo," and a continuous public "brawl." Mayor Ong and his P.A.P. colleagues in the Singapore Municipal Council so flagrantly violated all standards of official decorum that Dato Abdul Hamid, Deputy Chief Minister and concurrently Minister for Local Government, in mid-March stripped them of most of their powers and called for a full-scale investigation of their administrative record. Already, however, the P.A.P. had seized the initiative with demands for an investigation of certain financial involvements of the S.P.A., its top leaders, and their coalition associates. But that, basically, is the story of S.P.A. ex-Minister of Education Chew Swee Kee and of U.M.N.O. Deputy Chief Minister Abdul Hamid, both of them outspoken opponents of the P.A.P., Mayor Ong, and Lee Kuan Yew.

At a P.A.P. rally on February 15, 1959, Dr. Toh Chin Chye, chairman of the P.A.P. and Reader in Physiology at the University of Malaya, made a highly important "disclosure." It was an open secret, he said, that a certain S.P.A. minister had received M$500,000 (US$165,000) from

American sources for use in furthering political objectives, that the money had been put on deposit with an American bank in Singapore, that an income-tax investigation of the account had been started and then mysteriously suspended. The Singapore press headlined the story. The S.P.A., the United States Consulate General, and the First National City Bank of New York's Singapore branch issued denials. The P.A.P. stuck by its charges, with Lee Kuan Yew a few days later naming Minister of Education Chew Swee Kee as the recipient of the money and demanding an investigation. For three weeks Singapore speculated whether this was just another P.A.P. stunt, strategically timed for election purposes. Then on March 3 Chew Swee Kee resigned his post. Mr. Chew, a chartered accountant and long-time civil service employee in the police courts and in the Income Tax Office, also a leader of the trade-union movement and a former president of the Labor Front, was one of the last who might have been expected to stumble over the technicalities of financial accountability, but the conclusion seemed inescapable that Mr. Chew had stumbled.

On the next day, March 4, in a "drama-packed" session of the Legislative Assembly, Lee Kuan Yew declared that it was indeed Minister Chew who had received the money, not only the M$500,000 originally cited but M$300,000 at an earlier date, that Income Tax Office File Number 47909/GS was a key document in the case. Furthermore, he said Mr. Chew had recently purchased a M$30,000 house and the Acting Comptroller of the Income Tax Office had suffered a heart attack and died as a result of worry over the whole affair.

Chief Minister Lim Yew Hock, stung beyond endurance by Lee's attack, thereupon somewhat naïvely revealed that he had had Lee's assurance that if Chew resigned the P.A.P. would engage in no further "mudslinging." Now, he declared, since Lee had betrayed his word and was playing at "dirty politics," he, too, would play at the same game. "Now let the truth be told," he said. "The action this government took against subversives was an attempt to cleanse the P.A.P. for the good of the P.A.P." The antisubversive clause of the constitutional agreement— a clause which the P.A.P. and other political groups have never ceased publicly to denounce since it bars many P.A.P. and other political leaders accused of subversive activities from contesting the 1959 elections—was the result, said Lim Yew Hock, of a meeting with the British Colonial Secretary at which Lee Kuan Yew had been present. The strong measures which he, Lim Yew Hock, had taken against Singapore subversives, thereby calling down abusive criticism upon himself, had not been on his own responsibility alone. "I did so many things for the good of the country, and I did so many things for the good of the P.A.P. after discussions with the P.A.P. Such is politics in Singapore today."

It was Lee's turn to deny, and he did so, first explosively, then sadly. "It distresses me to see the Chief Minister in this state. In his agony as the final blow has landed, he resorts to countersmear." The Chief Minister, he appended later, was "a master plotter" and a "very cunning and very wily man."

All this excitement was prelude to the final stormy five-hour session of the Legislative Assembly on March 19 before it was prorogued for the elections and to a sensational set of investigations which followed. The debate covered all the recent developments in Singapore, and it resulted in appointment of commissions to investigate not only the Chew bank account but the leakage of secret income tax information, also the conduct of the mayor and the City Council.

During the next couple of weeks, as the newly-appointed investigation commissions started to work, Lee Kuan Yew himself directed a good deal of the cross-examination. By the adroit maneuver of challenging the impartiality of the chairman of the Commission of Inquiry in the City Hall case, Lee managed temporarily at least to stall the investigation and to focus attention not on accusations against the P.A.P. mayor but on accusations against the previous "colonial" city administration. By a combination of intuition and luck, he managed to bring out in the Chew hearings that the M$800,000 contribution had indeed been received, that the middleman in the transaction had allegedly been Archbishop Paul Yu Pin of Taipei and New York, and that the money, rather than being devoted exclusively to party purposes, had gone into some rather questionable private enterprises. One of these was a tin-mining company in which, to Lee's immense satisfaction, it turned out that free shares had been issued to one Madame Kartini binte Abdul Mulok, promptly identified as the wife of Deputy Chief Minister Dato Abdul Hamid bin Haji Jumat.

The S.P.A., which had been making real headway in forming an anti-P.A.P. Front, began to lose rather than to gain ground. The Liberal Socialists and others, who had already joined up or had been on the point of joining up, decided apparently not to risk affiliation with the S.P.A. but to go it alone. They entered their own candidates in electoral districts where S.P.A. candidates are entered as well, and what might have been a clear-cut contest between the P.A.P. and an Anti-P.A.P. Front has become a many-sided one in which, unless last-minute withdrawals occur, the anti-P.A.P. vote will be divided two, three, four, or five ways.

The Singapore U.M.N.O. branch, recently regarded as an almost certain supporter for the S.P.A., all but fell apart as a result of the "scandal." The Singapore U.M.N.O. executive committee, after long secret sessions, first cashiered Dato Hamid as party chairman and party candidate, then, after last-minute emergency consultations with representatives especially dispatched to Singapore from Kuala Lumpur, reinstated him. But both in cashiering and reinstating Dato Hamid, Singapore U.M.N.O. suffered loss of other prominent members and of public support. Despite its eventual appearance of solidarity, the party was unmistakably torn by conflicts such as re-emphasized its recent trend toward splits, defections, insubordination, and even cooperation on the part of individual members with the P.A.P., despite the central office ukase that U.M.N.O. cooperation with the P.A.P. was "unimaginable."

The week prior to April 25, when all election candidates had to register, was a period of most undignified, disorderly, and contradictory political maneuvering on the part of almost every party except the P.A.P., which made an ostentatious display of confidence, solidarity, and enthusiasm. It staged a total of thirty-two rallies on Sunday, April 19, as compared with very few for the demoralized S.P.A. It climaxed the week by fielding a total of fifty-one candidates, one for each electoral district, instead of the forty that had previously been intimated and predicted. The S.P.A. entered thirty-nine; the Liberal Socialists thirty-two; U.M.N.O./M.C.A. (Malayan Chinese Association) thirteen; six other parties two to five each, with thirty-four independents bringing the total to 194

The P.A.P. has acquired the reputation among Singapore conservatives and moderates of being a party of "wild," "angry" young men, or, in the words of official S.P.A. publications, "power-mad politicians who exploit the poor and the needy," "warped and twisted leaders," practitioners of "intimidation and blackmail," manipulators of a "regimented riffraff" which is utilized for "booing and heckling at mass meetings," "haters of foreigners and foreign capital," "instigators of riots and bloodshed," "Communist sympathizers" who are preparing "to fleece and squeeze the working classes" after misleading them with promises of a "workers' Utopia." The S.P.A. leaders, on the other hand, along with Liberal Socialists and others of the "so-called democratic forces," are being branded by the P.A.P. as the "despicable political pawns" who make "sordid deals" with "sinister and wealthy men"; they are the "stooges" of "anonymous foreign desperadoes" who are plotting to "terrorize and plunder" Singapore but whom the P.A.P. will "seek out and destroy."

The vituperative rhetoric of the campaign serves to obscure the underlying fact that all the parties and all the politicians make the same promises to the voter: greater prosperity, real independence, and union with Malaya. Even the P.A.P. spokesmen now tend to modify their earlier threats. They have repeatedly gone on record in the past as being in favor of chucking out the British, including British armed forces (and consequently severing relationships with SEATO), clamping down on foreign-capital enterprises, and prohibiting Federation "interference" in Singapore affairs. The P.A.P. has tended of late to stress the necessity for more gradual approaches and for accommodation to the desires of the Federation. Its new policy statements have introduced topics of little if any voter appeal—a "tariff system" and "industrialization" to replace free trade as Singapore's economic base, a "common market" with the Federation, "enforced savings and reinvestment of capital," quick adoption of the Malay language, and accelerated "Malayanization" of the civil service. Other parties, too, have been much given of late to talk of "tariffs" and "industrialization," "socialization," and "Malayanization." The ordinary voters are more interested in higher wages, better housing, and improved electrical, water, transportation, educational, and health services—all of which all of the parties promise them.

It has become apparent that a very great deal of the difference between the non-P.A.P. parties is not that of programs but of personalities. It could well turn out that a great deal of the difference between the P.A.P. and "the rest" is the difference between, say, an "angry" Lee, sobered by experience and steadied by responsibility, and a "calm" Lim, visibly shaken by political adversity. Should it come to power, as most people now predict, and should it really turn its energies to solving Singapore's problems, as its leaders promise, the P.A.P. may turn out to be able to capitalize upon the undoubted personal compeence of some of its top figures. It may turn out also to be far less reckless, extremist, and vindictive than most non- or anti-P.A.P. commentators now believe.

9

P. A. P. Record

September 19, 1959

DURING the morning of June 4, 1959, there occurred simultaneously in Singapore and Johore Bahru, just fifteen miles apart, two historic processions which could scarcely have been more dissimilar, although each in its way symbolized the end and the beginning of an era. From Changi Jail, outside Singapore City, came eight newly-released political detainees, all of them prominent members of the People's Action Party (P.A.P.). Liberating white pigeons as they emerged from the prison-gateway, they delivered prepared statements about "correct political analysis and principles" and "regret for the short breach in the true and correct leadership in the party in August 1957"—when they themselves were at the helm; they pledged total support for the present party leaders and acknowledged the roar of "*Merdeka*" from thousands of disciplined P.A.P. enthusiasts as they rode in a long motorcade past waving banners and popping firecrackers into downtown Singapore.

The eight had been put into jail thirty-one months earlier for involvement in Singapore's 1957 series of strikes and riots. But on May 30, 1959, the P.A.P. won a landslide victory in the elections for the Legislative Assembly of the new and largely autonomous state of Singapore, and the leaders refused to form a government until their Changi comrades were freed. British Governor Sir William Goode capitulated to the ultimatum, gave the order for release, then officially promulgated the new Constitution and prepared to install the new government. Thus, after 140 years, British colonialism was backing down and out in Singapore, and P.A.P.-type state socialism was roaring in, confidently, vigorously, and triumphantly.

In Johore Bahru that same morning the remains of Major-General His Highness Sir Ibrahim Ibni Al-Marhum Sultan Abu Bakar, D.K., S.P.M.J., G.C.M.B., K.B.E.(Mil.), G.B.E., B.C.O.C. (I), etc., late Sultan of the State of Johore, were being transferred from the liner *Willem Ruijs,* which had brought the coffin from England, to the state palace on a hilltop overlooking the city and the Straits. As the P.A.P. leaders were celebrating at their downtown Singapore headquarters their reunion with their long absent colleagues, the Sultan's funeral cortege was beginning to move through dense crowds of his mourning Malay subjects. At the precise moment that the procession started away from the pier a black rain cloud, which had been following the tender up the Straits from ship to shore, unloosed a tropical downpour upon the mourners. "Even the heavens wept!" exclaimed the devout Muslims.

Such were the chief events of June 4. The autocratic but progressive old feudalist, Sir Ibrahim, no longer ruled in Johore, and across the causeway in Singapore there no longer remained, half allied with and half opposed to him, a government of British colonial gentlemen. And just as the new P.A.P. government is no benevolent paternalism like the British colonial system, so the new Sultan is no benevolent despot like Sir Ibrahim. The new P.A.P. government is still on the whole an unknown and unpredictable quantity, and the new Sultan has all the appearance of being a political nonentity.

The P.A.P. in Singapore and the various "people's" parties in the Federation of Malaya have replaced Sir Ibrahim in the role of gadfly to British complacency and, what is even more to the point, to British position and prosperity. But Malaya has now been independent for two years, and no dire consequences have ensued. Singapore has now been virtually independent for a hundred days, and no very dire consequences have ensued there either. The thought is passing through many minds that in historical perspective, which seems to come into focus more swiftly these days, the new regimes may ultimately appear—at least in comparison with possible alternatives—almost as mellow in terms of the mid-twentieth century as Sir Ibrahim's sixty-four-year reign now seems in terms of the late and post Victorian era.

So far as the P.A.P. regime in Singapore is concerned, however, developments have not yet been such as to encourage easy confidence. Still, the mere itemization of what has not happened is in itself reassuring. The new P.A.P. government has not renounced any of the terms of the negotiated Constitution under which it now operates and it has not given any evidence of proposing to overthrow constitutional processes. It has not turned in an exhibition of parliamentary irresponsibility, such as characterized the P.A.P. municipal administration of 1957-1958, and it has not, therefore, converted the Legislative Assembly into a political sideshow. It has not emptied the prisons of suspected subversives, subsequent to the release of the first eight, and it has assigned to only one of the eight a really high official position (as head of a new development board). It has not rescinded the special security measures under which action against political subversives is possible. It has not interfered directly in business operations, or stirred up labor or youth demonstrations, or "cuddled the hawkers" by permitting them further to congest the already busy streets and shopping areas, or agitated against the presence of the British armed forces, on whom Singapore security depends.

The very fact that the P.A.P. election victory was so conclusive was perhaps better after all, many people are beginning to think, than a mere majority or plurality win. The P.A.P. has gained and has accepted unequivocal responsibility for the peace and prosperity of Singapore. It does not have to engage in parliamentary antics to confuse its opposition and to consolidate its support. It has been forced to face and to explain the difficulties of good administration, no longer being free to promote unworkable nostrums of its own and to sabotage workable but politically vulnerable proposals of others. This does not mean that a P.A.P. government is going to be easy or agreeable for the capitalist class of Singapore or of the West to deal with. It does seem to indicate, however, that the rate of change is going to be less swift and the direction of change less sharply leftist than most P.A.P. opponents feared.

The constantly reiterated objective of the P.A.P. "to convert Singapore into a democratic, socialist, and non-Communist state" would seem from the present evidence to involve less democracy than the optimists hoped for, less communism than the pessimists feared, and a great deal indeed of left-wing socialism. The major hazard at the moment seems to be the reliance upon propaganda appeals and devices all too familiar in the "people's democracies," plus the threat that swift "socialization" may harm rather than repair Singapore's capitalist-based economy. For purposes of appraising the P.A.P. performance to date and tentatively forecasting its performance in the future, it seems useful, now that a hundred days have passed and the new government is getting into stride, to attempt to distinguish major trends in policy and action.

(1) *The P.A.P. Policy toward the Civil Service.* Singapore civil service employees, both state and municipal, local and foreign, have proved in

the past, from the P.A.P. point of view, to be distinctly intransigent. They have tended to align themselves with "reactionary" rather than "progressive" forces, to continue to stress British rather than Singapore orientation, and to resent P.A.P. interference in their hierarchy and privileges. Even before it actually assumed office, the P.A.P. made preparations for ousting "undesirable" officials and for evicting and then dismantling a lame-duck municipal administration. Then, on June 6, the morning the new P.A.P. ministers reported to their offices for work, came the first overt move. Mr. P. C. Marcus, chief administrative officer for the former municipal government and chief spokesman for the municipal employees in an old feud with the P.A.P., was informed that his services were no longer required but that his office space was—for the new Prime Minister, Lee Kuan Yew. Mr. Marcus had also been the chief agent of a rump anti-P.A.P. municipal government which had continued to function and had reversed P.A.P.-dictated decisions after P.A.P. members bolted the Municipal Council, to run in the state elections. Exit Mr. Marcus, who later started a law suit and then settled out of court for the better part of a month's pay.

Exit also during the next few days and weeks a number of "expatriate" officials (mainly British) who found their new P.A.P. supervisors and colleagues uncongenial. Enter a new apprehension on the part of the "English-educated," "English-oriented" local officials who have had it pointed out to them repeatedly and emphatically that they themselves and their psychology are relics of the colonial past. The official emphasis is now to be upon "Malayanization" of the civil service, as of the Singapore citizenry in general.

"Malayanization" is nothing new in Singapore. It has been the policy and objective of the government for the last few years. Local persons have been promoted to replace "expatriates" as rapidly as possible, and local loyalty and patriotism have been stressed in contrast with colonial or even with Commonwealth ties. But the new P.A.P.-type Malayanization now involves frequent polemics against the "English-educated" who, according to the Prime Minister, are "devitalized, almost emasculated, as a result of deculturalization." The civil service of the future, the P.A.P. officials declare, must look to the new class of "Malayans," who may be "English-language-speaking" but who will not be "English-oriented." They must be people who will have the "vitality," "self-confidence," and "integrated culture" which the present generation lacks and the new state itself will now inculcate.

The most painful assault upon the civil service, however, has not been upon its anglophilia but upon its paychecks. The ministers themselves set the example and gave the tip-off by voting themselves salary reductions. In the case of the Prime Minister, the cut came to M$450 out of a former M$3,500 (US$1,166) monthly stipend. The other ministers lost M$350 out of M$2,500 and also a M$150 monthly transportation allowance. Other civil servants were advised on June 19 that, as of July 1, their take-home pay would be reduced by a minimum of about M$10 for menial employees and a maximum of about M$400 for those in the higher grades. The cut, it was explained, would not affect base salaries but the "variable allowances" which have in the past constituted prime civil service perquisites. By this measure, it was further explained, the government would save approximately M$14 million per year, thus making up for the "extravagance" of the previous government and bringing the 1959 budget into balance.

The government has given evidence of intention to reduce other salaries that come out of state funds, those of University staff members, for instance, many of them foreign, who protest that they are contract employees whose contract terms cannot be arbitrarily and unilaterally rescinded. Government spokesmen have announced that there are plenty of qualified, competent people, local and foreign, eagerly applying for jobs in Singapore, so that anyone who doesn't like the pay cuts is welcome to resign. Many Singapore civil servants suspect that they are being encouraged to resign and that recruitment of competent replacements will not be easy. In any event, the first few rounds, perhaps the crucial rounds, of the conflict between the P.A.P. government and the civil service which it inherited from the colonial and semicolonial administrations have gone indisputably to the P.A.P.

(2) *The P.A.P. Policy toward Labor.* The second major P.A.P. move, in order of chronology, has been the initiation of a new labor program, announced by the energetic Labor Minister, Mr. K. M. Byrne, on June 7, the second day of the P.A.P. regime. The government proposed, said Mr. Byrne in the course of his original announcement and of later amplifications, to unify the labor movement under direct government auspices. It will therefore establish a labor court for settlement of labor disputes, assert its control over the "splinter and yellow unions" (undefined), dissolve unions which "operate against the interests of the workers," and build a big new trades-union house to accommodate labor headquarters, meeting and recreation rooms, a library, and other facilities.

The actual effects of the new labor program are as yet far from clear.

If the P.A.P. does manage to impose discipline upon the unions, including the "splinter and yellow unions," then it can prevent labor-union violence from being used against itself as it was used against previous governments. On the other hand, if it dissolves and reconverts the more conservative unions, leaving only the more leftist, the P.A.P. may find the labor movement rebelling against its own control.

(3) *The P.A.P. Policy toward a "Malayan Culture."* The third major P.A.P. move was the beginning of the long-promised P.A.P. drive to promote a new Malayan culture, as distinct from the Colonial British or Overseas Chinese variety. Much of the emphasis to date, however, seems to be upon drives to reform and to rally the general public, rather than upon any more transcendental enterprises.

On June 8, for instance, there came from the Minister of Home Affairs a ban on eight Singapore publications as an opening move in an "anti-yellow culture campaign." The publications in question were for the most part rather luridly written and suggestively illustrated jobs, bordering on the mildly pornographic, and their demise was no loss. On June 9 there began a shake-up in Radio Singapore, designed to correct the former Western emphasis and to introduce a "Malayan" tone to newscasts and other programs; also to substitute serious music for popular music and rock 'n' roll, and to increase information-education broadcasts to replace a more frivolous fare. Then came decisions to ban jukeboxes—on the unexceptionable grounds that they constitute a public nuisance—to outlaw pinball machines, to clamp down on dance halls, night clubs, and gambling houses, to "protect bar-girls from exploitation," and to investigate "guest houses" and "massage parlors." Decision was taken also to ban movies which "glorify colonialism" or "bring the so-called colored people into ridicule," and to apply uplift to Singapore's own trashy motion-picture industry, the latter project getting off to a not altogether exciting start with a stiff twenty-minute documentary to introduce the new P.A.P. Cabinet.

The government embarked simultaneously upon a series of programs to enhance the "cultural appreciation" of the public. One of the results was the first of a promised series of "people's concerts," staged in the Botanic Gardens—itself one of Southeast Asia's landmarks of enlightened city planning, albeit a colonial landmark. Another was a "good will" visit in mid-August from an Indonesian cultural mission of forty-five musicians and dancers. The group was invited by the Singapore Government and sent by Djakarta as a move toward creating "friendship and understanding" to offset the record of suspicion and bickering that has marred Singapore-Indonesian relationships in the last few years.

Potentially the most significant of the new moves relating to a "Malayan culture" is the promised development of a new educational program in which the emphasis will be upon "Malayanization" and upon education, therefore, not for British examinations but for the conditions and needs of modern Singapore. As of January 1, 1960, the schools are to be provided with a complete new syllabus; as of the beginning of the 1959 fall term, they have gone on a six-day-per-week schedule, with hours of instruction correspondingly increased, and with new emphasis upon language (especially Malay), mathematics, the sciences, and civics. As an early move in implementing the new program, the government on June 22 opened a new institution to train teachers of the Malay language.

(4) *The P.A.P. Policy on Finance and Development.* The P.A.P. has frequently fulminated against the alleged incompetence and extravagance of the previous governments, their "reckless" expenditure of funds in excess of revenues, and their "failure" to implement significant programs of community and economic development. The P.A.P., accordingly, has taken the following relevant steps of its own: A) It has practiced "great economies" and avoided a "large deficit" by cutting about M$26 million (M$14 million in civil service pay) out of the earlier 1959 state budget of M$268,500,000. At the same time, however, it has added new expenditures for new ministries and new projects that bring the budget back up to M$253,900,000. By year's end, if revenues hold up—and world rubber prices indicate that they will—the government will at worst face only a slight deficit and may even show a substantial surplus. B) It has gained authorization from the Legislative Assembly to float local loans of M$100 million for development projects and has actually started to raise the first M$40 million. It has intimated that it may recall Singapore money now invested abroad and require its reinvestment in Singapore itself and has announced that its first move in this direction will be to require reinvestment in Singapore of life insurance premiums paid by Singapore citizens. C) It has announced its decision to raise taxes and has intimated its determination to tighten up on collection procedures.

The P.A.P., in its charges of mismanagement of Singapore's finances in the past and in its promise of proper management for state development in the future, is faced with a rather peculiar dilemma. Despite P.A.P. allegations, the previous Singapore governments were not only spectacularly solvent but were also extraordinarily active in development projects.

During the 1951 and 1956 rubber booms, the government met all ordinary expenses from current revenues and accumulated huge reserves totaling approximately M$325 million. Most of the reserves have now been spent on development projects, but as of mid-1959 approximately M$75 million remained to offset anticipated deficit spending in 1959 and 1960. The government had not only accumulated reserves at home but had used pension funds and other government money in an overseas investment program which now provides credits totaling about M$273 million in the United Kingdom, British Colonies, and Commonwealth countries. To be sure, there is a Singapore state public debt of M$120 million; but there is also a Singapore municipality debt of approximately M$267 million, for a good M$75 million of which the P.A.P.-dominated City Council of 1957-1958 was responsible.

(5) *The P.A.P. Policy on Public Security.* Singapore has been suffering from open gang warfare of a scale and frequency which makes the city, despite the apparent orderliness of its modernized areas, a jungle of lawlessness once one gets behind the brightly lighted streets. The chief offenders are the Chinese secret societies which have flourished ever since the city was founded, gangs of thugs who operate either in conjunction with the secret societies or on their own, and, more recently, gangs of juvenile delinquents who compete with their elders in violence and sadism. British police officials declare that such lawlessness has risen by 100 per cent in recent years.

The problem, of course, is not unique to Singapore; but rising unemployment, plus increased political tension, make it one of peculiar local urgency. Murder, acid-throwing, vandalism, arson, beatings, and occasional kidnappings have caused the new P.A.P. government to adopt a new Criminal Law (Temporary Provisions, Amendment No. 2) Bill. The law makes possible quicker, surer action against the gangs, the secret societies, and other forces which make for "communal" strife and are more dangerous to the state, according to reiterated P.A.P. announcements, than are the forces of communism.

According to P.A.P.'s opponents, the new Criminal Law Bill gives sanction to police methods which are incompatible with human dignity and freedom. It allows for discretionary application of police authority against individuals who may be guilty more of political than criminal offenses. But to date, at least, the P.A.P. has given evidence of determination and sincerity in attempting to stamp out the long-standing evils of secret society intimidation and gang warfare. It has maintained in force the old public security regulations under which, while non-P.A.P. sympathizers may now go to jail, P.A.P. sympathizers still remain in jail. Furthermore, it has upheld the British governor (now the Yang di-Pertuan Negara) in his refusal to pardon Malay extremists involved in inciting the race riots of December 1950.

(6) *The P.A.P. Policy toward Mass Action.*   The People's Action Party is committed to the principle of mobilizing the masses to public displays of civil and political enthusiasm. The leadership in this drive falls to ex-Mayor Ong Eng Guan, now Minister for National Development, who inspired the 1957–1958 P.A.P. municipal administration's three-anti's campaigns and worked out its propaganda emphasis on covered bus stands, water standpipes, and cheap electric current for "the people."

In mid-July Minister Ong thought up a "Lungs for Singapore" project. The announced purpose is to develop and to beautify an extensive downtown sea-front property, the larger part of which was once the former Singapore airport, a small part of which is marshy tideland alongside a new water-front highway. The implementation of the project calls for the "voluntary" contribution of Sunday labor on the part of civil servants, P.A.P. members and supporters, students, and the general public. The call for volunteers has resulted to date in a turnout of crowds of some 2,000 to 10,000 persons and is expected to result in a permanent "voluntary labor corps" of some 50,000. The first volunteers, unsurprisingly, were party members and employees of Minister Ong's own ministry; then came other civil servants, with women presently appearing in the majority, after it had earlier been ruled that women volunteers were not required since the lists were already filled with eager male candidates. The Sunday volunteers assemble on the *padang*, hear an inspirational talk, generally by Minister Ong, then march to the labor site, at times with Mayor Ong in the lead, followed immediately by a battalion of women workers. Other ministers turn out to visit the projects, give talks, wield a shovel, and pose for the photographers. The Indonesian cultural mission turned up one Sunday to perform and then, very briefly, to lend a hand. P.A.P. ladies' auxiliary members prepare and serve refreshments (workers bring their own lunches, though); public address systems broadcast encouragement and entertainment; and ribboned P.A.P. leaders roam the site by jeep to direct operations according to the master plan. The rapid completion of the leveling and filling job on the original project site is already noteworthy, and here one day there may be sod, trees, flowers, ponds, a children's playground, and other civic improvements. As work on the site progressed, a seagoing task force took off from the main job on at least one Sunday to visit the off-lying islands, there to bring new cleanliness and exhortation to the impoverished inhabitants. But mutterings have been heard that there are quicker, cheaper, better ways of getting the work done. Civil servants whose pay has just been cut exhibit perhaps less ardor than might seem exemplary. Students are apt to believe they have better ways to spend their Sundays. Nevertheless Minister Ong's squadrons go marching on.

(7) *The P.A.P. Policy on Foreign Relations.* The new state of Singapore remains dependent upon the United Kingdom in matters of internal and external defense and foreign relations, and the new P.A.P. government has given assurances that it does not propose to press for revision of these conditions. Both the United Kingdom and the Singapore Government have openly declared, however, that Singapore's long-range stability depends upon merger with the Federation of Malaya—a proposal about which there is much less enthusiasm in Kuala Lumpur than in Singapore. During the period of separation, which may be a prolonged one, the P.A.P. government is setting about the job of clarifying its immediate relationships with the three countries of most concern to it— the United Kingdom, the Federation, and nearby Indonesia.

The present P.A.P. concept of diplomatic conduct is revealed almost as well, perhaps, in incidental matters as in formal external relations, specifically in its attitude toward some of those matters which ordinarily weigh heavily upon a nation's officialdom—the minuter details of dress and protocol. The P.A.P. has adopted as its uniform the open-collared white shirt and white trousers in which its leaders staged their election campaign, a costume well suited to Singapore's climate and similar to that which Sir Malcolm MacDonald, then Commissioner-General, tried unsuccessfully to introduce into Singapore clubs and drawing rooms a good ten years ago. When the P.A.P. leaders deviate from their habitual informal dress and informal conduct, they generally do so for calculated purpose. The Prime Minister, for instance, dressed himself in a sober business suit on one occasion when he went to call on the British Yang di-Pertuan Negara, conceivably for no other reason than to provoke a reporter's question to which he had a ready answer. Inside, he said, it had been "rather cool." He dressed himself again in a business suit to receive the official call of his predecessor, ex-Chief Minister Lim, who had carefully turned himself out for the occasion and the photographers in white shirt and trousers. Other P.A.P. officials make a point of dressing themselves in correct jacket and tie for the Singapore diplomatic functions. But only one minister turns up per function and according to a rotation system which has not yet been figured out by the diplomatic bookmakers. The others, it is to be presumed, busy themselves with more essential matters. Hard work and little if any cocktail drinking is what the P.A.P. promised the voters. To date, it is what they are delivering, and they are still rather ostentatious about it, also about restricting the use of official limousines, refraining from lavish social expenditures, and staying aloof from foreign contacts such as might prejudice their relations with Djakarta and Kuala Lumpur.

P.A.P. official relations with the British have been correct but formal. The Prime Minister has made it clear that he thinks display of the Queen's portrait, the playing of "God Save the Queen" (also of the marching song from *The Bridge on the River Kwai*), flying the Union Jack, and other such evidences of Commonwealth solidarity are "dated" and "inappropriate," but minor detail such as can be dealt with at leisure. The P.A.P. government accords to the Queen's representative all the honors which protocol requires and no more. The Prime Minister himself has tended to exercise his full official authority in dealing with local Britishers, private as well as official. He has tended, as a matter of fact, to be both prickly and peremptory. He lodged a sharp official protest, for instance, over a British general's rather casual comment to press representatives abroad regarding the P.A.P. He accepted an invitation to sit on a joint United Kingdom–Singapore foreign affairs committee, with the explicit proviso that he was not in any way committed thereby—a proviso which might normally seem uncalled for. But he has sent his Minister of Finance to London, there "to establish confidence in the P.A.P. leaders," and presumably to hint at Commonwealth aid. The London visit, like a recent government radio comment favorable to SEATO, might indicate that the P.A.P. is mellowing a bit. "We will welcome foreign aid," said the Prime Minister a few weeks ago, "but we won't go out of our way to get it." Now, it seems, he would at least make a slight detour via London.

The Finance Minister, presumably, will reiterate in London the point which seems to be crucial in the P.A.P.'s relations not only with the British but with the Western world in general.

As the Minister of Culture put it, addressing not the British but the more categorically anti-Communist American University Association of Singapore: "Whether you agree with the P.A.P. or not, the situation in Singapore today is that none of the old parties and political leaders are equipped organizationally or ideologically to succeed the P.A.P." The P.A.P., he says, has gone as far left as any Socialist party could without going Communist; this swing to the left is inevitable and irreversible, and if the P.A.P. fails, then sooner or later, perhaps with a disastrous interval of "rule by racialists and generals," "the people of Singapore and the Federation will turn to the Communists for help to complete the unfinished Asian revolution." In other words, support the P.A.P., for any other alternative is worse; a line of reasoning with which Americans are not unfamiliar, from the far right as well as from the left.

Singapore's priority problems in international relations concern Indonesia and the Federation. The Indonesian problem, from the Singapore point of view, is that Indonesian exports and imports, in which Singapore used to have a major share, are being deliberately diverted from the Singapore entrepôt trade, and that continuing Indonesian political and economic instability threatens Singapore's own position. The problem, from the Indonesian point of view, is that Singapore takes much too much profit already from the Indonesian trade, that it offers facilities to the smugglers and sanctuary to the rebels, and in general that it somehow constitutes a threat to Indonesia's national well-being and even existence. The P.A.P. government, hopefully looking to improvement in political and economic relations, has adopted a policy of getting tougher with rebels, getting stricter with smugglers, and promoting cultural exchange as a catalyst.

The Federation problem, as defined by the Prime Minister, is "to establish Federation confidence in the P.A.P. government" so that a merger will ultimately be possible and in the meantime cooperation can develop on such matters as trade, economic development, and cultural exchange. P.A.P. moves toward the Federation government, itself innately suspicious of the P.A.P.'s Chinese and leftist backing, have to date been tentative and diffident. Shortly after taking office, Prime Minister Lee himself led a mission to Kuala Lumpur to hold preliminary discussions with the Federation government and "to establish confidence." The Prime Minister and the whole P.A.P. government, furthermore, are committed to a policy of Malayanization which will bring Singapore closer to the Federation in language, culture, and outlook. They are planning to push ahead with proposals made during the campaign period for agreement with the Federation on economic development, taxation, a common market, and other matters of immediate and practical significance. Whether they make much progress with their proposals, and whether

Singapore consequently remains a truly viable state, depends to a major extent, however, upon the new Alliance government which has just taken office in Kuala Lumpur, where both the mood and the setting are very different from those in Singapore.

On September 12, 1959, just one hundred days after the P.A.P. ministers went to work in Singapore, the Yang di-Pertuan Agong opened the Federation of Malaya's first fully elective Parliament. The King and his consort, the Raja Permaisuri Agong, turned out for the occasion in full royal regalia. The King wore royal yellow and was escorted by golden-umbrella-bearing attendants and resplendently uniformed aides as he reviewed the smart Malayan troops before the Assembly Hall. The Queen was equally handsomely dressed, and she wore the diamond tiara and other state jewels. Inside the hall were the brilliantly clad Malay politicians, the local Chinese, and the diplomatic corps. Bewigged and gowned officials took their place on the dais just below the royal thrones. Opposition Members of Parliament—half a dozen of whom (the Socialist members) had created a scene the day before by attempting to attend the swearing-in ceremony in P.A.P.-style white shirts and trousers—turned up in impeccable suits or the colorful Malay national dress. They appeared to enjoy the pomp and to share in the triumph of political achievement as much as did the victorious Alliance.

The contrast between Kuala Lumpur and Singapore leads to sober reflection. Obviously the two must get together, but no one has been able as yet to devise a mutually satisfactory formula. Obviously, also, the problem is more urgent for Singapore than for the Federation and calls for both more immediate and more far-reaching accommodation. As and if the two do come together, the very process which may make for greater stability in Singapore may be disruptive in the Federation. All is by no means as friendly and placid in Kuala Lumpur as it appeared to be at the Parliamentary opening ceremonies. There is a growing political opposition, one important segment of which, specifically the Chinese "rebels" from the Alliance, may possibly throw in with the P.A.P. to hasten the mutual accommodation, although not necessarily through devices which will be altogether welcome in Kuala Lumpur. On the other hand, all is not as bleak in Singapore as it appeared to be on the day when the peace doves were fluttering and firecrackers popping and ex-subversives going free. The deliberate Malayanization program of the P.A.P. may serve not only to allay Federation fears but actually to transform the new state.

Whatever the developing situation, it will probably be one which would have diverted old Sir Ibrahim. Over a period of decades he extracted much pleasure and also much advantage from baiting both the Singapore British and his kindred Malay sultans. In the end he turned out to have performed valuable services to both. The P.A.P., which now replaces Sir Ibrahim as a major source of concern to many local men of moderation and also, perhaps, timidity, could conceivably do the same.

PART THREE

———

Economic Development

10

Elastic Profits of Rubber

May 28, 1960

JUST seventy-two years ago Henry Nicholas Ridley began experimental plantings in the Singapore Botanic Gardens of *Hevea braziliensis,* the "weeping wood" otherwise known as the Parà rubber tree or just plain rubber tree. According to popular account, Ridley's first seedlings, received via Ceylon from Kew Gardens in London, were the illicit offspring of Brazilian jungle trees, and Ridley himself, who predicted a bright future for a Malayan rubber industry, was considered mad. In each part of the account there are elements of truth and of exaggeration.

The seeds from which Ridley's twenty-two original trees germinated were not, technically speaking, smuggled out of Brazil as the romantics declare; they were quite correctly described to Brazilian customs officers as "exceedingly delicate botanical specimens"; by his personal presence a British consul lent his official endorsement to the plea of a British scientist that this small and curious shipment be cleared without delay; a British steamship, especially chartered for the run, hustled this minute cargo off to London, where rare orchids were exposed to the weather to make hothouse space for rubber seedlings.

Ridley himself did indeed have to endure public ridicule and official censure in Singapore where scientific curiosity rated low on the list of common motivations. Among his more outspoken critics was that usually discerning empire builder, Sir Frank Swettenham, in whose garden in Kuala Kangsar (state of Perak) were planted a few of the first and finest specimens. Sir Frank Swettenham waited a few years, then ordered skilled Malay cocoanut palm climbers to comb the trees for rubber fruit, pod, or flower, and when they reported that none was to be found, summarily

ordered Malaya's first little rubber estate to be cut down. Ridley, meanwhile, was patiently experimenting with various tapping methods, dem-
onstrating the remarkable properties of the dried crude rubber which
he produced, explaining that already more valuable uses had been found
for the commodity than the production of rubber balls which Columbus,
among others, had observed West Indians utilizing in sport, and attempting to persuade local planters to divert at least a few acres from coffee—
a crop already doomed in Malaya by reason of plant blight.

Ridley's first convert was a Chinese, one Tan Chay Yan by name, who
began planting rubber near Malacca in 1896. In the next several years a
few more planters took the gamble. By 1900 Malaya had a total of about
five thousand acres in young rubber. Then suddenly, following upon
the bicycle and the solid rubber bicycle tire of the 1890's, there arrived
the automobile age and the pneumatic automobile tire. The demand for
rubber far outdistanced the supply, which hitherto had been quite adequate for the production in minute quantities (beginning about 1770) of
India rubber erasers, then (after 1823) for the manufacture in larger and
larger quantities by a gentleman named Macintosh of two-ply rubber-
bound raincoats, and then (after 1850) in thousand-ton lots for manufacture of rubber rollers and other industrial equipment.

In 1830 rubber sold for seven pence halfpenny a pound on the London
market. In 1880 it sold for a shilling, in 1890 for two, in 1900 for four.
In 1909 the price shot up to twelve shillings nine pence (US$3.12) per
pound, and the pioneer rubber planters in Malaya became millionaires.
In 1911, for instance, the Linggi Plantations paid dividends of 237 1/2
per cent—calculated, of course, according to the British system of percentage of face and not market value of shares, but a formidable statistic
however reinterpreted. Other estates paid off on almost as grandiose a
scale, and planters, investors, and government officials needed no further
persuasion that rubber was fully as desirable as East Indian spices had
ever been.

The first great rubber boom was on and Ridley was vindicated. He was
not, however, enriched. He had invested skill, time, and effort but not
money. When he retired in 1912, he had little more than his government
pension to live on, plus a gift of M$6,800 from the grateful but not un-
controllably generous Malayan Rubber Planters' Association. He did
not, it would seem, have the financial vision to invest even this M$6,800
windfall in the rubber industry, for at his death in 1956—at the age of
a hundred—he was still a man of limited means. His widow even today

receives a minute M$4,304.93 annual pension from the Malayan Rubber Producers' Council. Or perhaps Ridley did invest in rubber after all and was wiped out, for between 1912 and 1956 the industry went through a series of booms and busts which demonstrated quite early on, and re-demonstrated frequently thereafter, that rubber profits, like rubber products, featured an almost instantaneous two-way elasticity.

Today the Malayan natural rubber industry, which is the world's greatest, is once again in a boom phase. Those who had the courage to invest their money in it in 1957 or early 1958 are today calculating their profits at a minimal 100 per cent, a probable 150 per cent, and a possible 200 per cent or more, depending upon how shrewdly they chose exactly when to invest in what plantation or brokerage firm. Rubber planters, brokers, investors, and speculators, however—most of them highly sensitized by previous experience with fickle rubber prices—quite naturally ask: "How long will it last this time?" Memory has not died out of the bleak year 1929 when rubber prices dropped to an all-time low annual average of US$0.0343 per pound. Memory is still vivid of the post-Korean War period, when rubber prices dropped from wartime heights of over M$2.00 per pound (in the first quarter of 1951) to a low of M$0.5345 in February 1954. Ever since early 1954 prices have been on the rise again, not without serious fluctuations, to be sure, but with an unmistakable upward trend. At present, rubber prices hover about the M$1.30 per pound level, susceptible to decline on rumor that the United States is dumping its rubber stockpile, equally susceptible to rise on rumor that Russia and China are making heavy purchases. Whatever the tremors of the market today, many people who were pessimistic about natural rubber a year or two ago now think that the price will go considerably higher, say to M$1.50, before it drops off again for any prolonged period.[1] They believe also that the industry is at last achieving a sound basis for long-range stability and profit.

Confidence, in other words, characterizes the Malayan rubber industry today. This confidence is born of the recent conviction, after years of hesitation, that Malayan natural rubber is still a good gamble and is likely for quite a long time to remain so. This confidence is based upon rectification of three interrelated errors of judgment—or errors they now seem—which led many professional and even more amateur experts to forecast the impending decline and demise of the natural rubber industry in Malaya and elsewhere. Error One was a miscalculation of the threat to

[1] It did and has, the June 1964 price being about M$0.60 per pound.

the natural rubber industry from the development of synthetics. Error Two was a miscalculation of the balance between world supply and demand. Error Three, which applies particularly to Malaya, was a miscalculation of the effect upon the rubber industry and upon Western investment in it of Malayan independence and of political developments in adjacent rubber-producing areas. These three miscalculations are best dealt with in reverse order.

Malaya achieved independence on August 31, 1957. The sequel was not, as the pessimists anticipated, prompt discrimination against foreign investors and managers—who control 40 per cent of the rubber land and a good deal more than 40 per cent of the local rubber industry—but reinvigoration of the rubber industry along with the rest of the Malayan economy. New problems have arisen, to be sure, problems such as political pressure for quick replacement of European with Malayan personnel on the big estates, but these problems have not as yet assumed really critical proportions. The new Federation of Malaya, rather than adopting ultranationalistic policies such as make for political and economic instability, has already achieved and seems to have a reasonably good chance of maintaining Southeast Asia's happiest and most prosperous economic system. Meanwhile, the nearby Republic of Indonesia, which used to be the world's biggest producer of rubber, has experienced and has indeed by its own chaotic policies induced steady political, economic, and military deterioration. Consequently Indonesian rubber production, which had already fallen off severely prior to mid-1957, has fallen off by another 10 per cent or more since then, during exactly the same period that Malayan production has risen by 10 per cent. Indonesia has now yielded first place to Malaya as rubber producer and exporter. The very decline in Indoniesan production and prospects, rather than constituting a pattern for Malaya as many feared, has enhanced—at least on the short-term basis—Malaya's market position.

Malaya's rubber production, to put it into statistical terms, came to 698,000 tons in 1959, as compared with an estimated 600,000 tons for Indonesia. Malaya's 698,000 tons—valued at about M$1,600 million—represented approximately 35 per cent of the total world supply of 2 million tons of natural rubber as compared with some 1.2 million tons of synthetic—1 million tons of the latter manufactured in the United States and 900,000 tons of it used there. Malaya's rate of production is increasing faster than that of any other rubber-producing country. Its production totals far surpass not only those of Indonesia but of its other competitors—Thailand with about 140,000 tons per year, Ceylon with about 90,000, Viet Nam and Cambodia together with about 110,000, West Africa with about 125,000, British Borneo and various other Asian countries with another 30,000 tons among them, and South America, the original producer, with a mere 25,000.

World demand for natural rubber, according to the latest calculation of the experts of the International Rubber Study Group—who have, to be sure, been seriously in error in the past—is likely to exceed world supply for the 1960-1965 period by at least 600,000 tons. This estimated gap between supply and demand could be filled by releasing the strategic stockpiles amassed by the governments of the United States and Great Britain, these now totaling something like 1.15 million tons and 150,000 tons respectively. Indeed, both governments have announced their intention of selling off large quantities of stockpile rubber, but mainly, it would seem, to keep rubber prices from continuing their upward spiral and to replace old stocks with new—a transaction which is not calculated over the five-year period to reduce the world deficit. Russia and China, whose requirements and intentions are unpredictable either to Western experts or Eastern producers, now seem likely to make large-scale purchases such as might more than offset American and British government disposals. The vigorous re-entry of Russia and China into world rubber markets in 1958 and again in 1959 was a major factor in precipitating the current boom. Russian purchases in 1958, for instance, totaled 209,000 tons as compared with 77,500 in 1957, and heavy Russian and Chinese purchases in November of 1959 and again in May of 1960 served to drive prices sharply and briefly upward to a point well above the present high.

Among the champions of natural rubber there is endless argument about the optimum price to allow reasonable profit and yet maintain industrial stability and discourage new synthetic developments. Interested industry spokesmen now say publicly that the current market price is much too high and that the optimum price is about M$0.80 per pound. They admit privately that they would not suffer hardship if the price dropped to M$0.70 per pound. They exhibit no signs of panic if anyone suggests that the price might drop to M$0.60 per pound. Theoretical break-even point is about M$0.25 per pound—but this calculation involves decreased payments to labor as prices drop, a contingency which is covered by present labor-management agreements but is not calculated to do any good to the over-all Malayan economy or morale. Perhaps the fairest way to represent Malayan natural rubber production costs and profits is to reproduce and annotate one table from a detailed study made by a professional economist of the relatively high-cost (but also high-profit) operations of a group of the biggest estates. (See table on page 127.)

It seems reasonably safe to conclude, as investors and speculators have long since done, that whatever the wild fluctuations in costs and profits, the Malayan natural rubber industry is one in which disastrous losses are unlikely, at least until such a time as science finally unveils that long-dreaded creation, a low-cost-as-good-as-natural synthetic. Despite all past alarms, natural rubber remains today superior to any commercially produced synthetic for many important manufactures—foam rubber products, for instance, and heavy-duty tires such as those for trucks and planes. For many other manufactures (including, according to some manufacturers but not others, standard automobile tires), a mixture of natural and synthetic remains superior to either product used alone. Nevertheless, the specter of some new miracle synthetic continues to lend mystery to the market and caution to long-range forecasts. This distillation of misery out of prosperity, a process which seems to characterize the natural rubber industry when it is not distilling misery out of depression, is not, to be sure, altogether unjustified on the basis of recurrent scientific announcements.

U.S. Rubber and Shell, for instance, by pooling their research facilities, have now put into pilot production a new "cispolyisophrene" which is acclaimed as a true "synthetic natural," chemically all but identical in properties with Malayan or other natural rubber and theoretically susceptible to large-scale production at about US$0.30 per pound. The question remains, of course, whether this new "cispolyisophrene" can really be put into factory production at low cost in large quantities and whether it will not turn out in the manufacturing industry, like all other synthetics to date, to be subtly different from natural and therefore more complementary than competitive. Australian experimenters have announced that they have accomplished what for all his optimism, effort, and outlay Henry Ford never brought off—the development of a rubber-producing weed which requires little effort for cultivation and only mechanical cutting, crushing, and straining for collection. If the new American "cispolyisophrene" or the Australian weed prove illusory replacements for natural, then no doubt some other alarm will quickly be sounded.

RUBBER PRICES AND PROFITS, ALL-IN PRODUCTION COSTS
OF DOLLAR COMPANIES IN MALAYA, 1947–1958 [1]

	Average rubber price [2]	All-in costs [3]	Price, less all-in costs	Company profits (net) [4]	Residual costs [5]
	(Cents per pound)				
1947	37.3	26.4	10.9	7.1	3.8
1948	42.2	29.1	13.1	6.6	6.5
1949	38.2	28.7	9.5	6.9	2.6
1950	108.2	38.2	70.0	37.2	32.8
1951	169.6	62.0	107.6	53.3	54.3
1952	96.1	63.4	32.7	23.6	9.1
1953	67.4	53.2	14.2	10.8	3.4
1954	67.3	49.1	18.2	17.4	0.8
1955	114.2	58.7	55.5	34.1	21.4
1956	96.8	60.5	36.3	32.1	4.2
1957	88.8	53.1	35.7	24.0	11.7
1958	80.2	47.9	32.3	22.8	9.5

[1] Source of table and facts: Ronald Ma, "Company Profits and Prices in the Rubber Industry in Malaya, 1947–58," *The Malayan Economic Review* (The Journal of the Malayan Economic Society), Vol. IV, No. 2, October 1959, pp. 27–44.

[2] Price is for R.S.S.1, or top-grade smoked sheet rubber.

[3] All-in costs include labor costs (in 1958 about 52 per cent of the total), export duties (about 17 per cent), administrative expenses, salaries, and depreciation (about 31 per cent).

[4] Company net profits are calculated prior to payment of company profit tax— 30 per cent prior to January 1, 1959, 40 per cent since then.

[5] Residual costs include staff bonuses (some years the equivalent of six to twelve months' salary), managers' commissions (some years the equivalent of twelve months' salary or even more, not uncommonly M$50,000), plus directors' fees and emoluments.

In 1951 the Federation of Malaya government, then still a British colonial government, embarked upon an immense scheme designed to expedite the replanting of the national total of some 3.5 million acres of rubber, much of it overaged and neglected as consequence of a decade of war and Communist terrorism. The replanting is being carried out with newly developed high-yield stock with which the big estates, well in advance of the government-sponsored program, had already begun to rejuvenate their holdings. The program has been successively modified and adjusted since 1951 and has been greatly responsible for the replanting to date of almost 50 per cent of the national rubber acreage—exactly 46 per cent, according to the official report, as of January 1, 1960, with a 4–5 per cent increase anticipated this year. Total replanting (plus large-scale new planting) is now in prospect by about 1967–1970. Since rubber trees come into production six to eight years after planting and into full production after twelve to fifteen years, the effects of the replanting program are already apparent in production statistics. Increased yield from replanted acreage now more than compensates for temporary curtailment of production while old trees are cleared and new trees cultivated.

The basic calculation on production is approximately as follows. Old rubber stock yielded, on the average, about 400 pounds of rubber per acre per year. New high-yield stocks, if properly cared for, yield 1,200 pounds; under very favorable conditions, they yield closer to 1,600 pounds; under exceptional conditions on several of the most efficiently operated plantations, they have already yielded as much as 2,000 or even 2,400 pounds. Not all rubber producers tend their plantings carefully or tap them efficiently, of course, smallholders being notably less scientific than big estate operators. Average yield from mature replanted stock, therefore, is as yet only about 854 pounds per year per acre—far below optimum yield but more than double the old average.

Allowing for suboptimum yield on many smallholder plots but also for rapid increase in the total acreage of new trees mature enough for tapping, it is probable that Malayan natural rubber production will at least double and perhaps triple within the next decade. Once the replanting is accomplished, the increase will call for relatively little extra outlay for labor or equipment. Even if prices fall by 50 per cent, the profit margin seems unlikely to fall off seriously; if prices fall by more than 50 per cent—which would be well below the foreseeable level of synthetic prices—the profit margin should still remain comfortable. Since research on new and even faster-maturing, higher-yielding stock and more efficient processing and manufacturing methods is going briskly forward, it would appear that natural rubber profits, like rubber products, have become as durable as they are elastic. And just in case world demand should show signs of dropping behind world supply, Malayan rubber interests are pushing forward with experiments on rubberized roads. If once they achieve a real break-through on that problem, they are assured of a virtually insatiable market so long as wheeled land vehicles are not themselves supplanted—for instance, by the new compressed-air cushion model.

The Federation of Malaya's rubber replanting program is financed for the most part by a "cess" of M$0.045 cents per pound on all rubber exports and in smaller part by special government grants which are far more than recovered from other rubber export duties. It is administered by several different agencies of the rubber industry itself under the supervision of government inspectors. It is divided into various complicated and overlapping "schemes" and "subschemes." Rubber estates receive lump-sum advance payment of M$400 per acre for replanting up to 21 per cent of their holdings. Smallholders receive installment payments totaling M$600 per acre for replanting up to 100 per cent of their holdings, if they amount to ten acres or less; 66 2/3 per cent of their holdings, if eleven to fifteen acres; 33 1/3 per cent, if sixteen to thirty acres.

The M$400–600 per acre subsidy, according to the standard estimate, covers at least two thirds of the actual cost of bringing the new high-yield rubber into production. Costs are less on big-scale operations, hence the lower subsidy for estates and for government land development tracts. Costs are higher for the scattered small holdings, hence the higher subsidy. Since smallholder operations are likely to be unscientific and inefficient unless closely supervised, payments are made on an installment basis after government inspectors have certified that the planting has been done according to specification and that maintenance meets at least minimal standards. Estate owners have required little persuasion to replant as rapidly as possible and by January 1960 had replanted 50 per cent of their total holdings, some of the biggest and best estates achieving 100 per cent. Smallholders and medium holders have lagged behind government schedule and by January 1960 had replanted only 26 per cent of their over-all total.

The differential in the subsidy paid to the estates and to the smallholders has of course led the inevitable sharp operators to figure out ways to make it work to their advantage. One result—to which there have been other contributory causes—has been a rash of "fragmentations" of big estates. Many estates are being divided up into twenty-five-acre plots; each plot is registered in the name of a new owner—frequently a dummy owner. The new owner applies for the M$600 per acre replanting subsidy. The replanting is carried out to meet the bare minimum in government specifications. The land, much enhanced in value by replanting, however substandard, and by the M$600 per acre subsidy installments, often passes from speculator to speculator, each time at a new markup. Partly in consequence of this maneuvering, prices of rubber land have risen 100 per cent to 200 per cent or more in recent years and continue their upward trend. Increase from prewar value of a few hundred Malayan dollars per acre to about one to three thousand dollars per acre today for good land, depending upon condition and location, plus fear on the part of European owners of nationalization, discriminatory taxation, or restriction on transfer of eventual profits and capital, has led many boards of directors to sell out and take their quick profits—capital gains profits which are not subject to tax either in Malaya or in the United Kingdom.

The problem of fragmentation, however, and the subsidiary problems which it introduces, are as yet relatively minor ones such as must be expected in any healthy industry. Just how healthy the Malayan rubber industry is today, and just what its other problems are, may be shown best by specific examples—one a big estate, one a small plantation.

The Big Estate.   The Tanah Merah (Red Earth) Estate near Port Dickson is almost exactly what any conservative investor would want to put his money into if he were buying rubber stocks today. It is one of forty-five European-owned estates of over five thousand acres which, along with seven Chinese-owned estates of comparable size, account for something over 10 per cent of all rubber plantings and a good deal more than 10 per cent of all rubber production in Malaya today. It is one of 646 European-owned and 1,845 Asian-owned (mainly Chinese, some Indian) estates of over a hundred acres which account for 2 million out of the 3.5 million acres of rubber land classified as big holdings. It is exactly 13,776 acres of healthy rubber trees, virtually 100 per cent of it replanted in new high-yield stock of which 8,569 acres are now mature and therefore coming into full production. It is being expanded by new plantings in fringe areas, until recently overgrown with jungle.

The Tanah Merah Estate is so beautifully gardened as to seem like rolling English park land rigorously disciplined into endless rows of trees uniform in size and shape. As painstakingly groomed a piece of real estate and as productive a one as can be found in Southeast Asia today, Tanah Merah features not only luxuriant growth where weeders, tappers, and replanters are constantly at work. It features also a big modern factory for the processing of latex and crude rubber into smoked sheet and crepe, a handsome manager's bungalow set on a landscaped hilltop, a couple of new laborers' settlements, a small hospital, a school, a sports field, a Tamil temple, and a market area. It is a thriving community whose prosperity spills out over the nearby countryside, where Malay, Chinese, and Indian employees and their relatives are putting up new houses, starting new businesses, and acquiring new possessions such as bicycles, motorcycles, and even—a few of them—automobiles.

Tanah Merah is the biggest single holding of the United Sua Betong Rubber Estates, Limited, incorporated in London in 1909. Sir John Hay, its Chairman since 1927, is the outstanding figure in the rubber industry today and holds, in addition to the chairmanship of United Sua Betong, many other chairmanships and directorships. Tanah Merah is peculiarly Sir John Hay's protégé, for he persuaded the company directors to purchase it from previous Chinese owners in 1925 and made it the basis for the company's remarkable growth. United Sua Betong stock today, thanks in large part to Tanah Merah, is a gilt-edge security, one of the few in a traditionally speculative market. Just how bright the gilt is apparent from the mere recital of U.S.B.'s performance on the London market during the last twelve months. A little over a year ago it was selling at 70 shillings for the £1 share. By early June 1959 it had risen to 92. On June 10, 1959, on the occasion of the fiftieth anniversary of the company, the directors announced a plan for capital readjustment under which each shareholder received one additional share for every three he then held. Also on June 10, 1959, the directors recommended and the company voted a final dividend of 37.5 per cent (of the £1 face value) on the original shares. Earlier in the year the company had paid a 12.5 per cent interim dividend. After dividend and split, United Sua Betong shares dropped to about 65 shillings, then started climbing again. Today they stand at about 98.[2] Anyone who invested in United Sua Betong in early 1958 and sold off today would realize about 150 per cent on his investment; but few are selling off, because most stockholders expect the finale to this year's performance to be as lucrative as the finale to last year's. Just in case rubber should become less profitable, United Sua Betong has long since diversified its interests to include tea and palm-oil estates, on both of which, to put it conservatively, profits are satisfactory.

Confidence marks not only investors and managers but the laborers as well. The estate laborer (male) on the Tanah Merah Estate today, in accordance with a nationwide industry-labor agreement, can count upon a guaranteed daily minimum of M$2.15 so long as rubber prices are better than M$0.40 per pound. In actuality he now draws a good deal more. He draws M$2.60 per day if rubber prices are between M$.60–.80 per pound, M$2.90 when prices are between M$0.80–1.00 per pound; M$3.25 when prices are between M$1.00–1.20 per pound, as they have been of recent months; M$4.00 if prices are between M$1.20–1.40. The female estate laborer gets 80 per cent of the standard for males.

[2] June 1964 quotations: about 60 shillings.

Tappers make out better than the ordinary laborers. A skilled tapper who is indefatigably industrious is able today, according to common report, to make as much as M$8.oo per day—which, if he is single, puts him into the income-tax-paying, middle-class income bracket. On the Tanah Merah Estate, as on others, the Category A tapper has received, at recent prices (M$1.20) for rubber, M$2.90 per day in basic wages, plus a premium for bringing in thirty-five pounds over the generally accepted fifteen-pound minimum of latex, plus a premium for collecting about six pounds of coagulated "scrap" rubber that has accumulated since the previous day's tapping—in all, just short of M$5.oo cash income per day. Some earn more, many earn less, for there is a wide difference in the amount of latex brought in by various tappers, even those working the same type of level or hilly land, the same type of old or new planting, and the same number of hours per day. According to industry-wide surveys, there is a marked difference in productivity and hence earnings among Chinese, Indian, and Malay tappers. Chinese monthly earnings average out the highest, Tamil earnings next, and Malay earnings lowest—partly, of course, because the Malay takes more holidays than the others. Compensation for estate laborers and tappers has increased more than 100 per cent in the last twelve years, and with the recent increase in rubber prices and recent or impending increases in rubber yields, it stands to rise still higher.

In addition to basic wages plus premiums, the estate workers enjoy an impressive number of amenities, such as provident funds (to which they contribute) which allow for a lump-sum payment at time of retirement, free medical services, free schooling, and free housing. The quarters now provided to estate laborers at Tanah Merah, as on many other large estates, are one of the demonstrations of joint government-industry efforts to raise the general standard of living. On Tanah Merah Estate the progress has been particularly noteworthy. Old "labor lines," in which lived a dozen or more families, each occupying one sectionalized compartment in a long row house, with communal toilet facilities some little distance off, have now been abandoned or reconverted. Materials from the old-type quarters have been utilized to build new semidetached two-story quarters which feature space, air, and sanitation as old "labor lines" did not. The show spot on the estate, however, is a new housing area where there have been built several dozen semidetached, two-family bungalows, with hollow concrete block walls, tile roof, concrete floor, louvered windows, two bedrooms, semidetached bath and kitchen, each bungalow placed in its own garden plot. The bungalows cost the estate

M$4,400 per two-family unit to build. The tenants, motivated by pride of occupancy, keep the buildings and the grounds in excellent order and compete in planting trees, grass, and flowers. Higher level personnel are provided with larger, better bungalows costing about M$15,000–20,000. The new housing areas more than meet government specifications. Save that the laborers' bungalows lack electricity, the developments are fully as modern and attractive as new low-cost and middle-class housing in the urban centers.

Management of the Tanah Merah Estate is a job which calls for a combination of scientific and administrative know-how. The present manager, a Scot, is a forester by education, an estate manager by long experience. He is now assisted by a couple of young Englishmen and is training Malayan citizens (Chinese, Malay, and Indian) to take over both estate and factory supervision. Estate management entails getting up long before daybreak to check the laborers out on their jobs—which are best performed in the cool morning hours. It also involves long daily rounds of inspection to make sure that new clearing and planting are being carried out by the most efficient methods, that various pests like lalang grass and root rot are detected and eradicated before they have a chance to spread, and that tapping is being skillfully carried out, plus long additional hours of paper work.

Upon the skill of the tapper depends to a very great extent the life expectancy and productivity of the tree. Without constant checking the tappers might resort to the slovenly methods that reduce productivity on a smallholder plot to about half that of the big foreign estate. The skilled and careful tapper—the great majority of the tappers are women—cuts a paper-thin strip of bark about one quarter of an inch deep from the bark of the tree, taking off no more than about a one-half-inch panel per month and allowing plenty of time, therefore, for new bark to grow smoothly over the wound before the tree must be tapped again in the same place years later. Prior to tapping, the tapper strips off whatever latex may have flowed from the tree and coagulated since the previous collection. A few hours after tapping, preferably still in the morning hours to minimize the hazard of rain diluting the latex, the tapper returns and collects in a large metal bucket the latex which has dripped from the tree trunk into the collecting cup. The scrap rubber and the latex, plus also such drippings as may have become mixed with twigs, leaves, or soil, are all accumulated at collection points and trucked off to the factory for processing.

The pure latex itself is mixed with acid, allowed to coagulate as thick wet slabs, pressed to squeeze out the excess moisture, then dried and smoked for easy shipment as sheet rubber in waffled sections resembling light brown rubber mats. In some new factories, but not at Tanah Merah, latex is merely concentrated for shipment in liquid form. At Tanah Merah, as at a number of larger factories in Malaya, some of the rubber is processed into crepe. For every drop of latex and every shred of scrap there is demand and economical use. Even the dried latex mixed with leaves and gravel is salvable and for that matter completely satisfactory for various rubber manufacturing processes, commanding a lower price chiefly because it is not so easily graded, shipped, or reprocessed as the purer rubber.

The Lee Family Estate.   The Lee Family Estate, located close to Tanah Merah, is as noteworthy for its differences as for its resemblances. It is a holding of just over 250 acres, one of the 1,608 "under 500-acre" estates accounting for rather less than one tenth of the total Malayan rubber acreage and less than a tenth, also, of total production. It is fairly typical of Chinese small estates and medium holdings. This means that it is the speculative operation of an absentee Chinese owner who has invested part of his capital in rubber, hopes for and frequently gets big returns, and takes with much more enthusiasm to improved scientific production methods than to improved management or labor relations.

The owner of the Lee family estate has placed a Chinese resident manager—a relative—on the property. He provides the resident manager with necessary materials and equipment. He himself takes 50 per cent of the proceeds from the sale of rubber and leaves the manager the other 50 per cent for labor, incidental costs, and his own commission. Since about half of the Lee estate is now planted in new high-yield rubber that is just coming into production and the remainder is rapidly being replanted as well, the owner can and does estimate annual production at the moment at something like 125,000 pounds of rubber worth at least M$150,000. He himself pockets, therefore, about M$75,000, less, say, an unlikely maximum of M$10,000 for new equipment and materials. Since his land is now worth about M$1,200 per acre on the average, or a total of M$300,000, his annual profit is well over 20 per cent, a relatively modest percentage as Malayan rubber profits go, but rising fast.

The manager and the laborers on the estate do not make out as well as the owner, and the rate of production, while good, is far from what it could be. The estate, while it is being rapidly replanted in new rubber, lacks the pruned, clipped, and well-groomed look of Tanah Merah. The ground under the trees is covered with coarse undergrowth such as makes tapping difficult and draws off soil nourishment. The trees are none too skillfully tapped, so that already the trunks of the new stock show scars and swellings. The manager has difficulty keeping the tappers from seriously over or under tapping and he has difficulty also in keeping the antiquated processing shed and smokehouse in operating order.

The workers—half a dozen Indian families, some of them numbering three generations, who have lived all their lives on the estate—occupy squalid, lightless sheds and look ill-nourished and impoverished. These Indian laborers, like other laborers on other small-scale holdings, lack the amenities provided by the large estates. They do not even draw the legal minimum wage, since on small estates like this one inspection is infrequent and circumvention of wage and other industry regulations is easily possible. The laborers do, of course, have schools, clinics, and other modern facilities at their disposal if they care to walk a few miles or pay a few cents bus fare to Port Dickson. They seem to prefer, however, to spend their effort and their money on weddings, temple ceremonies, and most of all upon palm toddy, a highly intoxicating beverage on which, coincidentally, the government realizes a big profit in taxes.

The life of the laborer on the Lee Family Estate is far from enviable. The best that can be said for it is that these Indian workers earn far more and have far more advantages than they could ever expect in India or in most Southeast Asian countries except Malaya, and that an occasional member of the group breaks loose and improves his circumstances elsewhere.

The life of the manager seems, at first glance, not so enviable either. His house is a bleak little bungalow, concrete floored, sparsely furnished, provided with little in the way of modern facilities except piped water, electric light and a refrigerator which function when the home power plant operates. Still, he does have his own car, he undoubtedly has his savings, and he is in all probability investing in rubber land of his own so that one day not long distant he too will be an owner.

Conditions on the estate as a whole may improve, once the whole area is replanted and starts bringing in even greater revenue. The Chinese owner may then appreciate the desirability of better maintenance, better housing, and better wages. It is being demonstrated every day right next door and in a thousand other places in Malaya that all these pay off in the end in surer, steadier profits—a point which is not indefinitely delayed in dawning upon the Overseas Chinese capitalist. The really big Chinese rubber owners—Sir Cheng-lok Tan, for instance—have long since adopted the standards of the European estates.

RUBBER BENEFITS AND PROSPECTS

The common feature of the Malayan rubber industry today, whether estate, medium holder, smallholder, or rubber brokerage firm, is the built-in profit escalator. "It can't last forever though," the cautious remind themselves and each other as they continue to plunge in rubber land and rubber stocks. But while it lasts, it is a bonanza whose proportions become most conclusively apparent not from examination of individual operations but from the national statistics.

Rubber—and in some years tin—has made Malaya the biggest dollar-earner in the British Commonwealth. Rubber has also made the Federation of Malaya, next to the minute but oil-rich Sultanate of Brunei in Borneo, Southeast Asia's most solvent state. Rubber accounts directly for about 25 per cent of the total national revenue; both directly and indirectly it accounts for well over 50 per cent. Rubber constitutes 50–70 per cent by value of the Federation's total export; rubber production accounts for 25–35 per cent of the gross national product; rubber plantings cover 64 per cent of the nation's cultivated land, employ 400,000 laborers —100,000 estate laborers, 300,000 smallholders—and give direct or indirect livelihood to at least 1.5 million out of the nation's 6.5 million people.

Various export duties on rubber, plus a 40 per cent tax on company profits, plus a 5 to 45 per cent tax on scaled segments of individual income earned from rubber, plus up to 25 per cent duty on the imports which rubber money buys, constitute by far the most important part of the national revenue. Direct export duty on rubber, assessed according to a sliding scale that rises with rising prices, brought in a total of M$184,-455,000 in 1959—almost three times what the budget makers had anticipated (on the basis of a M$0.80 price average forecast for the year) and almost 20 per cent of the total national revenue of M$874,063,000. Anti-inflationary "cess," which goes into operation when rubber prices reach the M$1.00 per pound mark, brought in an additional M$17,567,000. "Replanting cess," levied at the rate of two cents per pound on exports (raised as of January 1, 1960, to 4 1/2 cents, brought in M$32,175,000— more than enough to finance the 1959 replanting program. "Research cess," recently raised to three quarters of a cent per pound of export rubber, brought in M$12,093,000—easily enough to justify expansion of the

Rubber Research Institute's program from the previous M$8.4 million per year level to M$12.4 million for 1960.

Windfall profits from rapidly rising rubber prices resulted in 1959, as they have in certain previous years, in a very happy situation as regards the national budget. Although it had forecast a M$114 million deficit for 1959, the government found itself possessed at year's end of a M$4 million surplus. It could make its new budgetary calculations on the conservative assumption that prices would remain well above the M$0.80 per pound mark throughout 1960. It has been able, accordingly, to step up its general economic development program, for which rubber, naturally, pays most of the cost. There are lean years, too, and all too many of them, and such overwhelming reliance upon rubber, as the commentators constantly point out, is not in the long run a good thing. For the year 1959, however, and so far into the year 1960, it looks like a very good thing indeed.

11

Contained Profits of Tin

May 31, 1960

TIN AND elephants were two lures which brought both Asians and Europeans to Malaya in earlier centuries, when the little northern Malayan state of Kedah, for instance, supplied tin to China and Europe and elephants to India. The local market in elephants has now collapsed, what with changes in means of locomotion, the decline of princely pomp in India, and the amalgamation of Ringling Brothers, Barnum and Bailey. The supply of Malayan elephants, furthermore, has gone into sharp decline, despite the efforts of the late Sultan of Johore, for instance, to protect them against the reprisals of planters annoyed at their consumption of young rubber trees and of farmers who begrudge them bananas, durian, and papaya in ton-lot quantities. The elephant market, it seems safe to report, isn't what it used to be and, what is more, won't ever be again. Tin, however, is quite another proposition, one that is hedged about with some very prickly problems and also some very inviting profits.

Tin long ago displaced elephants as a really critical factor in the Malayan economy. It has itself been displaced to a very considerable extent by rubber. It is responsible, however, for endowing Malaya with a good part of its present riches and an even greater part of its present problems. Tin bequeathed to Malaya its potentially incendiary race problem—a 37 per cent Chinese vs. a 50 per cent Malay population, the rest Indian, European, and other racial groups. Chinese immigrants, attracted by tin or by the opportunities which tin created, largely built and populated the nation's principal cities, including Kuala Lumpur, the national capital, and Ipoh, the mining capital, and in the process they took over a major part of the nation's enterprises.

Tin also bequeathed to the new Malaya a great deal of the political residue of colonialism. Necessity to insure the steady flow of tin, un-interrupted by Malay feudal warfare and Chinese secret society feuds or the violent mixture of the two, led the British to impose the colonial rule of which both the happy and the unhappy vestiges remain. Tin shored up the shaky thrones of the Malay sultanates, particularly those of Se-langor, Perak, and Pahang. These ruling families, like those of the other Malay states, would long since have been deposed had not both the Brit-ish and the Chinese chosen, for the sake of maintaining stability in tin and other industries of the peninsula, to accept and to bolster feudalism in preference to the unpredictable alternatives. But tin remains today an important factor in the Malayan economy and a commercially sound proposition largely because of international cartel arrangements regard-ing production and pricing—arrangements such as any advocate of free enterprise is loathe to contemplate very closely and which even adherents to the cartel system regard as extremely chancy. Malayan tin, further-more, is a wasting asset, and the new Malayan Government, despite its declared policy of prospecting for and developing new deposits—which no one expects to rival the old—has as yet made little progress of signifi-cance to the industry. The reason, it appears, is governmental indecision and not, as it might well have been, fatalistic acceptance of the fact that world demand, given really world-wide application of present scientific know-how about tin-plating, might swiftly decline, and world supply, given really effective development of known or suspected resources in China and the U.S.S.R., might swiftly increase.

Tin, in other words, is an unusually unpredictable economic per-former, as investors in Malayan tin mines have found out all over again in the last few years. At the moment tin prices are high and tin shares are up on both the Singapore and the London markets, and any speculator lucky enough to have invested shrewdly in tin a year ago could realize a 100–300 per cent profit by selling out today. Tin prospects seem on the whole still to be looking up. There are plenty of investment counselors, however, who will tell you that you would be at least as well advised right now, unless you are prepared to watch the market closely and get out fast, to put your money in elephants.

The immediate state of the tin industry in Malaya, and elsewhere, is determined largely by the International Tin Council, set up under the International Tin Agreement of July 1956 to determine export quotas and manipulate a buffer stock to control prices. The International Tin

Agreement, signed by six producing countries (not including the U.S.S.R. and China) and by fourteen consuming countries (not including the United States, West Germany, and Japan), was designed, from the point of view of its signatories at least, to maintain reasonable equilibrium between supply and demand, reasonable stability of price, reasonable profit margin for the producer, and reasonable assurance of fair price for the consumer.

From the producers' point of view, the reasons for some sort of control board seemed compelling. Tin prices had averaged £1,077.3 per ton in 1951 during the height of the Korean War boom—double the pre-Korean War prices. They had fallen to £600 per ton during the first half of 1954. American stockpile purchases during the war and subsequent suspension of such purchases (1955) seemed to the producers a unilateral sort of manipulation calculated to ruin the industry. Various other manipulations, such as the dumping of tin by Russia, and even more complex maneuvers by various producing and consuming countries—each suspecting the motives of all the rest—had thrown the industry into a state of near panic. International consultation and limited international agreement were the consequence.

According to the 1956 agreement, which went into effect in mid-1957 and is up for reconsideration now in mid-1960, the Tin Council assigns to each member producing country a quarterly export quota which becomes, in effect, the production quota. This quota is determined on the basis of anticipated world demand and proportionate pre-1956 output of the producing countries. The Tin Council, furthermore, maintains a buffer stock of about 25,000 tons to which it adds when prices drop, from which it sells when prices rise, attempting thus to maintain a price floor of £730 per ton and a price ceiling of £880. The combination of quota system and buffer stock has worked well enough to date that, despite disgruntlement at times on the part of both member and non-member nations (recent rumblings of "discrimination" and "hardship" from Indonesia, for instance), it seems likely that the agreement will be renewed without drastic modification and that the non-member nations will maintain, on the whole, a benevolent attitude toward it. There are many unpredictable factors, however, not the least of which is total world demand and the ability on the part of all traditional suppliers to meet their quotas. Furthermore, Russia's performance, whether as purchaser or seller, is never predictable, and the United States' stockpile policies are scarcely more so. The profits of the tin industry remain, therefore, as in the past, a gamble and not a certainty, albeit a gamble which in the last year has paid off most handsomely.

Malaya, the world's largest tin producer, profited most richly from the tin boom of the early '50's, suffered most severely from the price decline of the mid-'50's, and is now successfully recouping as a result of a 1959 revival of demand and increase in price. During the Korean War boom and after Malaya had some 750 tin mines in operation employing some 40,000 persons (about 70 per cent of them Chinese). Tin profits rivaled rubber profits in bolstering the Malayan economy—then subject to the tremendous strain of military operations to put down the Communist terror. Tin production in 1956 set a postwar record of 62,295 long tons valued at about M$400 million. Of this amount, and of earlier and later export proceeds, approximately 15 per cent or about M$60 million went to the government in direct export duties, accounting for approximately 8 per cent of total government revenues, or 12–15 per cent if one includes company profit tax and income tax from tin earnings. Of the remainder a very great deal went into modern buildings and businesses in Ipoh, one of Malaya's richest and handsomest cities, and into various enterprises elsewhere in the peninsula, including Kuala Lumpur, the second tin center of the nation. In 1958, when tin export quotas were operative during the full year, in accordance with the 1956 agreement, Malaya's tin production dropped to 38,458 long tons, valued at about M$225 million; direct government revenue from tin slumped to M$30 million; some 325 mines closed down altogether and the remainder reduced their output; between 13,000 and 25,000 miners were either unemployed or underemployed. Tin profits dropped off so sharply that tin shares fell by 50 per cent or more on the Singapore and the London markets.

Curtailment of production resulted in improvement of prices, which rose from an average of £719.4 per ton in 1954 to about £790 per ton during the past year. Restriction of supply resulted in depletion of stocks overseas and in renewed demand. Total world export quotas—of which Malaya is assigned 37 per cent—were increased, accordingly, from 20 to 23 to 25 and then to 30 thousand tons, quarter by quarter in 1959. For the first quarter of 1960 the total was set at 36 thousand tons; for the second quarter it was raised to 37.5 thousand tons, or approximately 95.5 per cent of the immediate prequota period production figure. Today approximately 525 Malayan tin mines are in operation, approximately 25,000 miners are employed, good tin stocks have appreciated by 100 per cent or more in value since a year ago, dividends are being declared at the old rate of 30–50 per cent of face value of shares (often more than 10 per cent of market value). Few expect any really sudden change in the situation, although even fewer profess to see beyond the next quarter when the present quota seems likely to be maintained if not increased and the present profit rate to be sustained.[1]

The present market situation is comforting to those interested in the profits of the Malayan tin industry. But if the world markets are not to be alternately glutted and depleted of tin, if tin producers are not to go through alternating periods of boom and bust, if consumers are not to be confronted with wildly fluctuating prices, both national and international controls, it appears, must be stringently enforced. Yet the controls themselves create artificial profit-and-loss situations, artificial supply-and-demand equilibrium, and are subject to quick disruption as a result of developments in major tin-producing and -consuming nations either inside or outside of the cartel.

The U.S.S.R. and Communist China, for instance, suddenly appeared as sellers in mid-1958, dumping tin on the London and other markets, sometimes via Poland as intermediary, taking advantage of the high prices maintained as a result of self-restriction observed by other nations. The U.S.S.R. in January 1959 came to an informal agreement with the Tin Council that it would sell no more than 15,500 tons per year. The suspicion remains alive, however, that either Russia or China or both might suddenly disrupt the whole market and would willingly do so for either economic or political gain. The United States comes in for its share of suspicion as well, for American stockpile tin, if suddenly released for sale in considerable quantities, could be as disruptive as Russian or Chinese dumping, and despite all American reassurances there are many who believe or profess to believe that the danger is real. In any event, American advances in economical use of tin in tin-plating and development of new substitute metal products if they spread to other countries could cut consumption at least 10 per cent and perhaps a very great deal more. As for the producing countries, it is problematical whether Bolivia and Indonesia, for instance, could actually deliver their share of a much increased quota or whether Indonesia can be relied upon at all as a steady supplier. It is problematical also whether some producing countries—again Bolivia

1 The tin market has gone up, down, and up again since 1960. As of June 1964 tin is selling for over £1000 per ton, notwithstanding removal of production quotas and disposal of large quantities of U.S. surplus stock. Tin shares, however, are selling well under their 1961 high.

and Indonesia—would not, if they could, outproduce their quotas and dispose of their excess tin either in complete disregard of international agreement or via special barter arrangements such as the Tin Council tolerates but deplores. Finally, Malaya, the biggest producer of all, is depleting its richest deposits and seems unlikely to discover others that will really replace them.

The situation in Malaya, according to leaders in the industry, is already becoming serious, not as regards availability of tin to meet the demands of the near future, but as regards the long-term prospects of the industry. Malaya's known reserves of tin ore are estimated at about 1.5 million tons, a tremendous amount, but much of it, unfortunately, of relatively poor quality, expensive to exploit. Malaya's known reserves are about one third of known world reserves, and since they are enough to keep the Malayan tin industry operating at its present level for the next few decades, there would seem to be little cause for alarm. Malayan tin experts point out, however, that the industry must plan for the long-range future and that such planning is becoming increasingly difficult. They do not expect any new deposits to be located that are at all comparable, say, to the Kintah Valley deposit near Ipoh, which has been worked for the last fifty years and has provided a good 45 per cent of total Malayan production to date. Concerning possible new deposits, however, the industry leaders are only guessing on the basis of quite inadequate maps and surveys. They are not allowed to prospect or to develop new sites. The Federation Government declares that the Government itself, working through its Department of Mines, will prospect for new deposits. When and if such deposits are located, the separate state governments—which control most of the unexploited land—will "encourage" Malay individuals, companies, and cooperatives, as contrasted with the British and Chinese concerns which now control the industry, to apply for mining leases. Malays, however, do not at present have the experience, the capital, or the inclination to undertake the large-scale operations which are most efficient in extracting the maximum amount of tin from the deposits and the maximum profit from the operation. The big British and Chinese firms, meanwhile, are busily working the deposits for which they already hold mining licenses and are reworking deposits already processed once by the less efficient methods of a couple of decades ago. While ore and profits last, it is perhaps begging trouble to look twenty to thirty years to the future when tin may have lost much of its industrial importance anyway. But tin has been traditionally so important a factor in the Malayan economy that the long-range future of the industry inevitably demands attention.

The Malayan tin-mining industry today falls into these major categories: (1) tin dredge operations, carried out by big British companies, also by several American and Australian companies, a highly mechanized, large-scale capital-investment operation accounting for about 48 per cent of production; (2) *palong* (gravel-pump) operations, carried out by Chinese companies, a semimechanized operation requiring much smaller capital investment and accounting for about 41 per cent of production; (3) underground mining, carried out by only a few companies, mainly European, involving fairly large capital investment and accounting for about 4 per cent of total production; (4) *dulang* (hand-panning) operations, carried out by individual operators, mainly Chinese women but a few Malaysians as well, who work the streams near the other mine sites to recover ore that has been washed away, accounting for about 2 per cent of the total production; (5) other methods such as hydraulicing and open casting, accounting for the remainder of the tin produced.

The tin dredges are by far the most spectacular feature of the Malayan tin-mining industry. These enormous harbor-dredgelike installations— some eighty of them in all, costing in the neighborhood of £1 million to £2 million each to build and install—are mounted on barges and float about in small artificial lakes. They scoop or suck up ore-bearing soil to a depth of about 140 feet. They then process the soil through a series of settling troughs where water washes away everything but the heavy tin concentrate which is sacked for shipment to smelters in Penang. The artificial lakes are relocated to follow the tin lode. The dredges are operated in one area until they have quite exhausted the deposit, leaving behind them desolate expanses of "tin tailings" or gravel-like refuse so infertile that unless very expensive reclamation projects are undertaken, nothing but coarse lalang grass and a few particularly hardy but useless shrubs will grow upon it for a period of many decades. The dredges also leave behind them deep excavations which fill with rain water and constitute a serious hazard to youthful adventurers; some of these ponds are now being converted, as a result of government experiment and propaganda programs, into fish ponds capable of producing considerable quantities of fresh-water fish to supplement the Malayan diet. Once a deposit is exhausted, the dredges may be dismantled and reassembled elsewhere, or at times, such is the expense of removal, they are merely left to waste away like dinosaurs in the pits they have dug for themselves.

The tin *palongs* or gravel-pump installations consist of bamboo and timber scaffoldings built to a height of perhaps fifty feet, bearing a cascading series of settling troughs, each *palong* and its machinery representing an investment of about M$150,000. The *palong* is generally equipped with a small diesel electric generator to provide power for its pumping system. Laborers operating a large fire hose direct a powerful stream of water against the ore-bearing gravel. The water-borne gravel is then pumped to the top of the *palong*. From there it passes down the successive settling troughs from which, approximately once each week, workmen remove the heavy residue of tin concentrate. This type of operation, while far less expensive than the dredges, is also far less efficient. A smaller percentage of the actual tin content of the ore is actually recovered. Operators frequently concentrate upon the richest part of the tin lode to the neglect of deposits which may eventually be worked over at greater trouble and expense than would have been the case had they been mined in the original operation. *Palong* mining, like dredge operations, results in vast expanses of unsightly, infertile tin tailings which are a blight on the Malayan landscape.

Underground mining is restricted to a few areas where rich deposits of tin ore are to be found at depths or in locations which make dredge or *palong* operations impracticable. Of all the underground mining, some of the most profitable is carried out in the extensions of natural caves in Perlis, where underground mountain streams have already washed out the ore and deposited it in crannies among the rocks.

Panning operations are carried out in the streams flowing away from the mine sites, particularly from the *palong* sites where a significant percentage of the tin ore washes away with the gravel. Women operators stand in the streams, rocking broad wooden bowls, in much the same technique of California Gold Rush days. A really skilled operator may recover as much as M$10 worth of tin in a single day, and since the only investment is time, muscle, a shallow wooden bowl, and a small license fee, most of this represents clear profit.

At the present time most of the tin dredges are back in operation, some of them on a twenty-four-hour-a-day basis. Many of the *palong* installations remain idle, however, several years of disuse and neglect making new capital investment essential before they can be reactivated. The underground mines, like the dredges, are rapidly increasing operations, and the tin panners are back in the streams, gleaning what is for Southeast Asia an extremely lucrative reward for their efforts. There are complaints about past inequities in parceling out quota shares among the various mining concerns, and recriminations that these past inequities have resulted in present positions of relative advantage or disadvantage in resuming full-scale operations. There are complaints, on the other hand, that some concerns are not in fact able to meet the quotas assigned to them and that with Malayan tin-ore deposits running out, inefficient producers should be penalized and efficient producers rewarded. It would require a wise judge indeed to weigh the merits of the several arguments, but as the tin industry continues to boom, the arguments of the past decrease in volume and importance. What is really important is that the tin industry, which only a year ago seemed most precarious, seems once again a mainstay of the national economy.

Nevertheless Malayan tin, the nation's second most important export industry, lags far behind rubber in the contribution it makes to the national economy. Malayan tin production has dropped from 62,295 tons valued at approximately M$390 million in 1956 to 37,525 tons valued at approximately M$250 million in 1959, as compared with rubber production valued at approximately M$1.4 billion in 1956 and M$1.6 billion in 1959. Government revenue collected from export duties on tin (including duties on tin ore imported each year to the amount of about 17 per cent of local production and smelted for re-export) has dropped from M$61 million in 1956 to M$36 million in 1959, as compared with direct revenues of M$210 million and M$246 million from rubber.

The great discrepancy in value from year to year of tin output and revenue, including revenue from company and income tax, and the even greater discrepancy in the case of rubber—which shows up far more dramatically in years other than those cited above—constitute twin hazards to the Malayan economy and to Malayan budgetary planning. Tin prices, relatively stable for the last several years, albeit at a cost of greatly curtailed production, have perhaps ceased to fluctuate as widely as before, but so too, it seems, has tin production as a whole ceased to be as nationally lucrative an operation as in years past, when, with rubber, it was one of the "twin pillars" of the economy.

A very serious economic question, therefore, today troubles many Malayans. What is to be done to develop a new product or, better yet, a whole range of new products which will not merely fill the critical role once fulfilled by tin but also diversify the economy so that sudden world price fluctuations on one or two major products will not make the difference between prosperity and depression? To this question there is as yet no clear answer, and until there is one, Malaya remains, for all its present prosperity, in a highly vulnerable economic position.

12

Distant Profits of
Diversification

June 2, 1960

THE ECONOMY OF the Federation of Malaya today is at once overspecialized, underdeveloped, and ultraprosperous. A dual economy within a plural society, it is subject to all the built-in tensions of social and racial conflict. Modern European-Chinese-Indian enterprise for hugely profitable export and import overlaps increasingly upon Malay subsistence farming; it coexists with relatively low-paid Chinese and Indian labor and relatively inexperienced and highly paid Malay officialdom. This highly complex composite implies a state of balance so precarious that one stumble might lead to disaster. The miracle is that so far no one has stumbled. Having got safely through the first treacherous years of preparation for and implementation of independence—years of crisis in world affairs and consequent fluctuations in world markets—the Federation cannot yet afford to relax. Its economic anomalies demand intelligent, concerted effort at resolution if the nation is not to be overtaken by the critical difficulties which block progress in various other Southeast Asian countries.

Thanks to windfall profits in recent years from high rubber and tin prices, thanks also to an enlightened administration during both the colonial and the postcolonial period, the nation has achieved the highest over-all standard of living in Southeast Asia. In doing so, however, it has intensified rather than ameliorated the discrepancies among social and racial groups. Malaya today is a land of high-salaried European estate, mining, and business operators (US$400 minimum monthly income is a prerequisite to resident status); Chinese tin and rubber millionaires; well-to-do if not actually rich Chinese and Indian merchants and professional

148

men; well-paid Malay government officials (US$300 to $1,000 monthly in upper grades); wealthy Malay royal families—nine of them, with involved collateral branches and expensive government stipends; plus, of course, the great bulk of the population of ordinary Malays, Chinese, and Indians who exhibit widely varying degrees of enterprise and prosperity at a much lower level.

In Malaya in 1958, to take one good indicator of the distribution of wealth, a total of 19,195 Chinese paid M$11.701 million in income taxes; 5,538 Westerners paid M$8.784 million; 5,904 Indians paid M$2.024 million; and 3,596 Malays—mainly government officials—paid M$1.098 million. Tax dodgers, to be sure, are both numerous and agile, especially within the Chinese and Indian communities, and newly revised and tightened regulations may greatly increase both assessments and assessees. Even so, it does not appear that a really large number of the nation's 6.5 million population actually earn, let alone report, at the approximate rate of M$5,000 per year for a five-member family which would qualify them to move into the income-tax-paying social stratum. This M$5,000 per five-member family works out, incidentally, at just slightly above the M$900 per capita figure which makes Malaya's name lead all the rest on Asian income statistics, well above Japan at about M$675, almost beyond sight of India at about M$175. The difference between the actual income of the ordinary citizen of Malaya and the ordinary citizen of other Asian countries is considerable and it is dramatically to Malaya's advantage. It does not appear half so dramatic on the spot, however, as do the differences in income among the various social and racial groups within the country. The true dimensions of Malaya's economic problem and of the measures being taken to solve it begin to come into focus, however, through consideration in some detail of the rubber-tin economy, as in the foregoing chapters, and through a quick survey of other important economic factors, beginning with the rice industry, in the sections to follow.

RICE

Malaya has increased rice production from about 600,000 to 700,000 tons annually ten years ago to about 700,000 to 800,000 tons annually at the present time. Such is the increased demand for rice, however, as a result of population growth (3.4 per cent per year) that the Federation has been unable to reduce imports below an average of 350,000 tons per year (about 30 per cent of total consumption) and seems unlikely to do so in the future.

Malaya's rice-growing centers are the West Coast "rice bowl" states of Province Wellesley, Kedah, and Perlis, and the East Coast plains of Kelantan and Trengganu. On the West Coast, by extensive reclamation and irrigation projects, and by introduction of improved techniques and more extensive double cropping, the government has achieved its most notable improvements. On both coasts it has encouraged the use of artificial fertilizers and the planting of improved rice strains.

But for all its efforts and achievements, the government is confronted with certain unalterable or only partially alterable facts. Rice lands and potential rice lands are strictly limited in Malaya by reason of disadvantageous features both of soil and of terrain. About 900,000 acres of land are now planted in rice—almost 100,000 acres of it newly opened up since 1950. Only about half of the total has good drainage and irrigation facilities, and much less than half of it is suitable for double cropping. An additional 200,000–300,000 acres of land suitable for rice farming may eventually be opened up, but only with very large capital outlay. Malayan rice farmers, furthermore, although capable of tremendous output of labor during the relatively brief planting and harvesting seasons, are not otherwise notable for industry, skill, or adaptability. Even the best of Malaya's rice fields look somewhat unkempt in comparison, say, with those of Japan or of Indonesia. Rice farming, finally, whatever its appeal to the Malays because of tradition or new advances, is already losing out with the younger, better-educated generation whose job preferences are changing rapidly although their basic food preferences are not.

FISHERIES

Malayan fisheries hold out a reasonably good chance of rapid development such as will satisfy increased local demand and permit of an important export product. As yet, however, local demand has not greatly increased, foreign markets have not been developed, the annual catch remains static at about 110,000 tons, and seasonal variations in catch, plus difficulties in modernizing both fishing and marketing methods, raise formidable problems. A government campaign to encourage people to buy and eat more fish, particularly during periods of market glut, and a continuing effort to persuade Indonesia to lift its restrictions against import of dried and salted fish from Malaya, have as yet had little measurable result. Other problems, fortunately, are yielding to effort, and the industry, which employs 50,000 persons (35,000 of them Malays), is beginning to enjoy more stable, if not yet higher, profits.

Chinese fishing interests, which center on the West Coast ports and islands, operate the larger fishing ships (up to about a hundred tons), and bring in the bulk catches, have experienced cyclical boom and bust in recent years, partly as a result of their own speculative business methods. The Chinese operators have now put their own business affairs in better order, and they have profited from long-range government programs of improving communications facilities so that they can now shift more readily from one urban market to another as supply and demand shift. The Chinese sector of the industry, although it is still shaken by crises, such as the one which arose last summer when the catch was unusually large and prices fell to an unusual low, seems to have settled into a period of relatively sound financing and orderly marketing.

The Malay fishermen, the majority of whom concentrate on the East Coast, operating out of several scores of little fishing villages and river ports, are being gradually persuaded by government loans and government propaganda to motorize their boats, to improve their gear, to form marketing cooperatives, and even to acquire their own ice plants and trucking fleets. One index of results to date is that motorized fishing vessels, which numbered only about 800 ten years ago, today total 8,000, most of them small Malay-owned boats with either outboard or inboard motors. Registered nonpower fishing boats, meanwhile, have dropped from 22,000 to 17,000. One power boat now normally accompanies each small group of sailboats to sea, then when the catch is made, hustles the fish back to shore to be iced, shipped, and sold, commonly through the new cooperatives.

Malayan fisheries have been confined, until very recently, to inshore fisheries dominated by the Malays and offshore fisheries dominated by the Chinese. There came into operation in 1959 on Penang Island a new deep-seas fisheries enterprise involving local Chinese and Malay joint capital investment (51 per cent, including investment by a Malay cooperative) and Japanese aid (49 per cent) in providing ships, equipment, training crews, and at some future date a new ice plant and canning factory. The first ship has already gone into operation in the Indian Ocean and has brought back catches of tuna, swordfish, shark, and other fish suitable for the cold-storage and canning industry which, if present expectations work out, could rapidly grow into a big-scale enterprise, the anticipated catch being about 5,000 tons per year.

Malayan pond fisheries have never been of comparable value to those of other areas in Southeast Asia, but recent government projects may result in their rapid growth. With funds and personnel provided under the Commonwealth Development and Welfare Fund, there was built and put into operation near Malacca about three years ago a new M$2.4 million fisheries research institute. From the breeding ponds of the institute are now being distributed to nearby farmers large quantities of fresh-water fish fry, especially the fry of the *Tilapia Mossambica,* the "wonder fish that breeds faster than any rabbit"—beginning, in fact, at the age of about two months, reaching six- to eight-inch table size at the age of about six months. The tilapia was widely acclaimed a few years ago as an easy answer to Southeast Asia's protein-deficiency problems. It has since been discovered, however, that in many areas the tilapia threatens to become more of a pest than a boon. It multiplies so fast, spreads so promiscuously, and eats so ravenously that it starves out other fish and stunts even its own growth. The Malacca research station has achieved a noteworthy break-through in tilapia science. It has crossed the Southeast Asia variety with the original East African variety to produce fry that are exclusively male and no uncontrollable hazard, therefore, to their own food supply or that of other fish. Pond culture of Malacca research station tilapia and other fish may not soon result in any new commercial product, tilapia in particular being prized more for its home-grown nutritional value than for its market appeal. It may, nevertheless, become an important factor in Malayan farm-home economy.

AGRICULTURAL EXPORT CROPS OTHER THAN RUBBER

Natural rubber, say the pessimists, will soon go the way of coffee, gambier, and spices, which ceased to be really important economic factors in Malaya half a century ago. The possible alternatives to rubber seem at the moment to be palm oil—perhaps as vulnerable as rubber to world price fluctuations; copra—subject to palm blight in Malaya and more economically produced in nearby areas; tea—much of it of relatively poor quality as compared, say, with that of Ceylon; and cacao— a recently introduced crop in production of which Malaya is not likely soon to rival Ghana.

At present Malayan production of palm oil and kernels comes to a combined total of about 90,000 tons per year (70,000 and 20,000 tons respectively) valued at about M$60 million. The cultivation of the oil palm is spreading rapidly, mainly as an estate enterprise and a hedge against decline in rubber prices; but production still has a long, long way to go to rival rubber, and the crop has not yet exercised much appeal upon the smallholder since processing is both difficult and expensive. Copra and coconut-oil production at present amount to about 20,000 and 30,000 tons per year respectively, to a total value of about M$45 million. The great part of the production is accounted for by smallholders—who operate at a very low level of efficiency—including kampong people who harvest the coconuts from a few stray trees. Annual figures on quantity and value are falling off rapidly, partly because coconut palms are being cut down to make room for more rubber. Tea production, almost all of it an estate crop, amounts to about five million pounds annually, valued at about M$10 million, and is holding steady. Really significant increase in production is contingent, however, upon government alienation of new land to the big estate interests—an unlikely prospect—or substitution of tea for other crops on land already under cultivation—an equally unlikely prospect, at least while rubber prices remain high. Cacao, of which only about 1,000 acres are as yet under cultivation, much of it by smallholders who receive government encouragement, is as yet of no real commercial significance. With no other miracle crop yet in sight, there is hope that cacao might conceivably be it.

TIMBER

Malaya's rain forests, which cover 70 per cent (37,452 square miles) of the nation's land area, constitute a vast timber reserve which, unfortunately so far as its commercial possibilities are concerned, is extremely difficult and expensive to work. The terrain is rugged mountain, jungle, or swamp, often all but inaccessible. The stand of trees is highly miscellaneous. Only a scattered few, accounting for no more than 6 per cent by volume of the total amount cut, are good hardwood; about 20 per cent by volume is usable only for firewood or charcoal; none except a few conifers experimentally planted in highland areas are good for wood pulp. Most of the product is softwood, which commands a good sale at present on the local market but is running into increased competition on the international market from cheaper, better, Russian and Canadian exports. Still, at the 1959 level of production, Malaya was turning out some 550,000 tons of usable wood, 250,000 of it for export at a reported value of M$32 million. The timber industry is the nation's third biggest commercial employer, with some 20,000 persons engaged in logging and another 6,000 in sawmilling.

Malaya's timber industry, which is now largely in the hands of the Chinese and is restricted in part by the reluctance of the government to license new Chinese concerns to operate in government forest reserves, may soon receive new stimulus. The government now proposes to encourage Malays to take a bigger part in the industry. It proposes also, as part of its rural development program, to clear huge new tracts of land for agricultural use, the clearing process to involve preliminary lumbering operations. If these developments result, as there is some reason to hope, in decreased costs for increased output, then Malaya's large timber reserves might assume much greater significance in the over-all economy.

MINERAL RESOURCES

Should Malaya discover oil or uranium, the problem of replacement or supplementation of tin as the chief mineral industry would be solved. Discovery of oil, say the experts, is improbable; discovery of uranium, despite flurries of excitement, has not yet been announced. National mineral resources surveys, while sketchy as yet, are discouraging. For the time being Malaya pins its hopes on its iron ore, an inferior grade at best, mined in 1959 to a quantity of 3.76 million tons, 90 per cent of it sold to Japan where it supplies about 45 per cent of the requirements of Japan's iron and steel industry. Iron-ore production, with Japanese contractual encouragement, has tripled in the last five years and seems certain to go much higher. Latest contract negotiations between Japanese firms and Malayan producers call for delivery of 4.75 million tons in the year beginning March 1, 1960, for a price of M$150 million.

PROCESSING, MANUFACTURING, AND CONSTRUCTION INDUSTRIES

Development of new medium-scale industries has been one of the most conspicuous aspects of the Federation's economy in the last few years, and the rate of growth is steadily increasing. This development is largely the result of free private enterprise, Western and Chinese, and it is made possible by government policies that are almost unique among those of the newly independent Southeast Asian nations. The Prime Minister, Tengku Abdul Rahman, has drawn up and proposed for international adoption an "Investment Charter" which guarantees private enterprise, including foreign enterprise, against nationalization, discriminatory regulations, or confiscatory taxation—the specters which haunt the industrial establishments of most other Southeast Asian nations. The government has enacted legislation (1958) authorizing "pioneer status" for approved new industries of foreign, local, or joint ownership, such status involving two- to five-year tax holiday, quick amortization of initial costs, free transfer of profits, waiver on duties for imports essential to the enterprise, and application of protective tariffs to discourage import of competitive merchandise. The government, furthermore, has set aside large tracts of land for industrial concerns and has undertaken to provide adequate facilities such as power, water, and transport services, also to underwrite adjacent new housing developments. All in all, in view of the extraordinarily favorable official climate for industrial investment and development, Malaya is able to a noteworthy extent to offset some very serious handicaps. In comparison with other actual or would-be manufacturing countries of Asia, Malaya suffers from a shortage of raw materials, other, of course, than rubber and tin; it lacks experienced managers and skilled labor; it can count upon only a very limited market—its own 6.5 million population, but not the additional 1.5 million population of nearby Singapore which is emerging more as a competitor than a partner; it pays the highest wages of any Asian country and has to sustain the highest standard of living.

Small- and medium-scale enterprises in Malaya today—many of which got started under British rule but have been encouraged to expand since independence—now employ some 80,000 persons, as compared with 400,000 in rubber, 45,000 (in good times) in tin, 107,000 in commerce and finance, 120,000 in communications, and 209,000 in government service. These enterprises include the following, listed in approximate order of importance: rubber milling and the manufacturing of such rubber products as shoes, bicycle tires, and foam-rubber pillows and mattresses; sawmilling; construction and manufacture of construction materials such as roof and floor tiles; cigarette manufacture; printing; rice milling; soft-drink manufacturing; oil milling; pineapple canning; and the manufacture of biscuits and various other processed foodstuffs.

The proportions and limitations of the Malayan industrialization program become easily apparent from a tour of the nation's most extensive new industrial center, the new Kuala Lumpur satellite town of Petaling Jaya. In the fringe areas of Petaling Jaya, the government in 1954 allocated some three hundred acres of former tin-mining land for acquisition at US$.25 per square foot by new industrial concerns. Already, after about five years, most of the available land has been taken up, many of the sites have been built upon, and in the newly constructed factories and workshops, employing a few dozen to a few hundred people, production figures are soaring on such items as matches, soap, paint, bottled drinks, and locally assembled electronic and construction equipment. Two of the more noteworthy new industrial projects now scheduled for Petaling Jaya are a M$25 million Dunlop factory, with an initial capacity of 400,-000 automobile tires per year (200,000 for export), and a milk factory, to be set up by Americans to process Australian milk concentrates into condensed milk for the local market. On the nationwide basis, according to recent official figures, a total of thirty new industries has been granted pioneer status as of January 1, 1960, and many more applications are soon to be acted upon. For the thirty industries already approved, the total capital outlay for initial installations will come to M$22.536 million, the total eventual outlay to more than double that amount. Of the original M$22.536 million, approximately 60 per cent represents foreign investment (including M$823,000 by American concerns). These new industries will give employment to some 2,300 persons in the course of the next several years.

The proportions of the new Malayan industrial program are not such as to result in swift and extensive industrialization in the Western sense, but for a small nation they are significant, and for private enterprise in Southeast Asia—taken in conjunction with huge reinvestment in rubber estates—they constitute a most remarkable display of confidence.

OVER-ALL ECONOMIC DEVELOPMENT PLANNING AND PROJECTS

During the 1956–1960 period the Malayan government has been carrying out a five-year plan for economic development, one which is extremely difficult to pin down to comprehensive charts or schedules, however, since the government each year adopts an "ordinary" budget for recurring expenditures and a "capital" budget for development projects, and the two not only overlap but are subject to much reshuffling. It is some indication of the scale of the programs that the "ordinary" expenditures now run to about M$650 million per year, while "capital" expenditures were about M$200 million for 1959 and will be about M$250 million for 1960. Ordinary or capital development expenditures for the year 1960 include the following: M$51.4 million for rubber replanting; M$26 million for roads and bridges; M$11.3 million for water-supply projects; M$14 million for electric-power projects; M$6.4 million for primary-school buildings; M$12.6 million for port improvements at Port Swettenham and Penang; M$3.6 million for airport improvement, particularly at Kuala Lumpur; M$9.6 million for the operation of a newly established Ministry of Rural Development. It is worthy of special note that this development plan is being carried out without any major reliance upon foreign aid, without any really alarming evidences of boondoggle or corruption, and without any strident propaganda campaigns for the glorification of the politicians.

Examples of specific projects serve better than statistics to illustrate scale and scope. The Cameron Highlands Hydro-Electric Project, for instance, is designed to generate 80,000 kilowatts of electric power for distribution through the network of the Central Electricity Board, an autonomous, profit-making government agency. The project is financed by three loans negotiated in 1958: US$35.6 million from the International Bank; £400,000 from the Commonwealth Development Finance Company; and M$38 million from the Malayan Government. Contracts have been let to German, French, British, and local companies for work on the dams, tunnels, roadways, transmission lines, and generator installation. Work on all the preliminary operations, which got well under way in 1959, is proceeding so satisfactorily that despite a couple of bad accidents from cave-ins, the project is likely to be completed on or ahead of schedule in 1964, to cost less than the anticipated M$149 million, and to be amortizing within a relatively short time. The Cameron Highlands power project will soon be supplemented by another 25,000-kilowatt project in the same area. It is the newest and biggest of half a dozen power plants of impressive size which have been expeditiously and efficiently put into operation in recent years and have enabled the C.E.B. to keep well ahead of swiftly growing demands for electric power and to provide by far the most reliable service in Southeast Asia.

Swettenham on the West Coast and Kuantan on the East Coast, passing through Kuala Lumpur, the national capital, is a vital link in the nation's 6,500-mile road network. A road-improvement and road-building pro-
National Route Number Two, the central highway between Port gram to modernize Route Number Two in all its segments and, in particular, to put in a new, wide, thirty-mile stretch in the hilly central part of the peninsula, is a major part of the communications improvement program. Last year the new thirty-mile stretch was opened to traffic and the nation now, for the first time, has a good, hard-top, all-weather road linking the most important part of the as yet underdeveloped East Coast with the far better developed Western areas and cutting off seventy miles, two hours' driving time, and much uncertainty from the trip. Other projects involve widening and improving roadbeds, putting in new bridges, eliminating bottlenecks, sharp bends, and slow ferries. Malaya, which al-

ready has the best road system in Southeast Asia, is rapidly expanding and improving upon it.

RURAL DEVELOPMENT

For all its extremely impressive development and expansion in recent years, it would be a serious error to assume that the Malayan economy today is resulting in rapid enrichment or marked improvement in the lives of the poorer Malays, Indians, or even Chinese. Nevertheless, by Southeast Asian standards, most of these people are already well housed, well fed, well clothed, well provided with educational, health, and public services. They take for granted such amenities as cheap public transportation, accessible and operational telephones, expeditious government action on their problems of registration and licensing, and availability (at a price they can hope to save up for) of all necessities and even minor luxuries as well. Nevertheless, all too many of the Malays in particular still live in primitive thatched huts, work their rice fields or other land holdings most laboriously by inefficient methods, put to sea in paddle or sail-propelled boats to fish with antiquated lines and nets, own only an extremely modest supply of clothing and other personal property, any small excess of which they frequently have to put in pawn to meet the expenses of special ceremonies. They are relative strangers as yet to the teacher, the doctor, and the banker. For those a little farther up the economic and social scale the major inducement to educational or economic advancement is the religious inducement of reading the Koran and paying for a pilgrimage to Mecca. Even for the somewhat better-off Malay, as for the ordinary Indian laborer and for a large number of the Chinese, an elementary education, a bicycle, and a modest home-garden plot for his family represents as yet the limit of achievement. The problem of rapidly expanding the range of opportunity for the ordinary people, especially the Malays, is one to which the government today is giving priority attention. Not the least compelling reason for the government's new preoccupation with rural development is the fact that the opposition made great gains during the 1959 election period by accusing it of flagrant disregard for the people's welfare and of "selling out" to the Chinese and the Westerners.

The best evidence to date of the government's determination now actually to implement the rural development which it has frequently promised is the creation a few months ago of a Ministry for Rural Development, with Tun Abdul Razak, who is concurrently Deputy Prime

Minister, as its head. Tun Abdul Razak has already acquired extensive new funds; he has issued a series of new directives regarding renovation of old programs and innovation of new ones. Calling for the preparation of a master plan of development projects for every kampong in the nation, he has promised that bureaucratic delays will be eliminated, that necessary funds will be forthcoming, and that command-post operational offices will insure the efficient completion of projects on schedule. Meanwhile he has undertaken the complete reorganization and reorientation of the Rural and Industrial Development Authority (R.I.D.A.), an agency of government whose past record has been little short of dismal. The new R.I.D.A. is to concentrate upon providing credit, processing, and marketing facilities for a wide variety of rural enterprises such as smallholder rubber, timber, fisheries, and cottage industries, thus enabling the Malay sector of the population in particular to take an important place in modern economic enterprise. It is to set about correcting the "deplorable" situation disclosed by a 1959 official survey, which indicated that Malays numbered only 8,800 out of 89,000 registered businessmen in the Federation, that they had provided only M$4.5 million out of a total of M$400 million in capital investment, and that they paid only 4 per cent of the total income taxes.

Of all the economic problems faced by the new Ministry of Rural Development and the government as a whole, the most crucial is that of developing new land. According to official calculation there are now about 11,500 square miles of developed land in Malaya (780 square miles of it mining land) and approximately another 11,500 square miles that are potentially subject to development. The pressure to acquire new land is intense, both on the part of estate and mining interests, which would like to expand their operations and have the capital to do so, and on the part of ordinary individuals who are eager to acquire small private holdings but lack any capital at all. Until very recently the government has been evasive and indecisive in policy. By mid-1959, however, the government had eleven projects well under way and had moved a total of 3,882 families onto some 39,100 acres of newly cleared or partially cleared land. Each family will eventually be allocated about ten acres—six of it in rubber—as its private holding from which, according to official calculations, it should be able to clear an annual cash income of about M$7,000. Eleven new projects are scheduled for opening in 1960, with 4,226 families slated for settlement. Should the speed-up now result in swift allocation of land not to thousands but to tens of thousands of families, Malaya

PART FOUR

International Involvement

13

Suspicious Neighbors

May 10, 1960

"SINGAPORE is a dagger pointed at our breast. Singapore must be crushed." This unneighborly sentiment is authoritatively attributed to an Indonesian personage so high he had best remain nameless.[1] It expresses a point of view to which a great many Indonesians subscribe, at least as to the accuracy of the premise, if not as to the feasibility of the conclusion. It is a point of view which Singapore's politicians, long either incredulous or indifferent regarding Indonesia's animosity, have now begun openly to acknowledge and to attempt to offset by emphasizing mutual Singapore-Indonesian opposition to colonialism.

"In the past, when the government of Singapore consisted of British colonial officials, it was inevitable that the spirit of mutual cooperation and camaraderie between the two governments was sadly lacking," declared Singapore's Prime Minister Lee Kuan Yew last January when he arrived in Djakarta on a state visit intended to inaugurate a new era. [But now,] he added, "I feel that our relationship has undergone a fundamental change for the better. . . . The Dark Ages of Asia are slowly disappearing into the limbo of the past [—the period, that is,] when Indonesia and Singapore were arbitrarily separated and set at odds by colonialists who divided Asia up among themselves much in the fashion of modern gangsters who demarcate their territorial jurisdiction over a city."

"Indonesia is glad," said Prime Minister Djuanda in his own restrained if not indeed admonitory speech of welcome, "that Singapore is now

---

[1] It was, of course, President Sukarno, who announced openly in 1963 his intention to "Crush Malaysia."

willing to seek for a firm foundation for closer cooperation toward mutual benefit."

In recent years relations between Singapore and Djakarta, to put it
bluntly, have been bad. Djakarta, if left to its own devices, would probably keep them that way. Singapore, however, now that the People's
Action Party has come into power, is willing to accept retroactively on
behalf of the previous colonial governments the major share of the blame.
Djakarta is happy to join in the *ipso post facto* condemnation without,
however, committing itself to unequivocal exoneration of the new Singapore regime. Both governments—but the Singapore government by far
the more profusely, hopefully, and penitently—are announcing a brave
new start.

In the past Singapore has represented just about every anathema on
the extended Indonesian nationalistic roster. It has been a British colony,
a British (and hence SEATO) military base, a British and Overseas
Chinese capitalist enclave. It remains, of course, a Commonwealth member, also a British financial stronghold. It was and still is an Overseas
Chinese commercial center, its predominantly Chinese population attracted in part to communism, in part to anticommunism, in far greater
part to fence-sitting. None of these Overseas Chinese groupings are attractive to neutralist, anti-Overseas Chinese Indonesia, and yet all command immense influence among the powerful and unwelcome Overseas
Chinese community in Indonesia itself. Singapore, furthermore, has been
a refuge for Indonesian rebels, a center for large-scale smuggling both
out of and into Indonesia, a base from which foreigners of many descrip-
tions are believed by Indonesians to have been meddling in Indonesian
affairs, even to the extent of fomenting *coups d'état* and rebellions, and
of introducing to Indonesia such baneful influences as luxury goods,
"decadent culture," "blue films," the hoola hoop, and the cha-cha-cha.
Singapore has served also as the major Southeast Asian entrepôt through
which have passed huge quantities of Indonesian exports and imports, on
all of which the Singapore merchants, brokers, and shippers have exacted
what Indonesians regard as exorbitant commissions. Singapore, in other
words, has seemed to many Indonesians to be just about as wholesome as
would be a composite virus, parasite, and narcotic.

In the last year Singapore has become a semi-independent state within
the British Commonwealth. Its left-wing People's Action Party government is attempting to build up close political, economic, cultural, and

linguistic ties with neighboring Malaya and with Indonesia as well. In adopting a program to develop "a democratic, socialist, and noncommunist state," it has made as yet inconclusive moves to curtail or control British military base activities and British or other Western and Chinese capitalist operations and considerably more effective moves to curtail Chinese Communist expansion. It has started to clamp down on political fugitives, smugglers, and even ordinary businessmen who, by their easygoing operations, give offense to the rather easily offended Indonesian Government. The new Singapore Government, in fact, in devising its various policies, has had one very watchful eye on Indonesia, one eye on the neighboring Federation of Malaya; Cyclops-like, it has had a big, central eye on all others, including the well-informed Singapore citizen who is disposed, with reason, to regard Indonesia as an extremely erratic and irascible neighbor.

From the point of view of the Singapore man-in-the-street, or it might be more accurate to say, the Singapore Chinese-in-the-godown, it is reasonably fair to describe Indonesia as follows: it is a huge, potentially rich and productive neighbor that is wretchedly misgoverned, one that is perennially on the brink of complete political and economic chaos and is worsening its own situation immeasurably by squeezing out the Overseas Chinese. All the same, it is an immensely profitable market, so long, of course, as one is realistic about its unworkable import-export regulations and relies more heavily upon principal than principle. Singapore's former Chief Minister, Mr. David Marshall, spoke more truthfully than tactfully when, in the course of a good-will mission to Indonesia in 1955, he declared: "We do not want to kill the goose that lays the golden eggs. We prefer goose eggs forever rather than goose soup today." The trouble, as Singaporeans often fail to comprehend, is that Indonesians don't like to be regarded as candidates either for the goose soup kettle or the gilded goose cage or, for that matter, as geese rather than as garudas.

The complex Singapore-Indonesian relations, if they are either to be comprehended or ameliorated, must be placed in a combined historic and current events context. It is also convenient for ease of analysis to identify the multiple problems in individual categories as follows: Historic Fact vs. Fiction; Colonialism vs. Nationalism; Trade vs. Smuggling; Confiscation vs. Piracy; Sanctuary vs. Interference; and Diplomatic Reserve vs. Spontaneous Reaction.

HISTORIC FACT VS. FICTION

Indonesian politicians, like the earlier Dutch colonialists before them, have chosen to believe that the Indonesian archipelago and the Malay Peninsula—including the island of Singapore—constituted in centuries past a geopolitical unit which British power nefariously split apart. The ancient Indonesian and Malayan empires and kingdoms, and even the early colonial domains (Dutch, Portuguese, and British) did in fact sprawl shapelessly across the equator and the Straits of Malacca. But the earlier contact between the archipelago and the mainland was intermittent, tenuous, and marked by more suspicion and rivalry than mutual accommodation, despite the fact that the predominant racial group in each area was Malaysian by origin and sea-nomadic by predilection.

The really sharp break with the past and the new start came in 1819 when Sir Stamford Raffles, having been defeated successively in his efforts to revitalize British Penang and Malacca and the Netherlands Indies, outwitted both the British and the Dutch colonial bureaucracies and founded Singapore, not as a new barrier but as a new link in area development. In the course of a very few years Raffles achieved the highly successful application of some startlingly revolutionary colonial ideas: efficient administration, free trade, welcome to foreign immigrants of all races, and relief from such local scourges as Malay piracy and indigenous or European exaction of transit tolls. In consequence, the little island of Singapore (225 square miles) became recognized as the most strategic, prosperous, stable, healthful, and hence desirable piece of real estate in Southeast Asia, the focus of Southeast Asian sea trade. The Dutch, who resented its acquisition and development, adjusted realistically to the facts. A combination of British administrative and Chinese commercial genius in Singapore afforded their own island empire a convenient and well-run free port, a bastion of defense supported by the British taxpayer, and an agreeable resort in times either of relaxation or of trouble. The independent Indonesians have inherited the Dutch resentment without inheriting their realistic acceptance. Singapore, today, by its astounding prosperity and progressiveness, makes Djakarta seem squalid and static. The Indonesian inclination, naturally, is to attribute Singapore's advances to Indonesia's misfortunes. Singapore's present-day progress seems to many Indonesians to be the mid-twentieth-century consequence of an early nineteenth-century imperialist plot, one that cut Singapore loose to enjoy most of the advantages and few of the disadvantages of Indonesia's own colonial and revolutionary development.

NATIONALISM VS. COLONIALISM

A great deal of the past trouble between Indonesia and Singapore has stemmed from differences of political frame of reference, that of Indonesia being nationalistic, but of Singapore being colonial. Of late, however, the nationalist versus colonialist positions have been curiously inverted. From the Singapore point of view, Djakarta has seemed to be manifesting a new sort of colonialism. It has forcibly restrained the outer islands of Sumatra and Sulawesi from cutting loose from the central government to determine their own political and economic policies—developments which would have involved much closer, probably better relations with Singapore. From the Indonesian point of view, Singapore has been developing some undesirable nationalistic attitudes of its own. It is displaying ambition, for instance, to equal treatment in the councils of Southeast Asian nations and pretensions to "Malayan" or independent Singaporean, rather than dependent Overseas Chinese, status.

Add two additional phenomena: Indonesia has been discriminating against and expelling Overseas Chinese, many of whom, whether of the political right, left, or center, have close family and business connections in Singapore. Singapore has been adopting a paternalistic attitude toward its Malay minority, a great many of whom are Indonesian by origin or descent. Indonesians instinctively mistrust Singapore's "Malayanization" policy as one of camouflage, while at the same time they must officially applaud it. Singaporeans instinctively reject Indonesians' claims that its Overseas Chinese policy is one merely of assimilation, not of elimination, and regard Indonesia's recent anti-Chinese measures as arrogant and oppressive. Dispassionately viewed, both objectives—the absorption of the Overseas Chinese in Indonesia into the Indonesian population, and the adaptation of the Overseas Chinese in Singapore to the cultural, linguistic, and political milieu of the area in which they live—are worthy goals in remedying the centuries-old conflict between Overseas Chinese and indigenous peoples. The trouble is that in each case the motive is suspect.

The Chinese in Singapore have recently been treated to some pretty convincing evidence that Indonesia's intentions are not altogether pure. Singapore has been flooded with news reports and personal accounts of the hardships endured by the Indonesian Chinese. Their businesses have been closed out; their properties have been in effect confiscated; their means of livelihood have been destroyed. Through Singapore's harbor are now passing many thousands of forlorn Chinese refugees. They are permitted to leave Indonesia with little more than they can carry in a suitcase and a packing crate; they have been subjected to concentration-camp type of treatment prior to departure; they have been repeatedly searched to see that they carry virtually no valuables and none of a long, long list of contraband; they are headed back to China, where they will be converted from the status of the once prosperous shopkeeper to that of the peasant or factory worker. "Colonial injustice was rarely so ruthless," remarked one Singapore Chinese, "although, to be sure, there was the infamous Dutch massacre of the Batavia Chinese back in 1740."

The Indonesians have been kept advised of some recent Singapore moves in the process of "Malayanization": the appointment of a local Malay of Indonesian descent as the new Yang di Pertuan Negara (Chief of State), replacing the British governor; the promise of free education through university level for any Malay who qualifies academically; and preferential treatment for local Malays who wish to enter the civil service or even commerce. But this is interpreted in Indonesia not as genuine effort on the part of the Singapore Chinese to transform themselves but as a series of window-dressing maneuvers whereby Singapore hopes to gain admission into the Federation of Malaya, which upon being admitted, it will promptly dominate. It is worth noting, incidentally, that in the Federation it is sometimes interpreted as a series of maneuvers whereby Singapore can win Indonesian approbation and hence play Indonesia off against the Federation, seeking greater and greater concessions from each.

TRADE VS. SMUGGLING

Singapore-Indonesian difficulties show up most frequently and expensively in the area of commerce. Since Indonesia, even under the Dutch, never developed the banking, wharfage, warehousing, and merchandising facilities adequate to its own vast trade, enterprising little Singapore became a major entrepôt and grew rich on commissions. In recent years, for instance, Singapore has handled a good half of Indonesia's rubber exports; it has supplied a large percentage of the textiles and sundries which Indonesia buys abroad. The Indonesian Government, however, has undertaken repeatedly, if not very successfully, to divert its trade from Singapore by working out direct barter deals, particularly with Communist-bloc countries which are eager to replace the traditional buyers and suppliers. Despite expensive muddles, it has achieved enough success to disrupt the even flow of Singapore-Indonesia trade and to reduce it somewhat in total annual volume. Singapore now experiences recurrent and acute shortages of Indonesian rubber with which either to steady the local market—which is the world market—or to supply the local rubber-milling industry. It experiences also recurrent gluts of textiles and sundry goods purchased in anticipation of quick resale in Djakarta on deals which do not come off. Then suddenly and unpredictably, with accompanying signs of panic when its import-export schedules get badly out of phase, Indonesia will ship rubber to Singapore or buy textiles from Singapore. It thus creates a market situation adverse to its own interests and builds up renewed resentment at home against Singapore middlemen, who continue to act as if the ancient law of supply and demand takes precedence over recent assurances of "closer cooperation toward mutual benefit."

Indonesian officials threaten repeatedly to put Singapore out of business in retaliation for Singapore's "uncooperative" attitude. They can do so, they declare, by systematically depriving it of that one third of Indonesia's exports and one tenth of its imports which continue, despite all disruptions, to flow through Singapore's port. This one third and one tenth might indeed make all the difference between prosperity and poverty for an overpopulated and economically vulnerable island, dependent upon world trade. Indonesian threats lose a great deal of their punch, however, when Indonesian officials proceed to define their master plan —the reliance upon more and more direct barter deals, although previous barter deals have been demonstrably unprofitable to them, and the establishment within Indonesia itself of a free port area. Few people with any knowledge of Indonesia believe that the government could ever bring itself to renounce its whole economic philosophy to the point of creating an enclave free of red tape and corruption, or even if it did so decide, that it could act upon its plan and duplicate Singapore's facilities within the next decade—or two, or three.

Since present Indonesian import-export regulations are complicated beyond the ability of man to comprehend or the arm of the law to enforce, the annual Indonesia-Singapore trade volume—despite over-all decline—still remains comfortably high, Singapore remains hopeful, and Indonesia becomes more and more outraged. The Indonesian Government has had to tolerate and indeed to legalize—with recurrent attempts, nonetheless, at revocation—a brisk Indonesia-Singapore barter trade. Since the barter itself cannot be effectively regulated, legal or semilegal barter is extensively supplemented by outright smuggling. Much of the barter and the smuggling both have fallen into the hands of the Indonesian regional civil and military authorities, some of them loyal to Djakarta, some of them in open or semiopen defiance of Djakarta, few of them amenable to Djakarta's attempts at supervision, many of them, of course, closely associated with smart Chinese businessmen both in Indonesia and Singapore.

The ordinary pattern of the barter trade is for authorized or semiauthorized Indonesian exporters to deliver local produce to Singapore middlemen, who supply them in return with 30 per cent of the value in merchandise and 70 per cent of the value in hard Singapore currency. The transactions come under the scrutiny, presumably, of the Indonesian port authorities, the Indonesian currency control board, the Indonesian check-point authorities, the Indonesian Consulate-General in Singapore, plus innumerable other Indonesian agencies, in addition, of course, to the Singapore harbor authorities. There is many a slip-up and many a payoff, however, and the barter trade constitutes a major loophole, indeed a gaping breach, in Indonesia's badly regulated economy. Valuable raw materials pour out of Indonesia; unessential luxury goods pour back in; and much hard currency ends up not in the Bank of Indonesia but in private accounts in Singapore and Geneva.

When Indonesians, including regional military commanders, choose to disregard most if not all of the presumed controls, then barter trade becomes outright smuggling. Both loyalist and rebel military commanders of the outlying provincial areas have managed over the last few years, thanks to industrious smuggling, to finance themselves, their troops, their regional civic improvements, even the regional insurrections. Needless to say, such barter-smuggling is not the most efficient way to conduct trade. Indonesian military commanders in Borneo, for instance, have been known in times of urgent need to exchange rubber for rice in equivalent weights, despite the fact that on world markets a pound of rubber is worth at least five times as much as a pound of rice. It is estimated that in the year 1958 smuggled Indonesian rubber amounted to perhaps 150,000 tons, or more than one fifth of Indonesia's total rubber exports. The smugglers were lucky, after paying off for protection, to get one half the value. Nevertheless, with rubber selling recently in Djakarta at the "controlled" price of Rp. 40 per kilogram and at the same time fetching M$2.50 per kilogram in Singapore, and with M$2.50 readily convertible into Rp. 500 on the black market in Raffles Place, the incentive to smuggling is even greater today than in 1958, although the hazards are considerably greater too.

The barter-smuggling trade has attracted both big and little businessmen, both big and little shippers, and to everyone's advantage except that of the Indonesian Government and people. Much of the smuggled rubber has traveled by 10,000-ton ocean-going freighters, loaded under military guard in Indonesian ports and provided with flawlessly falsified manifests. Much, too, has traveled by the ordinary Singapore-registry 500-to-1,000-ton coastal freighter, which carries legal barter goods legally or semilegally documented, smuggled goods casually or cunningly concealed, or a combination of all types. Some has traveled by the fleets of ten-ton motorized junks which slip back and forth across the Straits of Malacca or the Makassar Straits, providing lucrative occupation to owners and crews. Sumatra and Sulawesi have been the chief Indonesian areas in which barter trade and smuggling have prevailed and overlapped. The Djakarta port of Tandjung Priok, however, has featured in some of the largest transactions and some of the biggest scandals, with military officers prominently featured as principals.

Barter, smuggling, and barter-smuggling, it should be pointed out, have dropped off by an estimated 50–75 per cent in the last year or so, but there are many both in Indonesia and in Singapore who believe that this unfortunate trend could be swiftly and happily corrected. The reasons for the decline are numerous and complicated. The Indonesian Government has re-established control over many of the insurgent areas and in doing so has either more successfully channeled or more effectively interfered with production and export trade of any sort. The Indonesian patrols have increased their vigilance and their velocity. The regional civil and military authorities have become more cautious if not more docile in their acceptance of Djakarta's decrees. And the Singapore Government—which used to say in effect that what is smuggling for Indonesia is free trade for Singapore, and welcome by whatever name or device—has now acceded to Indonesian requests and demands for cooperation by tightening up on its own check points. As regards this latter development, there is much suspicion in Djakarta that the Singapore Government is interested mainly in preventing the smuggling into Singapore of tobacco, liquor, and oil—in other words, traffic in the few items dutiable in Singapore, rather than traffic in the innumerable goods dutiable according to totally incoherent scales as they enter or leave Indonesia.

CONFISCATION VS. PIRACY

The problem of barter-smuggling is further complicated by Indonesia's unilateral declaration of a twelve-mile limit for Indonesian territorial waters and its offhand disregard for Singapore's own three-mile limit or for freedom of the high seas. One result has been a series of small-scale maritime crises—almost all of them, it should be stated at the outset, of a year or more ago, none of very recent date. Several years ago Indonesia acquired fast, well-armed patrol boats—some of them from the Communist bloc—and it makes use of them with what Singapore traders call a "trigger-happy" abandon. Indonesian naval patrols staged a series of swoops upon unarmed trading craft, whether of Indonesia or Singapore or other registry, whether plying Indonesian, international, or Singapore waters. The gunboat crews towed such craft into Indonesian ports, confiscated cargoes, intimidated and manhandled the crews, relieving them in the process of such personal property as watches, cigarettes, lighters, money, and outboard motors. "Legitimate confiscation for infringement of Indonesian regulations," said the Indonesian authorities, when they admitted to any knowledge whatever of the events. "Piracy," said the Singapore and for that matter the Indonesian traders. "Piracy indeed," Indonesian officials at times agreed, but went on to point out that since piracy is a long-established profession in these waters, what more natural than that modern Malay pirates should masquerade in Indonesian military uniform?

Two instances out of a long series will serve to give the general picture. On May 18, 1958, according to reliable Singapore press and official reports, an Indonesian gunboat raced to within two to three hundred yards of one of Singapore's offlying islands, Pulau Senang. There it captured a prahu loaded with some M$1,500 worth of copra, presumably of Indonesian origin and destined without export clearance for Singapore markets, and towed the craft off toward Indonesian waters. On the gunboat's approach, the crew of three jumped overboard, swam ashore, and gave the alarm. By the time the Singapore marine patrol reached the spot, gunboat and prahu had vanished, but eyewitnesses gave an account which could scarcely have been complete fabrication.

On December 12, 1958, the Singapore-registered trader, *Honesta* (2,776 tons), was captured by an Indonesian gunboat in international waters. It was boarded by a party of twelve fully-armed soldiers who sealed the radio, searched the ship, and ordered the captain to sail to the Indonesian island port of Tandjong Uban. There the ship was detained and the crew held incommunicado for ten days. Finally, after being kept in the harbor for twenty days more, the *Honesta* was released without explanation and permitted to continue its voyage to Singapore, still loaded with some two thousand tons of copra.

SANCTUARY VS. INTERFERENCE

The Indonesian regional rebellions of 1958 created a long-continued crisis in Singapore-Indonesian relations which intensified all other conflicts and remains today, despite change of government and change of policy in Singapore, an extremely disquieting memory. The regional insurrection leaders made Singapore one of their major bases of overseas operations and the communications center for coordination of activities in Sumatra and Sulawesi. Long before the insurrections had reached the stage of armed conflict, the rebel leaders had set up offices in Singapore. They had entered into business contracts with Singapore traders who took their rubber and copra and provided them with logistic support, including arms and ammunition. Presently they rented Singapore apartments into which their wives, children, and supporters moved when the fighting started to go against them. Later they organized a relay speedboat service between Singapore and Sumatra and a charter air service (reportedly with C.A.T. planes) between Singapore and Taipei. Also they established a publicity office and vigorously cultivated press and public contacts.

On all of these activities the Singapore Government looked with tolerance—according to common Indonesian accusation, with approbation. The travel documents of the rebel leaders were in order, stated Singapore officials; most of the rebels held valid diplomatic passports, and to refuse them the courtesies of the port would be an affront. Their finances were also in order, what with a reported M$40,000,000-plus in local banks and more money being deposited to their accounts daily as more rubber and copra were smuggled out for sale on Singapore markets. There was nothing to prevent them from renting offices, purchasing and shipping materials, or for that matter chartering boats or planes. As Indonesian official outrage and pressure mounted, and as the rebel cause languished, the Singapore Government began to backtrack a little. It had already (February 1958) declared itself strictly neutral in the Indonesian domestic conflict. It announced presently (March 1958) that for "humanitarian reasons" it would not permit the sale or shipment of "warlike materials." Later (April 1958) it began to refuse landing rights to chartered planes and to inquire carefully into the arrivals and departures by night at remote beaches of anonymous envoys. It announced after many months (January 1959) that it would no longer grant political asylum to "persons known to advocate the overthrow by force of any government." But it did not do any of this quickly enough, vigorously enough, or apologetically enough to appease the Indonesian Central Government, which had already decided that Singapore was deliberately interfering in Indonesian domestic affairs.

Djakarta sent a brigadier general, recently in command of operations against the rebels in West Sumatra, to assume the post of Consul General in Singapore and to adopt a firm line. It sent also a motley lot of special agents who, by their conspicuous counterespionage, counterbalanced the conspicuous wheeling and dealing of the rebels. All was on a relatively modest scale, so far as big-league international intrigue is concerned; but it was sufficient to create again and again in Singapore the atmosphere of a Hitchcock thriller. The top leaders of the Indonesian insurrection— Natsir, Sumitro, Sjafruddin, Warouw, Pantouw—and some of their wives and children arrived and departed in a manner which ingeniously combined furtive cocealment with motorcades escorted by strong-arm squads. Sinister-looking Djakarta agents shadowed them and were shadowed in turn by equally sinister-looking local types. Again and again Singapore customs or immigration offices gave offense to one side or the other—and thus further stoked public interest—now by letting a top rebel leader slip through unquestioned, now by finding that the papers of a loyalist agent were not in order. Things were not simplified by Djakarta's compilation of a black list and its presentation to the Singapore authorities accompanied by demands for deportation. Djakarta also made sporadic efforts to clamp down on all travel out of Indonesia to Singapore in order to prevent incipient insurgents from escaping with the same sort of special and diplomatic passports the others carried.

Gradually the excitement died down. The collapse of organized fighting in Sumatra resulted in the speedy withdrawal, via Singapore, of numbers of the top rebel leaders and the sharp curtailment of rebel agent activities in the colony. Anticipation of a P.A.P. victory in Singapore's 1959 elections, and knowledge that the P.A.P. proposed to win friends in Indonesia by alienating rebel sympathizers, was another factor leading to the depletion of the rebel community. Its leading members found new refuge in Manila, Hong Kong, Macao, and Taipei. Then came the expected P.A.P. victory and immediate P.A.P. declarations of intention to assist Indonesia in every possible way, including the denial of facilities in Singapore to enemies of the Djakarta regime. Since the day of the P.A.P. election victory, residence permits for known rebels have not been renewed, and any remaining rebel agents have gone underground. Change of attitude in Singapore has resulted in announcements, a few in Djakarta, but mainly in Singapore itself, that a new era of confidence and cooperation has set in and that the unhappy memories of the previous era are now beginning to fade. It has resulted in dispatch from Indonesia to Singapore of a good-will cultural mission of Balinese dancers; of acceptance by Singapore's Prime Minister, Lee Kuan Yew, of an invitation to pay a state visit to Indonesia; and of subsequent "agreement in principle" that Indonesia's First Minister Djuanda will return the visit. It has resulted also in several actual or proposed visits of trade missions. It has not, however, resulted in much else.

DIPLOMATIC RESERVE VS. SPONTANEOUS REACTIONS

Indonesian-Singapore relations, then, have entered a new period of mutual self-congratulation, regarding improvement, and of mutual bewilderment, especially in Singapore, as to why improvement doesn't follow hard upon the self-congratulation. Bewilderment, in the past, has often led to harsh words, particularly on the part of Indonesian officials, who feel, rightly or wrongly, that they can afford them, and of these harsh words the memory is slow to die out. Present Indonesian diplomatic nicety is tempered by past Indonesian blunt admonitions. "If there is no good will toward Singapore from neighboring countries, Singapore will not exist," declared Foreign Minister Subandrio irascibly on a visit to Singapore in October 1957. If Singapore did not mend its ways, he added, he would himself "conduct a campaign in his country and other Asian countries against the colony." Foreign Minister Subandrio is busy conducting a campaign today against the Overseas Chinese in Indonesia, and it seems rather unlikely that he regards the Overseas Chinese in Singapore as a different breed.

"Singapore millionaires," said Indonesia's Prime Minister Djuanda, on passing through Singapore in April 1958, "flourish whenever there is chaos in Indonesia—political or economic." Chaos in Indonesia is compounded rather than diminished today, and Singapore millionaires, despite some pretty formidable obstacles, continue to flourish, to the annoyance of Indonesian observers.

"Do not mistake patience for weakness," the then new Indonesian

Consul General, Brigadier-General Djatikusumo, declared in late December 1958 when he announced that Indonesia was about to make some "basic changes in policy" toward Singapore. "How can anyone expect us to continue normal relations with our neighbors when they allow subversive elements to use their countries as bases against us?"

Singapore has now virtually closed its doors to Indonesian rebels, but it has opened them to refugee Chinese capitalists wealthy enough to invest in its vigorously-promoted industrial development schemes. It is vulnerable any day, therefore, to the charge that it harbors Indonesian subjects who are either passively or actively opposed to the Indonesian Government. It is still a center, furthermore, of financial and economic manipulation of the sort the Djakarta Government is attempting ineffectually to curtail. One of the biggest and most recent of Indonesia's long series of economic scandals involves a refugee Indonesian capitalist who made off to Singapore with a good part of the proceeds of a £3,000,-000 embezzlement coup. Singapore has cooperated with Indonesian Government agents in the detection and return of this particular gentleman, but the question quite naturally arises in Indonesian minds—just how culpable were Singapore Chinese capitalists in putting temptation in his way?

As yet, however, the Indonesian Government has exhibited more diplomatic restraint than open indignation in these and other recent episodes. Singapore officials, for their part, have exhibited a remarkable degree of caution in their comments on Indonesia. High P.A.P. government personages do nevertheless now and again let slip unguarded remarks which make it clear that despite their policy of friendship for Indonesia and of censure for previous colonialistic "provocation" of Indonesia, they are far from happy about the course of events just south of the equator. They are gravely concerned not only with the course of Singapore-Indonesian relations as such but with the critical deterioration in the Indonesian domestic situation which could, of course, swiftly and adversely affect Singapore too.

Singapore Prime Minister Lee Kuan Yew, in his New Year's message to the Singapore people, published just a few days before departing on his good-will visit to Indonesia, made this remarkable reference to his prospective host country: "What of our little world, Singapore, the Federation and Southeast Asia? . . . 1955 to 1960 were years of growing disillusionment with what has been made of the freedom so ardently fought for and won with such great sacrifice. . . . All said and done, India has moved forward, not backward in the economic, industrial, and social planes. This is more than can be said of the others. In Burma, Ceylon, *Indonesia* [emphasis mine], Pakistan, there is visible the gradual sag in standards, standards of public conduct, standards of public administration, and worse, standards of living. One thing is abundantly clear: It is not enough to have the will to be free. It is not enough to want to build up a happy, just, and prosperous society. Accompanying these sublime feelings, there must be the sustained discipline, the strength of social organization, the administrative skill, and the economic and industrial techniques to bring to reality the brave new world we all so ardently want to build for ourselves and our children."

Prime Minister Lee was spoken to very sharply by Indonesian editorial writers for his "insult" to Indonesia in this New Year's message. In his various messages to the Indonesian people at the time of his actual visit he chose to dwell upon the safer subjects of art and culture, in which the Indonesian unquestionably excels. On his return to Singapore, while various members of his party referred privately with some candor to the shocking evidences they had observed of the correctness of the Prime Minister's New Year appraisal of the Indonesian situation, the Prime Minister himself exhibited both caution and astuteness in officially summarizing his impressions as follows: "If Indonesia could match progress in the administrative and economic fields similar to the progress made in the cultural and linguistic fields, the second half of the twentieth century will see a powerful, industrialized, and prosperous Indonesia."

Of such administrative and economic progress, if it existed, he cited no evidence. He did, however, make a proposal. A M$600 million (US$200 million) steel manufacturing plant, to be built with World Bank money in Singapore, to be operated by Japanese technicians, to be supplied with iron ore from the Federation of Malaya and with coal from Indonesia, to supply Singapore, the Federation, and Indonesia in turn with its output: this was Prime Minister Lee's master plan for a significant beginning in regional economic planning and cooperation. The master plan vanished almost as soon as it was unveiled. The Indonesian Government, after indicating informal approval "in principle"—a virtually certain indicator of disapproval—decided to accept a new steel plant of its own from the U.S.S.R. The Federation, which sells to Japan at a good price all the iron ore it can now produce, saw little advantage in shifting customers. The Singapore Government is now planning a new steel plant all its own, international disinterest notwithstanding, and international cooperation, apparently, heavily discounted.

THE P.A.P. DILEMMA

To review Singapore-Indonesian relations in the recent past is necessarily to review a series of rancorous disputes. Such disputes, of course, might better be forgotten if it were not for the unhappy trick of history that new relations evolve out of old and not out of cosmic particles assembled either by design or at random. The Singapore P.A.P. Government has adopted as a primary point in its political platform the improvement of relations with Indonesia. The P.A.P. must make good on its promises or face formidable public criticism. The area in which it will be held strictly accountable by hardheaded Singapore merchants, and by the man in the street as well, is not culture, or athletics, or state visits, or even joint political manifestoes—witness the notably unenthusiastic response in Singapore when Prime Minister Lee, as a *de rigueur* climax to his state visit, endorsed Indonesia's claims to Netherlands New Guinea. What counts in Singapore is trade.

Progress toward improving Singapore-Indonesian trade relations can be gauged by the fact that Singapore-Indonesian trade is falling off, not sharply on the annual basis, but steadily, and by the further fact that many plans and starts in exchange of trade missions and conclusion of trade agreements have led to practically no meaningful action. An Indonesian Chamber of Commerce trade mission which was to have visited Singapore to resolve trade problems cancelled out last autumn when Indonesia instituted a drastic new financial and economic policy. A proposal for an exchange of trade missions was dropped when the Lee Kuan Yew state visit was planned, with trade talks to be part of the agenda—a highly inconclusive part of the agenda, as it actually turned out. Action on a new proposal for an Indonesian trade mission to Singapore was indefinitely suspended when the Muslim *Puasa* or fasting month approached—a calendar contingency which might easily have been foreseen. An exchange of visits is still proposed and the actual exchange will no doubt come off, perhaps even soon; but meanwhile Singapore-Indonesian formal trade agreements are just about where they stood five years ago when Singapore's former Chief Minister, David Marshall, achieved a much advertised "agreement in principle" which has never been translated into agreement in practice.

The critical fact for Singapore to adjust to is that the Indonesian economy is desperately disrupted, and the critical fact for Indonesia to adjust to is that Singapore is an essential entrepôt. Each must work out its own adjustment in its own way. The net result in the past of Indonesian economic debacle and Singapore economic enterprise has been an increase, not a decrease, in barter-smuggling-confiscation-piracy, all of which naturally exacerbate rather than improve Singapore-Indonesian relations. The pressure to rationalize the relationship is upon the P.A.P., not the Djakarta Government. It is in Singapore that trade still dominates politics, whereas in Djakarta politics dominates trade. The "Dark Ages" in relations between Djakarta and Singapore, despite Prime Minister Lee's declaration of a renaissance, are not yet past.

14

Strange Estrangement

May 11, 1960

THE NEWLY independent, formerly British-ruled Federation of Malaya, and the recently independent, former Dutch colony, the Republic of Indonesia, have shared a common or closely similar historical tradition, racial background, language, religion, and culture. They have also shared common or closely similar problems of economic overspecialization in raw export commodities, of subordination of indigenous to alien Chinese or European economic enterprise, and of necessity for rapid development of diverse regional and racial groups into a unified nation. Logically, then, one might expect to find in Djakarta and in Kuala Lumpur a large area of agreement on matters both of domestic and of foreign policy.

In actuality it would be difficult to find in Southeast Asia two more sharply contrasting capital cities and psychologies than in Djakarta and Kuala Lumpur. There exist in Kuala Lumpur, to be sure, elements of resemblance to Djakarta, and it is these very elements which constitute danger signals for the Federation: disposition on the part of some, especially those Malays most attracted to or influenced by Indonesia, to discriminate in favor of the Malay race, language, and religion at the great expense of the Chinese, the Indian, and the European; suspicion of unremitting anti-Malay intrigue on the part of all non-Malays; naïve conviction that it is better to wait for a spontaneous sort of local development than to entrust non-Malays with much real responsibility or privilege; willingness to risk deterioration, even bloodshed, rather than to tolerate any degree of alleged "exploitation."

Ultranationalistic concepts have not flourished in Kuala Lumpur, however, to anything like the extent to which they have flourished in Djakarta. Although there is danger that they will take hold both suddenly and disastrously, there seems to be a good chance that the tolerant attitudes of the present leaders will prevail. The very difference between moderate and ultranationalistic policies on the part of the top leaders in Kuala Lumpur and in Djakarta respectively has resulted in a noticeable coolness of relations between them—in what amounts, in fact, to a strange estrangement, not bitter on either side, but just bewildered.

In foreign relations, including, of course, relations with each other, the differences between Kuala Lumpur and Djakarta become especially apparent. In the first place, the very subject of foreign relations, which engrosses the attention of all Indonesian political leaders to the grave impairment of domestic administration, has been held distinctly subordinate to other matters in Malaya. The Federation Government, acting on the principle that Malaya would do well to consolidate its national position first, its international position afterward, has to date resisted opposition pressure even to open up a full-scale parliamentary debate on foreign policy. "There would be trouble," Prime Minister Tengku Abdul Rahman has explained with disarmingly undiplomatic candor, "if we said anything against the West Irian question. There would be trouble if anything was said against India. And there would be trouble from the Muslims if we said anything against Pakistan."

The Federation Government, accordingly, has declined to enmesh itself, Indonesian-style, in hour-to-hour debate on foreign policy and day-by-day release of communiqués condemning colonialism, imperialism, and capitalism throughout the non-Communist world. Unlike Indonesia, it has gone slow in setting up expensive diplomatic missions abroad and in dispatching and entertaining good-will missions heavily freighted with junketeering politicians. It has aspired, until very recently at least, when the Prime Minister became co-sponsor of a proposed Southeast Asia Friendship and Economic Treaty (SEAFET), to no role of leadership in any new bloc. It has felt under no compulsion to renounce the policies and the commitments of the colonial past— membership in the British Commonwealth, elimination of Communist terrorists, reliance upon outside military assistance, encouragement of foreign investment, adherence to liberal democratic principles in politics and free enterprise principles in its economy. It has no irredentist demands, no emotion-laden slogans, no mass movements, no—or at any rate, relatively little—oratorical fervor to expend upon such generalities as world peace, world tensions, world cooperation, or even atoms. It responds, therefore, rather lethargically to the great issues which Indonesia raises. On the few occasions when it raises an issue of its own, it provokes Indonesian dismay at its un-Afro-Asian statesmanship.

Some of the more important international issues raised or pursued to date by Indonesia in expectation of support from the Federation of Malaya, as from other former colonial areas, have been Indonesia's incessant claims to Irian Barat (Western New Guinea), its opposition to SEATO, its support for immediate Algerian independence, its campaign against the Overseas Chinese, and always its drive to organize and dominate an Afro-Asian bloc. The most important issues which the Federation itself has raised or pushed have been the condemnation of Russian aggression in Hungary, of Chinese aggression in Tibet, of Communist subversion in Laos, and a proposal for the formation of SEAFET, plus two others of more recent date on which not only Malaya and Indonesia but many other nations find themselves in unaccustomed agreement—condemnation of *apartheid* in South Africa and dictatorship in South Korea. The Malayan stand on the Irian Barat issue and the Indonesian stand on SEAFET are revealing of the contrast which ordinarily prevails in Malayan and Indonesian official psychologies.

Indonesia renewed its campaign in the United Nations for condemnation of Dutch retention of Western New Guinea at just the time that the newly independent Federation of Malaya took its place as a UN member. When the subject of Irian Barat came up for vote, the Federation's representative unexpectedly abstained—because, as the Federation Government explained, it had not yet had a chance to study the issue or to formulate a policy. Shock and dismay were the reactions in Indonesia, where it was a novel idea that a sister Asian nation would have to study the issue at all, since it was presented as one of nationalism vs. colonialism. "Incredible," exclaimed the *Times of Indonesia*. "It is to be expected that Malaya will now joint SEATO," editorialized the *Indonesian Observer*, voicing almost the most damaging judgment which an Indonesian journal can pass upon an Asian neighbor. The newly arrived Malayan ambassador to Indonesia, who had just a few years previously been an employee of the Indonesian delegation to the United Nations, experienced a sudden chilling of his welcome. The Federation has since then switched to support of the Indonesian claim, at least to the extent of branding Dutch administration of New Guinea as "vestigial colonialism." From the Indonesian point of view, however, Malayan support comes belatedly, equivocally, and without any of the resounding joint communiqués regarded in Djakarta as the *sine qua non* to real support.

In mid-1959 Prime Minister Tengku Abdul Rahman of Malaya was co-sponsor with President Garcia of the Philippines of a proposal for establishment of a SEAFET organization for regional cooperation in cultural and economic matters—and, as originally envisioned, before intimations of Indonesian objections were taken into consideration— in political matters as well. Indonesian spokesmen first rejected the SEAFET proposal out of hand, openly hinting that they did not like the anti-Communist overtones; they then explained that what they really preferred was binational arrangements first, multinational arrangements later, and in either event, arrangements within the Afro-Asian complex as defined in Bandung. The opinion prevails in Kuala Lumpur, however, that what Indonesians really prefer is for initiative to come from Djakarta, and that what they really fear is contamination by association with anti-Communist partners. As a result largely of Indonesia's opposition, nothing definite has yet come of the SEAFET proposal, although both Malaya and the Philippines continue to announce that planning is in progress and other nations—Thailand, for instance—have indicated willingness to join.

On various anticolonial issues the Federation has given mild support to the Indonesian position; in the case of Algeria, only to the extent of calling for negotiation and fair settlement, not to the extent of prescribing that the only "fair settlement" is immediate and total French capitulation. On the anti-Communist issues, such as Hungary, Tibet, and Laos, Indonesia has cautiously expressed concern, but only after much delay and without branding anyone an aggressor, always to the accompaniment of warnings that full-scale international debate will lead to increase, not decrease, of world tensions. Indonesia's fixation on anticolonialism and Malaya's commitment to anticommunism seem each to the other evidence of perversely wrong-headed misreading of the international facts of life.

If the Federation and Indonesia have reached no meeting of minds on subjects of broad international significance, they have reached no real meeting of minds either on subjects of dispute or at least of misunderstanding between themselves. The major issues are these: Indonesian complaints that the Federation has tolerated contraband trade with Indonesia and has afforded sanctuary if not outright encouragement to Indonesian rebels; and Federation complaints that Indonesia has not only obstructed normal trading and fishing operations but has both frequently and deliberately violated Malaya's territorial waters in pursuit of alleged smugglers and fugitives. The specific episodes which have led to frequent formal and informal exchanges of complaint or protest are very similar to the episodes which have exacerbated Singapore-Indonesian relations over the last few years.

Briefly, the Indonesian Government indignantly declares, citing abundant supporting evidence, that rubber, copra, coffee, and other produce smuggled out of Indonesia have been freely admitted into Federation ports and that Indonesian rebel agents, traveling to or fleeing from Sumatra, have gained easy entry into the Federation and even in some cases—here the evidence seems inconclusive—have gained audience with Federation officials (including the Prime Minister) and have taken up semipermanent residence. The Federation Government mildly and quietly declares, also citing abundant supporting evidence, that Indonesia has blocked normal Federation exports to Indonesia—notably fresh and salted fish—and that Indonesian gunboats have repeatedly pursued, captured, imprisoned, intimidated, and looted the crews of small Malayan trading and fishing craft in international waters, within the Federation three-mile limit, or actually within yards of the Federation shore line. Neither government has received any very explicit satisfaction from the other regarding its charges. The Federation, however, has tightened up on its customs and immigration checks—which reveal, among other anomalies, that there is a regular business in running lepers from Indonesia for free hospitalization in the Federation. The Indonesian Government has exhibited a willingness to ease up a little on obstruction of imports from the Federation and on assertion of its self-arrogated prerogative of patrolling Federation waters.

Although rancorous exchanges have been infrequent, several much publicized episodes have served of late to call attention to the possibility of really serious conflict. A thirty-ton Indonesian junk, loaded with thirty Indonesian rebels, some of them armed, slipped through Indonesian patrols in the Straits of Malacca a few months ago and put into a secluded river mouth on the Malayan coast near Port Swettenham—not for the first time, according to common report, and not without local assistance. The Malayan authorities on December 21, 1959, apprehended and imprisoned the rebels and held them for trial on charges of illegal entry and unauthorized possession of weapons and ammunition. The Indonesian Government requested—demanded would be the better word, according to informed reports—that the rebels be turned over to Indonesian custody. The rebels appealed for political asylum in Malaya. The Malayan Government, in the face of testy Indonesian insistence that the rebels be handed over forthwith, announced its determination to adhere strictly to local and international law, which in this case made provision for fine and prison sentence but none for what would have been the much more severe punishment of extradition. The rebels were tried, convicted, fined (M$225 each), and sentenced to imprisonment (six months). The question remains open whether Indonesia and Malaya will now work out an extradition agreement—as Indonesia is now eager to do—and if so, whether it will apply retroactively to the case of the thirty rebels. Meanwhile, at frequent intervals, come reports of "mystery gunboats" speeding into and out of Malayan waters. The suspicion persists that the mystery is by no means deep and that the intention is to intimidate.

Most widely publicized of the "mystery gunboat" episodes occurred, by a miracle of mistiming, just one week prior to the state visit paid by Indonesian Prime Minister Djuanda to the Federation of Malaya in mid-April 1959. The captain of a fast gunboat in hot pursuit of a Malayan craft, Singapore-bound from Sumatra, followed it into shallow inshore waters off the Malayan coast, commandeered a small local boat to continue the chase, finally captured the craft, confiscated its cargo, and abducted its captain. In the excitement of the raid, however, he left ashore one pretty conclusive bit of evidence of what had happened, namely, a member of his own crew, unmistakably an Indonesian in Indonesian military uniform. The episode did not really mar the Malayan welcome for Prime Minister Djuanda, but it did cast a shadow upon official conversations about a new era in Indonesian-Malayan understanding. It has since then come to mind each time new "mystery gunboats" are reported—as in early 1960—to be interfering with traffic between Indonesia and Port Swettenham.

Federation-Indonesian relations are influenced, both for better and for worse, by the presence in the Federation of some tens of thousands of Indonesians and the presence in Indonesia of several thousand Malays. The leading members of the Malay community in Indonesia are the group of onetime "Freedom Fighters," young Malays who went to Indonesia during the war and threw in with the Indonesian revolutionary movement, a few of them as officers, most of them as soldiers in the very loosely organized Indonesian armies. These "Freedom Fighters" or "Malayan Youth in Indonesia" have since then organized and constituted themselves a lobby. They have had two primary objectives: one is to achieve recognition both from the Indonesian and the Malayan governments of their services, including status and benefits as veterans; the other is to promote the idea of a Pan-Malayan political union in which Indonesia and Malaya would be the leading members. In neither of their campaigns have they met with very favorable reception as yet either from the Indonesian or the Malayan governments, neither of which seems anxious to take official cognizance of their claim or their proposal. These Malayan Freedom Fighters have become involved also in Indonesian party politics, in international conferences, and in a whole series of related activities which have identified them as potential troublemakers. At the Bandung Conference, for instance, the Freedom Fighters, together with several prominent opposition politicians from Malaya (Burhanuddin and Boestamam, heads of the Pan-Malayan Islamic Party and the Party Ra'ayat, or People's Party, respectively), were present as self-invited observers. They received scant attention from anyone else and have since aired their grievances against both Indonesian and Malayan officialdom. The Freedom Fighters have recently been put on notice by the Malayan Embassy in Djakarta that if they expect any Malayan Government consideration they must keep out of Indonesian politics and must register as Malayan citizens. This latter move will immediately make them subject, like all alien residents of Indonesia, to the Indonesian Government's alien head tax—a tax scaled far beyond the capacity of many of them to pay. Their state of mind and their state of finances is not at the moment a happy one.

If the Malayan Freedom Fighters in Indonesia have lately embarrassed both governments, so too, and not so very long ago, did a few other Malays of a very different political orientation—Malays of the anti-Communist right. Four Malay youth representatives, the founders of a "Southeast Asia Friendship Association," happened to be in Djakarta at the time of the assassination attempt upon President Sukarno in the fall of 1957. Along with other known anti-Communist operators they were rounded up, detained, and questioned. According to the report of their leader after his return to Malaya, they were accused of "subversive" activities as "SEATO agents," confined incommunicado in filthy cells, given food "fit only for pigs," and routed out for questioning, "Communist style," at any hour of day or night, then finally, after a month or so, permitted to "bolt for it" and get back to Malaya. Stories like this, perhaps not particularly significant in themselves, do contribute to the impression, now growing in Malaya, that all is far from well in neighboring Indonesia and that Malays are not necessarily regarded as brothers.

Indonesians in Malaya, or persons of Indonesian birth or descent, constitute in some areas, such as Southern Johore, an actual majority of the Malaysian population. By far the most of them regard themselves and are accepted by the Federation Government as Malayan citizens, and all of them have been encouraged by the Indonesian Government to accept such status. Ties with Indonesia have been greatly weakened by reason both of local acclimatization and of wartime separation and postwar travel restrictions. The feeling of kinship remains alive, nevertheless, and pride in Indonesian origin is revived by reason of Indonesia's achievement, despite critical domestic difficulties, of big-power status in Southeast Asia, also by reason of the prestige which attaches to Indonesian language, culture, and intellectual attainment. The feeling of kinship and pride might swiftly be even further strengthened, particularly if anything should come of recurrent proposals of opposition politicians that the Federation increase its Malaysian population majority of a fraction of 1 per cent by permitting the entry of tens of thousands of willing Indonesian migrants.

During the early postwar years Indonesians in Malaya or Indonesian-Malays were particularly active in stirring up local support for the Indonesian republic and in spearheading Malaya's own independence movement. Two Malays of Indonesian descent, Burhanuddin and Boestamam—the two unofficial Malayan representatives at Bandung and frequent visitors to Indonesia at other times—were among the most prominent organizers of Malayan revolutionary groups and parties. Boestamam, for instance, organized a youth group armed with miscellaneous modern weapons and sharpened bamboo spears and published for its guidance a revolutionary manifesto of distinctly Marxist content. Burhanuddin was prominent not only in political organization but in instigating Malay street demonstrations which ended in the Singapore riots of 1950. Both Burhanuddin and Boestamam were jailed by the British, and both emerged from jail to renew their political activities. They are the leaders today of two opposition parties which combine Marxist, ultranationalist, and in the case of Burhanuddin's P.M.I.P., fanatical Muslim elements. These two parties challenge the moderate policies of the present Alliance administration. At the time of the election campaigns last year Burhanuddin and Boestamam were both widely believed to be receiving Indonesian support, including, improbable as it may seem in view of the state of the Indonesian economy, substantial funds. The activities of the P.M.I.P., curiously enough, have given rise to speculation not just about Djakarta's encouragement but about Djakarta's suspicions. The party has been rumored to be favorably disposed toward the Darul Islam rebels in Indonesia and toward a Sumatran-Malayan alliance. Such rumors are impossible to substantiate and perhaps unfair to repeat, but they do add a dimension to one of the more impenetrable political mysteries of Malaya today.

Indonesian crises and insurrections of recent years have put the Federation Government in an extremely awkward position. Considerations of kinship and of proximity have led on the one hand to divided sympathies as regards the various Indonesian factions and on the other to fear that disorders in Indonesia might easily spread to Malaya. The Federation Government has adopted a very correct and consequently a not very dynamic policy. It has repeatedly declared that the Indonesian crises and insurrections were domestic Indonesian problems in which the Federation would not meddle. Such statements did not, of course, satisfy the Djakarta regime, which would have welcomed Federation declarations of support for itself and vigorous Federation effort to deny support to the rebels. On the whole, however, the two governments have managed to maintain better and smoother relations than might have been expected under the circumstances—circumstances which included some little feeling on the part of many Federation citizens of Sumatran origin that Sumatra might do well to cut loose from Indonesia and join Malaya.

Several minor developments during the 1958 Indonesian insurrection resulted in minor flaps but fortunately in no real disturbance of relations. A few Malays of Indonesian descent at one point proposed to petition the Federation Council of Rulers to use its good offices to bring about peaceful negotiations between the Indonesian Central Government and the rebels. The idea aroused no enthusiasm in Djakarta where the Malay sultans are commonly regarded as feudal anachronisms and good offices as intervention; in Kuala Lumpur it aroused little except apprehension. A few hot-blooded youths, mainly of Indonesian descent, proposed to volunteer for the Indonesian Army. They received no encouragement from Djakarta and active discouragement from Kuala Lumpur. Tengku Abdul Rahman, as a good-will gesture, headed a drive to collect food and clothing for Indonesian relief. The Malayan ambassador in Djakarta reported, however, after Indonesian acknowledgement had begun to seem unduly delayed, that the Foreign Office had informed him there was actually no shortage of food or clothing in Indonesia and that further collections were unnecessary.

The spectacle of Indonesian insurrections, and the accompanying spectacle of national economic, political, and social deterioration, all intensified by anti-Dutch and now anti-Chinese agitation and discrimination, has constituted for many persons in the Federation a handy object lesson in how not to achieve national development. Some of the leading citizens and officials of the Federation are now acutely aware that the Republic of Indonesia has by its own policies and actions converted what were merely formidable obstacles into virtually insurmountable ones, and that should ultranationalistic sentiments prevail in Kuala Lumpur, the same thing could happen in Malaya. Whether the object lesson of Indonesia will actually constitute in the long run an effective deterrent to policies of nationalistic excesses, many Federation citizens, particularly, of course, those of Chinese origin, are inclined to doubt. It seems safe to conclude, however, that already it has served at the very least to slow down the development of ultranationalistic sentiments and that the slowing down may serve to preclude some of their most dangerous manifestations during this crucial, immediate postindependence period. The leaders of the Federation of Malaya are well aware that the Indonesian show is a poor one and the Federation show a good one, and so, for that matter, is a growing number of Indonesians. Exchanges of official and unofficial visits and exchanges of press reports have taken care of that. Even large segments of the uninformed population in both countries are well informed about the difference in desirability between the Indonesian rupiah and the Malayan dollar and the relative advantages of selling rubber, earning wages, buying clothing, or looking for a house or office in Malaya as compared with Indonesia. Malayan self-congratulation leads inevitably to Indonesian annoyance and defensiveness, and Malayan-Indonesian relations suffer accordingly.

The knowledge that Indonesia is chaotic and Malaya orderly, that Indonesia is impoverished and Malaya prosperous, has served in the last several years to change the tone of official exchanges between the two nations. A few years ago, before Malaya achieved its independence in 1957, Indonesia was evidently proposing to play the role of big, protective, and perhaps possessive brother to its small, inexperienced neighbor. In 1955 Tengku Abdul Rahman paid a state visit to Indonesia, in the course of which President Sukarno put on an extravagant and impressive show of the big-little brother relationship. But Bung Karno, ubiquitous state visitor that he is, has not as yet taken Malaya up on its standing invitation to visit the Federation, just possibly because he is aware that not only the political attitudes but the economic contrasts and comparisons are not in his favor. Indonesian Prime Minister Djuanda, who did pay a state visit to Malaya in mid-April 1959, returning a visit to Indonesia by the Federation's Deputy Prime Minister Tun Abdul Razak, did so only after embarrassing postponement and with evident reluctance, getting himself quoted in advance to the effect that he did not relish the sort of "tea party" which was in store. The quotation was repudiated, naturally, but the visit itself, while it went off on both sides with punctilious correctness, was lacking in animation or enthusiasm. Tendentious subjects were rigorously excluded from official discussion, or at least from official report, and the visit came to a climax with the signing of an innocuous Treaty of Friendship but no joint communiqué on that one subject most vital to Indonesian communiquémanship—Western New Guinea.

In accordance with the Treaty of Friendship and with subsequent binational negotiations, the point on which both nations now feel that emphasis can be placed most profitably is that of cultural exchange, particularly in the field of language development. Joint efforts at achieving common standards in the well-advanced Indonesian language and the much-less-advanced Malay from which it originally derives—efforts which have been proceeding spasmodically for the last few years—have now received new stimulus. Exchange of language experts, convocation of language conferences, joint display of Indonesian and Malay publications, even agreement on certain linguistic technicalities such as standardized spellings—all have come as a result of newly intensified efforts toward cooperation.

Cooperation in matters of language may lead to rapidly increasing cooperation in other areas, but as yet the evidence is not at hand. Indonesia has offered scholarships to a few Malay students to study in Indonesian universities, but both scholarship students and private students from Malaya—about fifty in all—have suffered such difficulty in finding suitable accommodations and suitable programs that the effort has led to date to more complaint than contentment. Indonesia has also provided a few grants for Malayan air cadets, and this program, it seems, has worked out better than the ordinary scholarship program. A few starts have been made in the exchange of technical missions, but exchange visits of rubber experts, for instance, have not yet led to any new cooperation in rubber research and development, matters in which Malaya far surpasses Indonesia. A few incidental projects of technical and economic assistance have actually got more or less under way, but it was five years after an agreement was reached for Indonesia to supply Malaya with specimens of a superior Indonesian breed of goat before the first goats actually arrived in Malaya in early 1960.

None of this cooperative effort attracts quite so much public attention and public debate either in Indonesia or in Malaya as do the more unfortunate developments, such as rebel activity and piracy and also, to introduce a not-so-trivial new subject in this area of the world, where sport is a matter of high government policy, a fracas about Indonesian membership in the Asian Football Confederation, of which Malayan Prime Minister Tengku Abdul Rahman is honorary president. The confederation was organized in Manila a few years ago, with delegates from the Indonesian Football Association participating, apparently as co-sponsors. But then, over a period of years, Indonesia failed to pay its dues, to hand over the agreed-upon percentage of proceeds from international matches, or even to answer confederation correspondence. The confederation finally announced that it would take severe disciplinary action unless Indonesia complied with the regulations. Indonesia thereupon announced that it had never actually joined the confederation, that its requests for information copies of the constitution had been ignored, and that rather than itself being disciplined, Indonesia was prepared to boycott the association. It became apparent that both politics and pride were involved—politics because Indonesia had reservations about playing football with anti-Communist teams like South Korea's or anti-Arab teams like Israel's, pride because Indonesia resented being taken for granted. The impasse lasted for months, with both A.F.C. and I.F.A. accusations becoming gradually less heated. Finally, after many sensitivities had been assuaged, Indonesia applied for admission, was quickly voted in, and has presumably begun paying its fees since it has just competed and won third place in the Asian Cup contest in Kuala Lumpur.

The story of the Asian Football Confederation is perhaps a suitable and on the whole hopeful finale to the sad story of Indonesian-Malayan relations in general over the last few years. If illustrative of any memorable lesson, it is this one: not only Westerners who try to understand Asians, and Asians who try to understand Westerners, but Asians who try to understand Asians—even those with whom they have the longest and closest ties—are likely to run afoul of some very treacherous barnacles.

PART FIVE

Malaysia Scene

15

Malayanization of Malacca

July 8, 1957

THE MALAY Sultanate of Malacca in the year 1511 was the first point in Southeast Asia to fall to the newly arrived Europeans. The Portuguese, who then seized control, converted Malacca Town into a European stronghold of war, commerce, and religion, and from it they pushed gradually to the far reaches of the Orient. When Portuguese power declined, Malacca was captured by the Dutch (1641) who later lost it to the British (1795). The Dutch reoccupied Malacca between 1801 and 1807, lost it again to the British, recovered it again in 1818, and finally turned it over to the British for good in 1825. Save for the interval of Japanese occupation (1942–1945), Malacca has remained British until the present time. On August 31 of this year, "Merdeka Day" for the Federation of Malaya, the Settlement of Malacca will revert at last to Malaya. Four and a half centuries of European colonialism will soon be at an end, but in this birthplace of colonialism in Southeast Asia the ancient and the newer skeletons are invested, happily, with dignity and beauty.

Malacca Town today is a living reliquary of the European past in the area and of even older Chinese colonization. The city proudly preserves atop its former bastion hill the ruins of the sixteenth-century Church of St. Paul, where St. Francis Xavier preached and was later buried. It maintains what is perhaps the highest concentration of Chinese shrines and temples of any city in Southeast Asia and certainly the biggest Chinese cemetery outside of China itself. The massive Dutch Stadthuys (built between 1641 and 1660), painted a rosy terra cotta and now partially modernized and air-conditioned, remains today the center of Malacca Settlement government. The old Dutch Heerenstraat is still

195

lined with the mansions built by Chinese merchant princes who have flourished for centuries under European protection. Everywhere are to be found the monuments to British rule—hospitals, schools, churches, courts, markets, and office buildings; good roads, good sanitation systems, and a good police force.

Malacca's people, rather than bickering about ancient grudges and present fears, are living on the whole as though the present is considerably better than tolerable and the future can be handled when it comes. The British colonials are intent upon cricket and tennis in their clubs and villas along the beautiful seashore drive. The Chinese and Indians are intent upon a still lucrative trade and commerce. The handsome, well-dressed Malays seem relaxed on the verandas of their latticed houses where colored tiles decorate the front steps. The few hundred surviving Portuguese-Eurasians live in a "Portuguese Settlement" on the seashore where they practice their fisherman's trade as though in a tropical Azores. The city's broad water-front park and esplanade are crowded at sundown with multinational promenaders, the women presenting a colorful array of saris, flowered or plaid sarongs, pajamas, or *cheongsams* —the close-fitting Chinese dress. There the footballers practice, the children play, the strollers eat Magnolia ice-cream sandwiches and hot roasted chestnuts, drink saccharine orange crush, play American juke-boxes, and speak British English.

The town and state of Malacca,[1] long a Straits Settlement (like Singapore and Penang, a possession of the British Crown), will be fully integrated on August 31 into an independent Federation of Malaya (as also will be Penang, but not Singapore). Appropriately enough, it was in Malacca, scene of the first Western intrusion upon Malaya, that Tungku Abdul Rahman, Chief Minister of the Federation, in 1956 announced the success of his mission to London to negotiate for Malayan independence. In little Malacca Town today, perhaps better even than in big Kuala Lumpur, the capital of the Federation, or in any of the princely states that make up most of the Federation, it is possible to observe some of the adjustments which are having to be made as the many racial groups of Malaya prepare for Merdeka. In Malacca, the area which has been longest under Western influence, the inevitable process of Malayanization has for some time been under way, and both the prospects and the problems

[1] Malacca Town population: 65,000; Malacca Settlement population: 300,000; total area: 640 square miles.

have begun clearly to show. The problems, fortunately, do not now seem too formidable; they seem to be man-sized problems of the sort that can be coped with.

My wife and I decided to explore not just the old European and Chinese Malacca, which invites leisurely study, but also the newly emerging Malayan Malacca as well, and to try to see it through the eyes of some of its leading residents. We worked out a busy series of appointments, therefore, starting with a call on the British resident commissioner, the Honorable Mr. H. G. Hammett.

THE BRITISH RESIDENT COMMISSIONER

We were received on the top floor of the old Dutch Stadthuys, in what had been in Dutch times the banqueting hall—a long, high-ceilinged room, now painted in stylized floral panels in the Chinese manner. Great windows stood open along three walls. Through the trees we caught glimpses of the Malacca River and of the roofs of the town. Up the slope of St. Paul's Hill were the massive white porticoed Residency and the ruins of the Portuguese church. In the floors below us, in the arched and vaulted corridors and chambers of the Stadthuys, some still tiled and paneled much as the Dutch left them, the business of colonial administration was continuing. The effect of the setting was of an earlier century, but the feeling was of the mid-twentieth century swiftly moving in.

Mr. Hammett proved to be a man of about fifty-five, fit, ruddy and solid, a long-time colonial official who served in Malacca in prewar days as district officer and has served two postwar terms as resident commissioner. He is a British colonial official of the classical type: orderly, efficient, thorough, a man clearly in command of the office and firm in his direction for the administration of his area. With the coming of independence on August 31, Mr. Hammett will withdraw and retire. The program of Malayanization in government provides for the rapid replacement of British with local officials. Mr. Hammett, like others of the British, will qualify for lump-sum "compensation for loss of career"— which in some cases will run as high as U.S. $33,000. He can also claim a pension, and he would probably encounter no difficulty in securing a new official position in British Borneo, say, or in British Africa.

Our conversation with Mr. Hammett was largely about the status of Malacca in the new Federation. In most other states of Malaya the

British, in transferring sovereignty, are transferring it back to the hereditary princes. The princes are agreed to band themselves together into a
Federation to which will be delegated broad centralized authority. In
Malacca the situation is different. The Malacca sultanate has long since
died out. The Malays of Malacca, of all the Malayan people, are probably the least bound to the feudal tradition. For centuries they have been
adjusted to a considerable degree of self-government under a foreign
power. The legalistic question now arises: to whom will sovereignty be
transferred, and in whose name will it be exercised? The present plan is
for the Federation Government to appoint a governor of Malacca, who
will serve in essentially the same capacity as the British resident commissioner at present. Such a plan raises certain further questions, however,
as to the actual status of Malacca, whether it will be equal or inferior to
that of the nearby sovereign states. Certain unexpected complications
have already arisen, as, for example, the claims of the Dato Naning, the
traditional head of the small Naning sector of the Settlement, that
regional sovereignty over Naning should actually be transferred to him.

We also talked with the resident commissioner about the economic
situation of present-day Malacca. The town has lost its long-cherished
status as a free port; it is no longer a center of trade for the surrounding
areas; and it now falls within the Federation customs service, as Singapore and Penang do not. It has failed to receive government approval or
funds for extensive modernization of its port. Malacca Town consequently is now visited only by Chinese and Malay junks and by small
power vessels that can enter the shallow river mouth; ships of deeper
draft are serviced offshore by lighter. The center of the Federation's own
trade and commerce is shifting to Port Swettenham, now undergoing
rapid development over the protest of Malacca's businessmen that
Malacca is the historic and logical choice. But if Malacca Town is not
the busy commercial center it once was, neither is it exactly languishing.
Local business is excellent, with a number of estate and business interests
maintaining sizable Malacca establishments. The impending transfer of
British Commonwealth military headquarters to a big new camp in the
town's environs signifies an upsurge in local provision of supplies and
services. Under the British Commonwealth Development Plan there is
now being completed in Malacca a 162-acre, M$2 million Fish Culture
Research Station which, it is hoped, will ultimately serve not only
Malaya but other Southeast Asian countries interested in improvement
of methods for fish culture in fresh-water ponds.

Our second call was on Dato Sir Cheng Lock Tan, K.B.E., the most eminent Chinese resident of Malacca. Sir Cheng Lock, who was one of the earliest rubber planters and is now one of the leading figures in the industry, has long been a top Chinese political leader of Malaya. He is the founder, for instance, of the Malayan Chinese Association (M.C.A.), the foremost Chinese political party. Despite recent hospitalization, Sir Cheng Lock, now in his mid-seventies, remains extremely active. He is commonly mentioned as candidate for appointment as the first governor of Malacca (also for appointment as the first governor of Penang).

Sir Cheng Lock lives in the old Tan family home—one of the handsomest of the Chinese mansions of Heeren Street. Like its neighbors, it is fronted by a shallow portico extending the thirty-five-foot width of the house, and it stretches the full depth of a city block to the beach. Entering the front door, we faced a long vista of marble-floored, high-ceilinged chambers and courts, divided only by carved screens and ornamental archways through which blew a cool breeze from the sea. The narrow house was not only deep but tall, for through the open roofs of a courtyard we could glimpse the galleries of upper stories, their overhanging eaves lending further shade and coolness to these airy and dignified rooms. Sir Cheng Lock received us with great courtesy in one of the sitting rooms and then showed us through the length of the house. It was furnished in the massive, baroque southern Chinese style, to which had been added the treasures and travel souvenirs of past and present Tans—early nineteenth-century European furniture and engravings; Chinese paintings, calligraphy, embroidered hangings, and *objets d'art;* photographs; and cases of medals and honors awarded to Sir Cheng Lock. An extraordinarily fine portrait of an early Ch'ing Dynasty ancestress, the envy of any collector, hung over the family altar. A huge engraving of Queen Victoria with her consort and children held the place of honor in another room.

Sir Cheng Lock, who has lived almost all his life in Malacca except for an interlude as a refugee in India during the Japanese occupation and various periods of travel abroad, spoke of the position of the Malacca Chinese. Many of them, like himself, come from families which have lived in Malacca for generations, some of them for centuries. They have adopted English language and customs in status almost co-equal with Chinese. In many instances they speak almost no Chinese. They have few if any connections with China itself; very few of them now wish to travel back to China, and only rarely do their children go to China to study. The Chinese of Malacca in general take pride in their status as British subjects. One of the most urgent political problems of the present time, therefore, is the determination of their future citizenship status. Sir Cheng Lock's M.C.A. realizes that recognition of dual British and Malayan citizenship for the Chinese would create peculiarly difficult problems for the new Federation. It has taken its stand for one nation, one language, one nationality—Malayan. But other powerful Chinese groups are working for retention of British-subject status, at least for those born under British rule, and the conflict is a troublesome one within the Chinese community.

Sir Cheng Lock presented us with autographed copies of volumes of his published speeches and referred us to this impressive collection for his statements regarding the necessity for cooperation among Malaya's various races. The conversation then turned to other matters, such as the history of the Tan family in Malacca, and to arrangements for a visit another day to one of Sir Cheng Lock's rubber estates.

THE SPOKESMAN FOR THE MALAYS

We spent a good part of one day in Malacca trying to get in touch with Inche Hasnul bin Abdul Hadi, local chairman of U.M.N.O., member of the Municipal Council, and recognized spokesman for the Malay community. Mr. Hasnul was hard to find. Not only was he attending three or four different meetings that day and moving meanwhile between his several different offices, but he was making trips outside the city and paying calls at the municipal hospital where friends were recuperating from the flu epidemic. Just as we were setting out to trace Mr. Hasnul down to his Malay-style home, a few miles outside the city, he came in search of us. He found us at the logical center of all Malacca visitors, at the Government Rest House—a pleasant, sea-front establishment, one of a Malaya-wide chain which for something like U.S. $3.50 to $5.00 per day provides traveling officials—also, on a space-available basis, the general public—with good quarters and good food.

In the Rest House lounge we had an hour's conversation with Mr. Hasnul. We started by inquiring about the recent trip he had made to the United States under the U.S. Department of State's exchange-of-persons program. Save for the Asian's inevitable reservation—profound disapproval of discrimination toward the American Negro—he had been delighted with almost everything he had seen. We then asked for his views on the future prospects for an independent Malaya.

Mr. Hasnul believes that Malaya's biggest difficulties will be economic, not political. He is of the opinion that dependence upon world prices (meaning, basically, American prices) for rubber and tin is a chancy business. Local industrialization, he thinks, is indispensable to a healthy economy, but industrialization, he concedes, will be beset by major difficulties with regard to raw materials (other than rubber) and discovery of mass markets. Besides industrialization, he favors agricultural diversification as another solution to Malaya's economic problems. Here, too, he recognizes special difficulties, not the least of which is the Malay's insistence upon production and consumption of rice which, at best, is an uneconomic crop.

Mr. Hasnul, who follows closely the political developments in nearby Indonesia, declares that Malaya has a major advantage which Indonesia lacked from the start, i.e., a strong, well-trained civil service. He observes also that Malaya is adopting the administrative system which is natural and logical for the area—the federal system which Indonesia rejected because it had been backed by the Dutch. Mr. Hasnul is not particularly worried about the possibility of racial strife in the new Federation, but he is worried about political opportunists who may seek quick personal aggrandizement at the cost of national harmony. He is not particularly worried either about an internal Communist menace, although Malaya, he says, is easily vulnerable "to external attack from whatever quarter."

A personable young man still in his early thirties, Mr. Hasnul is an ex-schoolteacher turned politician by reason of recent national developments. Alert and dynamic, he is typical of the newly forming group of politically active young Malays. This group is still extremely small, he admits; but whether it can provide the quality of leadership that the Malays and the nation require, only the future can show.

THE LEADING INDIAN MERCHANT

In one of the government offices we had a meeting with Mr. Seth, leading Indian textile merchant of Malacca. Mr. Seth, now in his sixties and in theory semiretired, is still in active command of his business. He devotes the major part of his time, however, to civic affairs. He is an appointive (nonparty) member of the Municipal Council, the chairman of several dozen committees, and an active social-welfare worker. The morning we talked with him Mr. Seth was busy with arrangements for a forthcoming charity fair. He had just come from a long session in the Social Welfare Office, one concerning an Indonesian child adopted at birth into an Indian family. On her brother's instigation the child had recently run away, to join her natural mother who is herself a welfare case, and Mr. Seth's advice was being sought by the Welfare Office.

Mr. Seth has lived through critical times in Malaya and has watched from a not very great distance even more critical times in India. He faces the independence period with the assurance of a man who believes there are always difficulties ahead, just as there are always solutions. In his textile business he is having this outlook reconfirmed today. Now that Malacca has lost its free-port status, he himself has become involved in all the unaccustomed tangles and delays of customs formalities. He purchases textiles in Singapore at a price which he believes, after allowing for transportation and duties, will allow him to sell competitively in Malacca. The new Malayan customs office may assess the textiles at an arbitrary rate which will throw all of his calculations out of line. Nevertheless, as Mr. Seth points out, he is still in business on the old scale, in competition with very shrewd rivals, with time and energy to indulge his interest in social welfare. He has valued his British-subject status, but he regards Malacca as his permanent home and he is ready for whatever comes.

THE DATO NANING

In order to visit the Dato Naning—Dato Mohammed Shah—semihereditary, semielective chief of the 50,000 Naning Malays of the Settlement, we drove some twenty miles north from Malacca Town up into the low hills that mark the border between Malacca and the neighboring state of Negri Sembilan. There we found the Dato Naning in his Western-style official "bungalow"—a two-story concrete building built at a cost of M$50,000 by the Malacca government as a joint Naning Council Hall and Dato's Residency. The Dato received us in the council room, a formal parlor furnished in the Southeast Asian version of modern Western style and provided with glass cabinets in which were displayed Japanese tea sets and rather an astonishing collection of cotton Easter chicks. The Dato himself was dressed in traditional Sumatran style, wearing a short plaid sarong over a soft, pajamalike suit, conspicuously displaying two particular emblems of office: a gold velvet Muslim cap, and an ancestral kris sheathed in pure gold. The Dato is a man of about fifty. He spent most of his career in the Singapore Police Department where he was a police inspector from 1936 to 1951. He was installed as Dato in 1953, twenty-four Dato of the line, succeeding the twenty-third, who was kidnapped and presumably killed by the terrorists, and the twenty-second, who was killed by the Japanese.

The Dato Naning answered our questions about the relationships between the Naning people and the Minangkabau people of Sumatra, from whom they derive. The original Minangkabau settlers of the Naning area brought with them in the fifteenth century their matriarchal social system as well as their *adat* (custom) law, both of which survive today and give the distinctive coloration to the Malay-Muslim culture of the Naning area and of large sections of Negri Sembilan. Direct contacts between Naning and Sumatra are few these days, the Dato told us, but occasionally a prominent Minangkabau religious leader visits Naning and is received with great ceremony by the community.

The Dato told us also of the famous Naning War when the British misinformed by a civil servant who declared that the Naning people had been subject to the Dutch and hence were subject to the British, in 1831 blundered into a war of conquest, only to discover that they had not had the provocation they supposed. Once they had conquered Naning, however, the British retained it as part of Malacca, stripping the then Dato of all authority but setting him up in considerable style in Malacca Town. Some years later the position of Dato was restored, but with powers limited only to *adat* and religious matters. Largely because of British neglect, the Dato believes, the landlocked Naning area has remained one of the least developed sections of Malacca. Schools, for instance, are rather below the Malayan standard. Economic opportunity is limited to farming and estate labor. The Naning males, like those of the Minangkabau in Sumatra, whether driven by economic pressure, or by consuming ambition, or by adventurousness, or, perhaps, feeling themselves oppressed by a matriarchal society at home, have tended to migrate to the more or less distant cities, particularly to Singapore. There they have become small businessmen or members of the armed and police services.

The Dato told us that he and the Naning elders have made a series of representations to the British Crown and to the various commissions established to make recommendations regarding the future of Malaya. They have asked, in essence, that the traditional rights of the Naning community be given special consideration. Whether this consideration would involve restoration of sovereign rights to the Dato Naning as the traditional head of the community—making him, then, the equivalent of the sultans and rajahs, or at least of the *adat* chieftains of Negri Sembilan —the Dato Naning did not say. The general impression in Malacca, however, is that what the Dato actually seeks is recognition as ruler of the Naning community. That, and continuation of his M$600 per month stipend and the various perquisites—such as bodyguards and a mileage allowance—afforded him in the past by the Malacca British authorities. On these matters the Dato did not comment; but he did express surprise that until the present time he had had no satisfaction whatever from Malacca, Federation or British authorities.

A YOUNG CHINESE RUBBER PLANTER

In the course of the trip on which we visited the Dato Naning we visited also Mr. Boon Weng Siew, manager of three of the five divisions of Sir Cheng Lock's four-thousand-acre Malaka Pinda Rubber Estates, near Alor Gajah. Mr. Boon was waiting for us in the manager's modern bungalow, located in the midst of extensive rubber groves. Mr. Boon is an energetic young man of about thirty, a former office worker in Malacca, an active member of the M.C.A., and a leader in the party's youth activities. He became manager of part of the Malaka Pinda Estate during the Emergency when terrorists were making estate operation in Malacca a very risky business. Although terrorists are still holding out in the hills not far away, none have been known to venture recently into the estate area, so Mr. Boon can usually count on a sound night's sleep. His family still has not joined him, however; the windowpanes of his bungalow are still painted dark green—to deceive terrorists into thinking they are actually steel shutters; his constant companion is his handsome Alsatian dog who holds each new visitor on probation until the master gives the nod.

In his new Volkswagen—which replaces one he lost when floodwaters swept him off a highway in Johore a year ago—Mr. Boon took us on an extended tour of the estate and of the neighboring countryside. He called special attention to the forty-year-old sections of the estate which were Sir Cheng Lock's original plantings, the trees still in excellent condition. We also saw stretches where old, inferior trees—originally the plantings of smallholders—had recently been felled and new high-yield trees had been planted.

At various points around the estate we visited the "lines," the houses of the laborers—most of them new, airy, one-story, row houses of fireproof materials. Each family is assigned a small apartment consisting of a covered porch, a couple of bedrooms, kitchen, living room, and bath. Potable water is piped in, but full electrification of the lines is yet to come. We observed the school which the estate provides for the children of workers and where adults may attend evening classes, also the dispensary, where simple medical treatment is offered, workers being sent at estate expense to a nearby hospital if they require further attention. Mr. Boon also pointed out a big movie projection van, complete with generator, which brings regularly scheduled entertainment films to the line units. Strategically placed radio loud-speakers bring news broadcasts and other entertainment programs to the estate.

While their life is still far from idyllic, the estate workers of Malaya seem by Southeast Asian standards to be relatively well-paid, well-housed, and well-treated as regards educational, medical, and other social services. The workers who live not on the estate itself, however, but in the "new villages" constitute a special problem. These workers, many of whom formerly lived as squatters on estate or adjacent government land, were gathered up a few years ago and moved to bleak, fenced-in new villages as a measure to deny to the jungle terrorists access to food, comfort, and information. Now that the terrorists have been driven into the remoter areas, the former squatters still live in the new villages, many of them each day bicycling back and forth to work. Real progress has been made in improving their living quarters, in providing them with garden space, and in removing onerous restrictions on their movements; but many of the people of the new villages are not yet by any means reconciled to their new environment.

THE LEADER OF THE PORTUGUESE SETTLEMENT

We made a visit to the Portuguese Settlement, a beach area on the southern outskirts of Malacca Town, in order to call upon Mr. Lazaroo, leading member of the Malacca Portuguese-Eurasian community. The settlement turned out to be a group of small tin-roofed frame houses, built before the war by the Malacca Government in an effort to reunite and rehabilitate the descendants of the old Portuguese colony. In the centuries since Portugal lost Malacca to the Dutch most of the local Portuguese have declined to miserably low social and economic levels. There are a few prosperous Portuguese residents of Malacca today, but these tend to dissociate themselves from the others, the great majority being uneducated, impoverished fishermen and day laborers. The fishermen, who wade out to fish the tidal waters or venture out short distances by small boat, are no longer able to compete with the Chinese who now operate power boats and build expensive fish traps. The laborers can expect to earn only about M$3.00 per day by working on Malacca's road gangs or by pedalling Malacca's trishaws. But although their skins are as dark as any Malay's and their occupations are often more humble, their features tend to be strongly European, their pride and animation and graciousness are typically Latin, and they regard themselves as Westerners. They speak a local patois, which probably is to modern Portuguese a Louisiana Cajun is to modern French. They cling tenaciously to a few Portuguese customs; they are deeply devout; they intermarry among themselves, and they depend primarily upon the Church as a center of community life. Over the centuries and against what might seem like overwhelming odds they have managed to maintain a distinct identity.

Mr. Lazaroo received us in his tiny sitting room which was modestly furnished and decorated with photographs of his family and of distinguished visitors, such as British governors and resident commissioners, framed diplomas, religious pictures, and a small shrine of Our Lady of Fatima. Now in his mid-fifties, Mr. Lazaroo is a shorthand-typist in a government office. He is proud of the fact that he virtually educated himself, his family, like other Portuguese families, being too poor to send him to school. Studying evenings on his own, he managed to qualify for and to pass the exacting Junior Cambridge examinations, then to put himself through a course in shorthand and typing. He now takes poor young students into his home after office hours and gives them free instruction.

As one of the very few educated adult residents of the Portuguese Settlement, Mr. Lazaroo has accepted community leadership, assuming his responsibilities with vigor and imagination. He has organized various new community projects—such as projects to persuade the fishermen to take up home gardening in order to improve their diet. One special project to which he has devoted himself is a Joint Burial Society, to which member families subscribe fifty cents a month and from which, when death occurs, they receive the M$70 necessary for a decent funeral. In times past the Malacca Portuguese were so nearly destitute that when a member of a family died the rest of the family was obliged to beg money from their better-off Chinese and Malay neighbors in order to pay the funeral expenses, the corpse going unburied until they had raised the necessary amount. The community now takes pride in its ability to depend to a greater extent upon itself.

Mr. Lazaroo talked with us freely about the poverty, misery, and ignorance of the Portuguese Settlement and about the various efforts made in recent years to achieve advancement. The Settlement itself, where government-owned houses rent at the astounding sum of M$3.50 per month, was a major step forward. The construction a couple of years ago of a fine new government school—which children of all racial groups attend—was another. Occasional direct contacts with Portugal help to revive community spirit and confidence. The Portuguese Foreign Minister, for instance, visited Malacca Town briefly a couple of years ago. Soon afterward the Portuguese Government took two Malacca Portuguese girls—both schoolteachers—on a free one-month tour of Portugal. The Portuguese Government also sent out historic costumes for use in a grand pageant portraying the history of Malacca. That pageant, we gathered, was one of the most agreeably memorable events in recent generations. It was of particular interest to Mr. Lazaroo who is secretary of the Malacca Historical Society, an interracial association which has done a fine job of setting up descriptive markers on Malacca Town's principal monuments.

The Portuguese community today, its members still enjoying British-subject status until August 31 at least, is having anxious thoughts regarding its future prospects under the independent Federation of Malaya. The subject is a sensitive one and the experience of the next few years, not advance speculation, is what matters. This tiny backwash of a centuries-old European empire, the oldest surviving "European" community of the earliest European settlement in Southeast Asia, is once again due for a major readjustment, this time as it changes from European to Asian masters.

GENERAL OBSERVATIONS

In Malaya today there are many well-informed, sober persons who believe that the process of conferring independence has been too fast, that the risks are too great, and that loyal Straits Chinese, for instance, have been sold out to the Malays. Indeed, should the worst predictions be fulfilled, should Malaya fall victim either to fanatical Malay nationalism or to aggressive Chinese Communism, or to racial feuding, or merely to administrative lethargy, there will be many to point out that the British left too soon. At present, however, the chances seem rather better than just reasonably good that Britishers and Westerners, as well as the Overseas Chinese, while they will undoubtedly encounter real and even serious difficulties of adjustment, will be able to remain in Malaya without prohibitive difficulties and that everyone, including the Malays, will continue to prosper.

16

Tengku's Home State

June 6, 1960

THE STATE of Kedah has special claims to distinction among the eleven members of the Federation of Malaya. Located in the relatively remote north on the Thai border, modest both in size and in population—3,600 square miles and 700,000 people—Kedah has a long history of close contacts with outside civilizations, including those of China, Indonesia, India, Indochina, Siam, and the Western world, and it is the birthplace of a disproportionately large number of the top Malay officials of the new nation. Displaying neither the wealth nor the poverty which are to be found in the southern and eastern states respectively, it is making one of the happier transitions observable in Southeast Asia today between the feudal and colonial past and the cosmopolitan present.

It is no mere accident, say the people of Kedah, that the state enjoys special advantages and provides far more than its per capita share of top national figures. During the period of British colonialism Kedah remained resolutely outside the British-dominated Federated Malay States, accepting British advice and assistance on a highly selective basis. Although it employed Britishers in technical positions, it built up its own civil service and reserved the key district-officer posts exclusively for Malay incumbents. It profited from the opportunity to send its bright young men to study not just in England but to understudy in Thailand, so that the Kedah youth frequently benefited by British and Siamese experience and by the British and Siamese sense of equality and mutual respect. The big, rich, Federated states, such as Perak and Selangor, argue some of Kedah's citizens, lethargically accepted outright British administration and acquired a sense of dependence upon Britain. The big, poor, non-Federated states of Trengganu and Kelantan, they say, lethargically accepted inefficient local administration and developed a sense of futility. Only the big, rich, non-Federated state of Johore, they say, exhibited any comparable ability to manage its own affairs and to train a considerable corps of men capable of assuming national as well as state responsibilities.

Exhibit A in the Kedah gallery of favorite sons is Tengku (Prince) Abdul Rahman, leader of the independence movement and now Prime Minister. Tengku Abdul Rahman, the fifth surviving son of the late Sultan Abdul Hamid Halim Shah and the Siamese consort who was the sixth and favorite of his eight wives, displays the qualities which Kedah leaders in general both possess and admire. He is, of course, an aristocrat but an aristocrat with the common touch. During the 1959 election campaigns he visited the smallest villages, stopped over in the most modest homes, associated with the ordinary people, and what was more, he seemed genuinely to enjoy it. He is convivial, at times to the point of frivolity; generous to the point of improvidence; relaxed to the point of being politically indiscreet in his offhand remarks; and racially unprejudiced to the point that his first wife (now divorced) was an Englishwoman, that his numerous adopted children include some of Chinese parentage, and that his familiar associates are as likely to be Westerners, Chinese, or Indians as to be Malays. His private home in Alor Star is a modest frame house in an unstylish part of town, right on the bank of the muddy river, close to a busy wharf and a noisy Chinese amusement park. His private fortune, according to common report, has long since been squandered, a good part of it during his marathon academic career which was distinguished more by his sight-seeing in Siam and his extracurricular activities in London night clubs and at the race tracks than by his final, rather anticlimatic achievement of a law degree in 1949 at the age of forty-six after twenty-five years of intermittent effort.

In Tengku Abdul Rahman are combined those characteristics which constitute the distinctive inheritance of the Kedah people—a blend of Malay and Siamese humor, tolerance, patience, vivacity, and self-confidence, with a minimum of either the hostility or the arrogance toward Westerners which frequently characterizes Asians newly emancipated from colonialism. He is no great organizer or administrator, but he commands respect, loyalty, and most of all, liking. For a nation in which delicate interrelations among Malays, Chinese, Indians, British, and other racial groups are the key to progress or debacle, he comes close to being the ideal intermediary.

Another important exhibit in the Kedah gallery of local boys who made good is a commoner, Inche Senu bin Abdul Rahman. Inche Senu, then a young teacher in a Malay school, informed his wife and children one day in 1948 that he was setting out to see the world. He shipped on a British freighter, jumped ship in San Francisco, posed as a Filipino to avoid difficulties with immigration officers, and worked his way through high school and university. Upon graduating from the University of California (U.C.L.A.) he worked for a time with the Indonesian delegation to the United Nations, then returned to Malaya via London and entered politics. He quickly became joint secretary of the Alliance Party and of the United Malay National Organization, which dominate the Federation Government. Inche Senu, now thirty-eight, has for the past three years held the post of ambassador to Indonesia, one of the four top assignments (along with London, Washington, and Paris) of the Malayan diplomatic service. Since the London and Paris ambassadorships are likewise assigned to sons of Kedah (the ambassador to Great Britain being a half-brother of the Prime Minister), the suggestion has been made that Kedah birth is just about the best possible start for a Malayan diplomatic career.

Of the sons of Kedah who remain in state service, the Mentri Besar (Chief Minister) is an outstanding example of the well-trained, long-experienced civil servant who has eased the transition in Malaya from colonialism to independence. Dato 'Syed Omar bin S. Abdullah Shahabuddin, a member of an aristocratic Kedah family and the husband of Tengku Abdul Rahman's sister, was educated in law in England. He rose through the ranks in the Malayan civil service. He is now president of the state organizations of the Alliance Party and of the United Malay National Organization, and as a result of the clean-sweep Alliance victories in the 1959 state and national elections, he has been named Mentri Besar. Dato 'Syed Omar, incidentally, has been twice in the United States, once to attend a session of the United Nations, once for eye surgery at Johns Hopkins University Hospital. He now finds time, in addition to performing the increasingly onerous duties of office—in which he must have much of the paper work read to him—to make frequent rounds of the state, meeting the people, observing and encouraging all aspects of state development.

The state of Kedah, whose administration Dato 'Syed Omar now heads, has shrunk greatly in size since the days when it was perhaps the greatest of the Malay states. Kedah history is only now being laboriously

reconstructed, but the area south of the 3,987-foot Kedah Peak, a conspicuous navigator's landmark both in ancient and modern times, was
almost certainly a transshipment point for goods being moved by land
across the Malay Peninsula, an important link, therefore, in the ancient
India-China trade and pilgrimage route. Here the archaeologists have recently rediscovered and partially restored a little Hindu temple dating
from about the seventh or eighth centuries A.D.—Malaya's oldest historical monument. In the succeeding centuries the various empires of Cam-
bodia, Indonesia, Siam, and China contested or divided control over the
region. When Islamic traders arrived in Southeast Asia in about the thirteenth century, it was in Kedah that they seem to have made some of
their earliest contacts and converts. The Portuguese and the Dutch put
in their appearance in the sixteenth century, attracted like the Hindus,
the Indonesians, the Siamese, and the Chinese before them by the convenience of Kedah's port, a river mouth near the present capital of Alor
Star, and by the availability of two highly prized export commodities,
tin and elephants.

The British were the first Europeans actually to open up regular trade
with Kedah, which was the first point of their own penetration into the
Malay Peninsula. A British sea captain from Madras, one Francis Light,
visiting Kedah in the late 1760's and finding the Sultan both friendly and
propositionable, established a permanent trading post. The Sultan, it developed, was eager to gain promises of British protection against his
enemies—the Siamese to the north, the other Malay sultans and the Dutch
to the south. After attempting unsuccessfully to extract clear-cut authorization and commitment from the British East India Company at Madras,
Captain Light exercised his own discretion and on March 2, 1772, signed
a treaty whereby the Sultan ceded the island of Penang to the Company,
which in turn guaranteed him military alliance.

A few months later Captain Light took formal possession of Penang
and started to build the present city of George Town. The Sultan soon
called upon the British to fulfill their part of the bargain by providing
him with military aid against the Thais, who were threatening invasion.
When none was forthcoming, relations between the Sultan and the
British became rapidly less cordial, so uncordial, in fact, that the Sultan
at one point staged an unsuccessful attack to repossess the island. It was
perhaps just as well that he did not succeed, also that he was sufficiently
softened by a promise of annual rental to cede the strip of mainland now
known as Province Wellesley, for in 1821, when the Siamese launched

their long anticipated attack, the Sultan precipitately took refuge with the British. He managed thus at least to survive, although not for long, for he died in exile in Penang a few years later. Penang and Province Wellesley remain British, and at this writing the government of the state of Penang, honoring the old British East India Company obligation, still pays the government of Kedah M$10,000 per year in "cession" money. Kedah itself became a tributary of Siam. Each year it sent specially wrought "silver trees," a highly esteemed product of the Kedah silver-smiths, along with other gifts to the Siamese king, whose concurrence it always awaited before investing a new sultan. Then in 1909, in conse-quence of a feckless but happy interlude of which the very memory still gives pleasure in Alor Star, came a drastic change in relationships.

The Sultan of Kedah (Tengku Abdul Rahman's father) discovered in 1906 that five of his children were all at once of marriageable age, so as a device of convenience and economy he staged a seriatim wedding ceremony and festival which lasted day and night for all of three months. His loyal and willing subjects, together with most of the neighboring royalty and many of their retainers, devoted themselves enthusiastically to the festivities to the exclusion, so far as the state of Kedah was con-cerned, of virtually all productive labor and to the total depletion of the Sultan's treasury. Thirty cases of champagne per day constituted the liquid ration for the more sophisticated celebrants, whose Muslim prin-ciples of abstemiousness evidently did not interfere very seriously with their inroads upon the royal cellar. Forty water buffalo were slaughtered each day to provide more substantial fare for almost any who cared to partake. When the party was over and the reckoning came in, it turned out that the Sultan owed the Indian moneylenders of Penang something in the neighborhood of three to four million (Malayan) dollars. His im-portunate creditors, to whom the Sultan at first listened rather inatten-tively, began hinting at foreclosure, intimating also that they had British sanction. The Sultan appealed to the Siamese Government to bail him out. The Siamese agreed to advance him money at 6 per cent but stipu-lated one preliminary condition: that he accept a financial adviser. Even the Sultan agreed that this was a good idea. The adviser who was then sent to Kedah from Bangkok turned out to be an Englishman, an advance party of one preceding British extension of protection.

In 1909 Kedah formally accepted status as a British protectorate and the Siamese reluctantly concurred. The finances of the Sultanate im-proved remarkably, and with them its public works, education, and sanitation systems and the social and economic situation in general. While Kedah remained relatively poor and underdeveloped as compared, say, with the Sultanate of Johore, nevertheless it opened up river ports, roads, bridges, rubber estates, tin mines, schools, and a hospital. Then in 1941 it was overrun by the Japanese; in 1943 it was handed over to Thailand; in 1945 it was liberated by the British; and in 1957 it achieved its full independence as a member of the Federation of Malaya. State sovereignty is clearly invested in the Kedah Sultan and national sovereignty in a new Paramount Ruler in whose election the Sultan participates along with eight other traditional rulers. In Kedah the memory of the British period is still pleasant and Britishers remain welcome, some of them still holding official positions.

The royal house of Kedah, which claims descent from Alexander the Great via its traditional founder, a Persian prince shipwrecked in Malaya on his way to China about 1,500 years ago, is represented today by His Highness, Sultan Abdul Halim Mu'azzam Shah. His Highness, or "H.H.," as he is commonly referred to in Alor Star, has yet to establish himself as a positive personality like his father or his grandfather. His father instituted the un-sultan-like practice of keeping regular office hours and devoting himself personally to administration; his grandfather distinguished himself, despite recurrent and serious attacks of mental and physical illness, by the number of his wives (eight officially), of his legitimate children (forty-five) and of his grandchildren and great-grandchildren (ninety-two). The Sultan, like other traditional rulers of Malaya, is now more a symbol than a power, his responsibilities being restricted principally to religious, traditional, and ceremonial affairs, his prestige being confined primarily to the Malay community whose younger, better-educated members are not altogether uncritical of feudal institutions.

The young Sultan of Kedah follows his father's practice of keeping regular office hours. He rides to and from the office in an ancient and resplendent Rolls-Royce painted royal yellow with a black trim. On his arrival at the Secretariat Building he flicks a gilt "In-Out" indicator on the ground floor and retires to his modestly furnished, air-conditioned office on the second floor. He makes it a practice to read all state papers and is undoubtedly interesting himself in administration. Like certain of his illustrious relatives, he also allows himself to be distracted by more frivolous pursuits. His scholastic career, for instance, was even less glorious than that of Tengku Abdul Rahman's, for he failed his Senior Cambridge examination and then "read" rather inconclusively for two and a half years at Wadham College, Oxford. After office hours almost every afternoon, rain or shine, he is to be found on the Alor Star golf course, where he perseveres but does not excel. He is skilled at billiards and at photography, and he rarely misses a Saturday night dance at the club. A sports-car buff, he particularly fancies his Jaguar, which he got up to 115 miles per hour in England but propels at a much more sedate pace in his home state.

For those interested in the modern economics of feudal royalty, it is worth reporting that the Sultan draws a state stipend of M$10,000 per month, tax free. The Sultanah, an extraordinarily beautiful young woman with excellent taste in clothes and jewelry, draws a personal stipend of M$1,000 per month. Both Sultan and Sultanah are reliably reported to have private means with which to eke out their official allowances.

The total cost to the state of maintaining the institution of the sultanate works out to about M$650,000–750,000 per year. Of this M$400,000–500,000 is the cost of maintaining the Sultan, the Sultanah, their personal and official staff, and their several residences—a Victorian "palace" just outside Alor Star, a seaside mansion in Penang, a hill bungalow on Kedah Peak, and a modern "palace" in Kuala Lumpur. This sum allows for an entertainment allowance (M$10,000 per year), utilities, automobiles, and motorboats, salaries for an aide-de-camp, various attendants, gardeners, cooks (five), a Koran teacher, the twenty-six musicians of the *nobat* or royal orchestra, and a special civil service allowance of M$18 monthly for the Sultan himself for proficiency in the Siamese language. An additional M$250,000 provides for "political pensions" and "compassionate allowances" to 153 members of the royal family or of the royal household, most of them princes and princesses. The allowance for Tengku Abdul Rahman, for instance, comes to M$3,600 per year, the standard amount for a prince of the first generation. The total of $M650,000–750,000 represents about 10 per cent of the normal revenue of the state and about 5 per cent of the normal expenditures, state funds for over-all administrative purposes being supplemented by a nearly equivalent amount from the federal treasury.

Alor Star, to a greater extent than the capital of any other state of Malaya, has about it the air of a royal town. Kedah was never a great or wealthy kingdom, but its royal monuments, if modest, are numerous by comparison with those elsewhere in Malaya; they are also both conspicuous and well preserved.

Facing the *padang*, or Malayan town green, stands the most noteworthy of the royal buildings, the Balai Besar, an ornate seventy-year-old audience hall of modified Siamese style recently expanded by two wings of unfortunate and unpedigreed "modern." Here on February 20, 1959, in the presence of the other rulers or their representatives, high Federation officials, and the diplomatic corps from Kuala Lumpur, was held the enthronement ceremony for the present Sultan. The occasion was highlighted by display of the state regalia and of extremely handsome brocade costumes, krises, and the crown jewels, the latter including a new US$16,000 platinum and diamond tiara presented to the Sultanah by the Kedah schoolchildren.

Near the center of the *padang* stands a small tower which houses the instruments of the *nobat*, an ancient orchestra derived from Hindu antecedents. The *nobat* is played at all court occasions, also for Friday worship and daily call to prayers. All about the *padang* and the older part of the city stand the "palaces" built by the Sultan's grandfather for himself and his many wives and children. Most of these now dilapidated mansions are devoted to the commercial uses of new Chinese owners, but several of them still house royal tenants. In a serenely beautiful spot a few miles outside the city is located the royal graveyard, where the well-cared-for tombs date back a good 250 years.

The present palace of the Sultan is set in a handsome park a few miles out of town. The road to the palace, which is the main road of Alor Star, is shaded by some of the finest rain trees which have anywhere survived modern traffic. It is lined by some handsome specimens of British colonial achitecture, including the residence of the Mentri Besar, a former palace of the old Sultan, built in tropicalized Georgian style.

The town is notable also for its grand mosque, facing the Balai Besar across the *padang*, a well-maintained Siamese *wat*, an assortment of large Hindu and Chinese temples, a new Roman Catholic and several Protestant churches, an impressive collection of Malay-, Indian-, Chinese-, and English-language schools, a hospital with a new nurses' residence in brightly painted modern style, an infusion of new houses inspired by Singapore ultramodern, a Government Rest House built originally by the Japanese as an ice factory, and the Kedah Club, where the British still gather for their sundown *stengah*, with the Indians, the Chinese, and some of the Malays now joining them. All are reminders that Alor Star is no mere backwoods upriver town but a modern state capital, one that is both growing and changing fast, but not so fast as to lose its original identity.

The people of Alor Star speak proudly today of their new Transport Building—the "biggest in the Federation," capable of handling fifty buses at once, providing office space, hotel rooms, and a huge banquet hall in its upper floors, the whole structure completed just in time to house the influx of visitors for the installation of the Sultan. They also point out a new Malay provisions market which affords increasing competition to the Chinese-dominated main market. They need scarcely call attention to an impressive line-up of eight jewelry shops, among the biggest, show-iest, and busiest in Malaya. Ornaments of gold and silver, for which Kedah is especially famous, are widely favored as an investment, since they allow for display along with security and liquidity—90 per cent being the guaranteed redemption rate in case of urgent need for ready cash, a contingency which, for the Malays in particular, is seasonally re-current. Even more conspicuous than the jewelry stores are Alor Star's three recently built movie theaters, which lack only air conditioning to compare with Kuala Lumpur's, and its "Great World" amusement park, where the male patron of the *joget* dance hall can take his choice of danc-ing with a hostess—without touching her, of course—or of summoning one to perform solo while he relaxes at a cabaret table. Alor Star still ob-serves the Thursday noon to Friday evening religious holiday, with all entertainment suspended from 6 P.M. Thursday until 6 P.M. Friday. But it no longer observes as it did in the good old days, both the Thursday-Friday Muslim holiday and the Saturday-Sunday Christian holiday, plus all British, Chinese, Indian, and Malay festival days as well. Alor Star and the whole state of Kedah give the impression of being hard at work—but not too tediously hard at work, especially not the Malay farmers who relax for months after the strenuous harvest period is over.

Kedah's basic problem, which is that of all Malaya, is to improve the standard of living of the Malay population, also that of large numbers of the Indians and some of the Chinese, and to achieve cooperation among the Malay, Indian, and Chinese communities. According to the 1957 census, Kedah's total population of a little over 700,000 is distributed approximately as follows: Malaysians, 475,000; Chinese, 150,000; Indians, 65,000; other racial and national groups, 15,000 (including 10,000 Siam-ese, 1,000 Pakistanis, 700 Ceylonese, 500 Britons, and 3 Americans). The Malaysians (including 5,000 Indonesians) are mainly rice farmers, rubber tappers, and fishermen. The Chinese are mainly small businessmen (and moneylenders) and smallholder rubber planters. The Indians are mainly estate rubber workers. The British are mainly rubber planters, plus perhaps a dozen or two who remain in the civil service. The three Americans are technicians at a U.S. Rubber Company estate.

Kedah has a much higher percentage of Malaysian population (66 per cent) than does the Federation as a whole (50 per cent). This fact simplifies the basic problem to the extent that the Malaysians feel themselves somewhat less crowded and less exploited by the Chinese. It complicates it in that the traditional and therefore also the reactionary Muslim influence is strong. The ready-made appeal of the opposition parties, particularly the Pan-Malayan Islamic Party (P.M.I.P.), to Malay and Islamic racial, religious, and nationalist intolerance can readily be exploited. Although the P.M.I.P. failed in the 1959 elections to win a single victory in Kedah, it managed to make alarming inroads nevertheless into the Alliance vote, and it is making vigorous postelection efforts to consolidate its position.

In Kedah the P.M.I.P. is working especially hard in the *pondok*—scores of little *asrama*-type institutions where Malay boys in their late teens or early twenties take up residence and pursue religious studies for a period of months and sometimes years. P.M.I.P. propagandists have been busily at work converting the teachers and through them the pupils, so that in these closely knit little bachelor communities politics now feature prominently in instruction and conversation. In another Kedah institution, an Arabic-language high school, students are being qualified to continue their studies, if they wish, in Cairo. There is some question in the minds of the less devout citizens, however, whether closer affiliation with Cairo will prove any more wholesome a religious and political influence than the P.M.I.P.-dominated *pondok*. The real hope for racial development and racial harmony, most of the better-educated people believe, lies in the rapidly growing but still noncompulsory public education system. The better schools now carry the student through secondary level, but all of them, and especially those providing education in English, are besieged by far more applicants than they can admit.

The Malay population of Kedah, except for a minority in the towns and in the hilly areas where rubber is grown, is concentrated in the coastal plain known as the "rice bowl" of Malaya which extends up into Perlis. This stretch of coast, only about fifty miles long and twelve miles wide, accounts for 33 per cent of Malaya's *padi* land and 36 per cent of its rice crop. The land becomes flooded in the rainy season; it grows parched and cracked during the dry season. The new silt carried in by the floods, the deep aeration caused by the cracking, and the liberal application of fertilizers, traditionally the bat guano from nearby mountain caves, combine to make the rice yield per crop per acre the highest in Southeast Asia. For lack of any elaborate irrigation system, however, the land yields for the most part only one crop each year. By tradition the Kedah peasant concentrates his year's labor upon production of this one crop and relaxes after it is harvested, but the population is now increasing at such a rate that unless farming methods are changed, the land will be unable to support the people at their present standard of living.

The state government, with federal assistance, is making extensive efforts, therefore, to increase and to diversify the Kedah plain agricultural production and at the same time to introduce other improvements. It has recently completed several large-scale drainage and irrigation projects which provide for flood control during the rainy season, protection against unseasonable drought, and the possibility in some areas of raising two crops of rice rather than one per calendar year. While working to introduce new and better strains of rice, it has begun also to interest the peasants in modern fruit, vegetable, and poultry farming. Meanwhile it has provided important state services, including extension of a piped water system so that kampongs stretching along the main road as far as twenty miles from Alor Star no longer have to depend upon unreliable and unsanitary wells. It has also expanded medical services by building clinics and activating mobile units, some of them water-borne, and has established a farmers' cooperative which has already to a marked extent freed the farmer from reliance upon usurious Chinese moneylenders. The inescapable fact remains, however, that the 65,000 Malay peasant families which now populate the Kedah plain are far too many and that at least one third of them will soon have to be supplied with new land and/or new occupations. Fortunately in the state of Kedah the land is available, and another occupation—smallholder rubber production—can readily be developed. After much delay and hesitation, for which the Kedah state administration like the national administration has been subject to serious criticism, the government has at least made a start. New land is now being opened up and plots of about ten acres each are being assigned to carefully screened applicants for the planting both of rubber and of subsistence crops.

Pending the development of an impressive smallholder rubber industry such as the new land program may provide, the showplace rubber plantings in Kedah are those of the big estates, and the showiest of all is that of the Harvard Estate, a U.S. Rubber Company operation. Located a few miles south of Alor Star, The Harvard Estate is six thousand acres of beautifully kept rubber, most of it replanted with new high-yield stock that is just coming into full production. On the estate has been built a modern factory to process latex for shipment in concentrated liquid form. In the center of the estate stands a workers' settlement, an imposing Hindu shrine, a school for Indian and a school for Malay students, a clinic, and a group of relatively good "labor lines" that are soon to be replaced by modern quarters for the workers. On a ridge nearby stand half a dozen ranch-house-type homes for Western staff employees. These homes, which command an unobstructed view of the green slopes of Kedah Peak, look out over mathematically precise rows of dense green rubber trees that have been pushed off to just sufficient distance to allow space for a nine-hole golf course and a small tiled swimming pool. The life of an estate manager, now that the terrorists have been driven off the fringes of the estates and the price of rubber has risen by 50 per cent in the last year, seems not to be without its compensations.

Kedah, which originally attracted foreign settlers by reason of its tin, has now almost exhausted its known resources. Only some small Chinese-owned mines continue in production. The big Western concerns have closed down operations, abandoning a couple of multimillion-dollar tin dredges that are impossibly expensive either to maintain or to remove. Along with its tin, incidentally, Kedah has nearly exhausted its supply of elephants, the few survivors having now retreated into the less accessible jungle along the Thai border.

Kedah's fishing industry, fortunately, is in better shape than its tin. Based mainly on the Langkawi Islands a few miles off shore and at a couple of small river ports, Kedah's fishing fleet of Chinese-owned, motorized boats of some twenty to thirty tons each now bring in a generally satisfactory haul. A new M$2 million government program to expand the industry and to improve the condition of the fishermen, the majority of them Malays, may soon work major improvements, especially if the program is quickly redoubled, as the government suggests, and if it results in really widespread modern developments on the Langkawi Islands, as the government definitely promises.

Kedah's fishing industry introduces some complications which keep Kedah in touch with the international politics of Southeast Asia. When Kedah fishing boats venture too close to what Indonesia regards as its own national waters, they are subject to seizure and prolonged negotiation for release, and also, on various occasions in recent years, to acts of piracy for which the responsibility is exceedingly difficult to pin down. When they venture unauthorized into Siamese waters—carried there, the fishermen protest, by wind or tide—they are subject to seizure and confiscation or else the extortion of bribes, the near equivalent sometimes of confiscation, but at least a more expeditious settlement than is ever possible in Indonesia. The people of Kedah, who have had close relations with Thailand and Indonesia over the centuries and indeed share and blend the racial strains, are likely to remark that, much as they esteem their kinfolk in neighboring countries, they are inclined to think that Malaya and Kedah handle their affairs much better. An Indonesian or a Thai ship's master, they say, has only to report himself at a conveniently located customs office in Kedah to receive quick, courteous, and efficient treatment. Only if he is actually importing any goods will he be charged any fee and then only a modest one in accordance with honestly enforced regulations.

The procedure at customs, it is fair to say, is representative of Kedah's administrative procedure in general. There are areas of inefficiency and even neglect, to be sure—particularly with regard to the land-development program which has been seriously bottlenecked. Even here, however, the deficiencies are openly admitted and the resolution to correct them has become apparent. The state of Kedah has had less than three years as yet in which to work out new procedures for state administration and new relationships with the national government. The exact division of authority and responsibility as between state and federal government is still far from clear, but the machinery of government, nevertheless, continues to operate smoothly. The visitor to a government office in Kedah is not confronted with the bureaucratic obstruction and indifference which has become all too familiar in nearby nations, Burma, say, or Indonesia. In Kedah, as in the rest of Malaya, the majority of the civil servants seem to know what their duties are and to be willing both courteously and expeditiously to discharge them.

One of the most serious problems in the new state of Kedah has already been surmounted. It was the problem of Communist terrorists who imposed a ten-year-long "Emergency" throughout the nation. The terrorists have now been all but eliminated as result of determined military action in which the local people cooperated with the British. A band of the most tenacious and the most daring of the survivors still hold out in the fringe areas between Kedah and Thailand, an expensive nuisance but no longer a serious menace to security. The Thais, who have frequently

17

Malayan State in Miniature

June 9, 1960

OF ALL the states of Malaya, the state of Perlis is the smallest, the least known, and just possibly the happiest, if by no means the most advanced. It has never had any real trouble, for instance, with Communist terrorists, and it experiences a minimum of interracial friction. It enjoys all the advantages of full-fledged membership in the Federation; its Raja has just been elected Deputy Paramount Ruler; in local government more and more of its own citizens hold positions of responsibility; grants from the Federation amount to quadruple its own revenues. Perlis, consequently, has a good road network, a good school system, and a good medical service, none of which it could afford on its own resources alone. It also has an ambitious program for improving public utilities so that electricity and water, now provided only for the capital town of Kangar (population 6,000) and the nearby port town of Kuala Perlis, will be extended far and fast, and a general program of economic and community development is already beginning to show results.

The minute state of Perlis (area, 316 square miles; population, 91,000) is one of the few states in the world about which a visitor may write with some assurance after not just a three-day but a one-day whirlwind trip. I myself propose to do so. I shall adopt the organization and labor-saving device of the travelogue, starting at the point where my wife and I drove across the Kedah-Perlis boundary on our way to the royal capital of Arau and the administrative capital of Kangar—only a couple of miles apart, and about thirty miles from Kedah state capital of Alor Star.

The coastal stretch of Perlis through which we drove was little different from the nearby areas of Kedah save, perhaps, that it was even wetter, greener, more crowded with Malay rice farmers and their families, and more proximate to the blue-green foothills of the interior mountain range. It is studded with astonishing little limestone peaks rising several hundred feet skyward out of the rice fields and riddled with caves from which bat guano is gathered to fertilize the rice crop. The southwestern monsoon season was at its height. The rice fields were flooded and the heavily loaded rice stalks were beginning to bend with ripe grain. The drainage ditches alongside the road were awash, and every otherwise unemployed man, woman, or child seemed to be happily splashing or fishing in them. The stilted Malay houses by the roadside stood in inches of water, and flotillas of ducks competed with rather badly handicapped chickens for the household scraps. The rice harvest would soon begin; this year it would be a bumper crop as compared with a poor one the previous year; the sense of expectancy and elation was contagious.

We stopped at the Government Rest House on the edge of Kangar—a new building of brick and concrete, brightly painted, modern in design and materials, providing a dozen rooms with spring beds, foam-rubber mattresses, and private baths. The Rest House, set within a quiet, shady garden, costs about US$7 per person per day for room and board. Over-all cost would go up, however, if instead of eating the standard Rest House fare of tinned asparagus soup, roast kampong chicken, french-fried potatoes, tinned peas and carrots, and tinned fruit cocktail, one ordered Chinese specialties of fresh local sea food, fresh vegetables, and fresh fruit. From the Rest House, after ordering in advance the day's table d'hôte luncheon, which was as predictable in timing as in content, we drove a few miles to the town of Arau to pay a call upon His Highness, Syed Putra ibni Al-Marhum Syed Hassan Jamalullail, C.M.G., Raja of Perlis.

The Istana is a prewar, foreign-style residence set in a gardened compound behind a stone wall built originally to screen a Siamese-style palace which has now disappeared. It is dignified but undistinguished in its architecture; in its furnishings it is noteworthy mainly for the predominance of royal yellow in upholstery, draperies, and cushions, and for a striking display of lances, krises, and elephant tusks.

The Raja, a plump but handsome man of thirty-nine, dressed in Malay costume of loose-cut silk jacket and trousers and a brocaded sarong, wearing a kris at his waist, received us in the entryway and showed us into a drawing room. His consort, the Raja Prampuan, an attractive and animated young woman, joined us presently, announcing in almost the same opening sentence that she had just been putting manure on her orchids, that she had been very busy lately organizing the National Poppy Day, and that she was the mother of ten, two of whom were now at school in England.

The Raja, who has taken a direct and continuing interest in the actual administration of his state, gave me what would rate in Western bureaucratic circles as an expert briefing on the situation and the problems of Perlis. Then, over cake and coffee, the conversation turned to his travels in Europe, Japan, Australia, and Indonesia; his interest in sports—particularly in tennis, which he plays daily; his relations with the other traditional rulers of Malaya; and his own good fortune in having an elected local government of persons who have both training and experience in administration and a knowledge of both the Western and the Eastern worlds.

The Raja, by way of an economic sidelight—available to anyone who cares to examine the published state budget—draws a state stipend of M$5,000 per month, the smallest of any of the traditional rulers. The total cost of maintaining the royal family amounts to about 25 per cent of the state revenue. To the state's own revenue—estimated at M$580,000 for 1959—is added a total of M$2,085,862 in "capitation" and "road building" grants from the federal government, the highest per capita grants for any state in the Federation.

Both the Raja and his consort, according to various local informants, have made themselves active in Perlis community affairs and have come to be regarded as a democratic couple, keenly interested in the welfare of their people. They frequently visit the Malay kampongs, where they are known personally to their subjects, and they associate freely with the Chinese and the Indian communities as well. Their prestige is further enhanced by the fact that during the Japanese occupation the Raja risked his succession to the throne by refusing to collaborate, preferring to occupy himself during the wartime years in private business in the east-coast state of Kelantan. Prior to the war the Raja put in a few years in the Malayan civil service in Kuala Lumpur. He had received his schooling in the English-language Penang Free School; he is now sending his own children first to the local English-language school in Perlis, where they mix freely with the other children, and later to higher schools in England. Somewhat incongruously for a progressive young ruler of Western training and orientation, the Raja has taken a second wife, by whom he has two children. The Raja Prampuan has since then redoubled her activities in public affairs and is now one of the outstanding leaders of the national women's organizations.

From the Istana we went to the Government Office Building in Kangar to pay a call on the Mentri Besar (Chief Minister). The Mentri Besar, a long-time member of the civil service, received us in his air-conditioned office and gave us a further briefing on the affairs of Perlis. The problem, he declared, as do virtually all other Malayan leaders, is one of rapid development for the benefit of the ordinary people, particularly that of the Malay population which lags far behind the Chinese in education and economic advantage. Perlis being a small, poor state, it experiences special difficulties. Real improvement of the rice-growing areas, for instance, would require a drainage and irrigation project costing, according to the estimate of a Swiss engineering firm, the sum of about M$400 million. Even if the project were carried out, it would result in little actual increase of acreage but mainly in improved flood control and the possibility of more extensive double cropping. In view of the shortage of present or potential rice lands, Perlis needs to convert rice farmers into rubber planters and resettle them, therefore, on new land-development projects. Even if the money were available for resettlement projects, however, the amount of state land readily subject to new development is strictly limited. Continued progress in Perlis, therefore, is inextricably linked to nationwide increase in opportunity.

The Mentri Besar presented us with a copy of a history of Perlis which he himself had written. The history, to condense recklessly, is one of common background with Kedah, then separation from Kedah (ca. 1821) and direct attachment as a vassal state to Siam; mediation between Siam and Kedah (ca. 1840) for restoration of a high degree of independence to both Kedah and Perlis as separate states; protectorate status under the British (1909); occupation by the Japanese (1941); liberation from the Japanese (1945); then independence as a member of the Federation of Malaya (1957). The princes of Perlis, like those of Kedah, declined to join the prewar Federated Malay States. They maintained close contacts with Siam but accepted nevertheless the advice and assistance of the British, recognizing the value of Western institutions but retaining a spirit of independence.

We left the Chief Minister's office to go to meet a Chinese member of the State Council who had offered to accompany us on a quick tour of the area about the capital. After pausing briefly to view the *padang*, or central green, where a big government hospital occupies one side of the square and nearby sites are reserved for new government offices that are soon to be built, we drove a few miles from Kangar to the port town of Kuala Perlis. On one bank of the wide river on which the town is built stands a new Chinese quarter with conspicuous schools, a theater, and numerous office buildings. On fishing wharves that stretch along the river front are located the offices and the processing plants of the Chinese fisheries operators. Across the river stands the predominantly Malay town, built on stilts above the mud flats. To both the Malay and the Chinese sections in recent years have been brought electric current, piped water, and improved medical and social services. Since Kuala Perlis serves not only as a fishing port for the state of Perlis but also as a communications center for the off-lying Langkawi Islands, it is due to double in population in the next few years, and everywhere the signs of new building operations are apparent.

Returning from Kuala Perlis to Kangar, we visited a newly developed area across the river from the main town. The one reminder of the old days is the mansion of the Mentri Besar, once the British Residency, elegant and airy, set in a well-tended garden among fine rain trees. Two new English-language schools have been built nearby, one Roman Catholic, one government sponsored, and both are hard pressed to admit increasing numbers of applicants. Adjacent to the schools is located a newly opened low-cost housing development. Some fifty houses, built in a modernized version of the traditional Malay style, with two bedrooms, veranda, living room, kitchen, bath, and garden, are provided by the government to approved tenants on rental purchase terms of about M$30 per month.

After returning to the Rest House for luncheon, we went to see smallholder rubber plantations, many of them newly replanted with highyield trees, and then continued our drive until we came to the end of the road, close to the Thai border. There we were met by a young Chinese who had arranged to show us the Kaki Bukit tin mine, which is unique in Malaya. The approach to the mine is by a thousand-foot-long natural cave that tunnels through a rugged ridge of hills. Inside the cave, just above a rushing stream which sometimes rises fast, the mine owners have laid a boardwalk provided with a flimsy handrail and lighted by an occasional dim electric bulb. The cave opens into a small mountain valley in which are located a Malay kampong of a few hundred people, a Chinese rubber estate of a couple of hundred acres, and a series of small lakes—abandoned tin mines now stocked with pond fish. In the hills or in the valleys just beyond, our Chinese guide informed us, are still to be found elephants, tigers, anteaters, wild boar, and even a few stray aborigines. Dug into the ridge are the new tin mines, sometimes merely enlargements of natural caves, sometimes shafts angling off from the natural tunnels. The ore to be found in the scattered pockets between the rock formations is the purest in Malaya, the metal having been washed and concentrated by underground streams before being deposited among the rocks. After being still further purified at a small processing plant at the mine, the tin is taken through the tunnel to the road terminal by Chinese porters who carry out something like a 150-pound load, then bring back diesel oil to power the mine's generators. If they survive this strenuous life for many years without falling victim to tuberculosis, the porters sometimes accumulate enough capital to turn business operators themselves.

In Perlis, said our informant, opportunity is still open to the Chinese, whether the coolie or the *towkay*. In this small state, where the Malays outnumber the Chinese five to one, the Malays feel secure enough to be relaxed, and the Chinese are confident of their ability to supply services which the Malays will not dare dispense with. Our guide, the son of a wealthy family which had sent him to school in Penang, where he had had a taste of big-city life and big-city ways, seemed content to return to an isolated valley in Perlis. He fully expects to profit from opportunities which are relatively much more inviting here than in cosmopolitan Penang, where competition is keener and discrimination more probable.

In Perlis, as in Kedah and elsewhere, the racial and religious agitators are at work, improving their position against the day when discontent may make public disorders easy to stir up. The P.M.I.P. in particular is busy proselytizing the Malay youth of the traditional Muslim schools, attempting to divert them from religious to political indoctrination, with basic appeal to intolerance. Among the Chinese there exist, in Perlis as elsewhere in Malaya, those who are susceptible to suggestion from Peking, and if not from Peking, then from the leftist political groups and the terrorist secret societies of Penang, Kuala Lumpur, and Singapore. Among Malays, Chinese, Indians, and others, including the minute Siamese minority, there are unemployed or underemployed youths who are beginning to adopt the long haircut, the tight, low-waisted pants, and the jukebox jargon which are the recognizable marks of youthful troublemakers and troubleseekers. Still, Perlis remains today far from the center of such contagion, and sporadic symptoms need not signify that the malady will become endemic.

18

Land for the Landless

June 11, 1960

In MALAYA practically everybody agrees that the government should swiftly fulfill its long-standing promise to open up for the benefit of the less privileged segments of the population that 50 per cent of the whole land area which is now national or state reserve. Serious disputes have arisen, however, over the procedure by which the land is to be developed and allocated; the extent and source of financing; the relative rights and responsibilities of the Federation and the state governments and of the traditional rulers and the people; also the proportion of Chinese and other non-Malays who may be permitted to participate in the direct benefits. During and after its recent election victories the government reiterated in much more vigorous and convincing terms than ever before its resolute determination to cut through all impediments and to get on with a big-scale program. A few pilot projects are now under way, and from present indications it seems not unduly optimistic to conclude that a nationwide program would not in fact be prohibitively difficult or expensive and might well prove to be highly successful.

One particular project which has now advanced far enough to afford sound basis for judgment is the Bukit Tembaga resettlement area in the state of Kedah, about fifteen miles from the capital city of Alor Star. The project, curiously enough, was virtually self-generating and now turns out to be almost self-amortizing. It has served, along with later projects of the same type, virtually to demolish many of the bureaucratic arguments for caution, delay, economy, and legalistic niceties.

The Bukit Tembaga project got under way in late 1955. The Kedah politicians had just conducted the 1955 election campaign on a promise of land for the landless and state aid in enabling worthy people to improve their livelihood. After the campaign nothing much happened that seemed to fulfill the political promises. A few indigent farmers, noting that the government had recently completed lumbering operations on a stretch of rolling land near Alor Star but had then abandoned the partly cleared land to regrowth of jungle, decided to move in. Before the authorities were really aware of what was happening, approximately a hundred families settled in as squatters, threw up flimsy thatch shacks, parceled the land out among themselves, continued the clearing operations, and then attempted to bring the land into cultivation.

After the first brave start things didn't go so well. The physical drudgery of clearing the land without mechanical aids was itself appalling; the soil proved unsuitable, once it had been cleared, to the wet rice culture with which the farmers were familiar. The beasts of the jungle exhibited a ravenous appetite for whatever crops and fruits got started. The mosquitoes proved not just vexatious but malarial as well. Nobody had any real financial backing, and the government provided no subsidy. During the next several years 70 per cent of the squatters dropped out or died, only a few new settlers moved in to take over their holdings, and the development seemed doomed to failure.

In January 1959, when the state government was preparing to stage a new election campaign on the basis of the same promises as before, it finally felt impelled to act. It designated Bukit Tembaga as a state project to which it appointed a manager and two assistants. This three-man team proved competent and resourceful. The state public health service, on their prompting, cleaned out the mosquitoes and treated the settlers who were already ill. The state treasurer put up enough financial backing that the project manager was able to distribute M$300 worth of building materials to each settler. With the project manager holding them to rigid specifications in construction and sanitation, the settlers then built themselves new houses of approved design. The government, furthermore, granted each family of settlers a monthly living stipend of M$50, the total amount eventually to be repayable, as were the costs of the building materials. The project manager then mapped out a coordinated scheme of land development according to which each settler would acquire six acres of rubber, two acres for other crops, plus a quarter-acre plot about his own house for vegetables and fruit. The whole project, it turned out, would go a long way toward paying for itself, for the National Rubber Replanting Board would pay on an installment basis for each acre of new rubber that was planted the sum of M$400, almost enough to meet the M$506 per acre cost of development.

Bukit Tembaga, a forlorn wasteland a year and a half ago, is now a tidy, bustling settlement. Neat wooden Malay houses dot the rolling landscape. Built high on stilts, they are covered with aluminum roofing, provided with nearby well and toilet, and surrounded by flowering trees and shrubs which testify to pride of ownership. A few thatched huts serve as storage shelters and as reminders of what the settlement used to be. Good strains of fruit trees, chosen for suitability to the soil and supplied at cost by the agricultural department, are already beginning to yield bananas and papayas and will soon yield the slower-maturing fruits. Chickens and ducks are multiplying rapidly, and water buffalo, cows, and goats are not uncommon. If the fruit trees and the livestock are thriving, so, too, are the families. A visiting midwife now finds much more employment than does the resident religious leader who conducts the funeral ceremonies.

At the project center there now stand a new administration building, a set of modest bungalows for the supervisors, a new school, and a long building which serves as warehouse and cooperative store. The resident manager, who has recently completed construction of his own new home, can point out on the blueprints of the project area the proposed site for a full shopping center and even for a parking lot. Already a small mosque has been built to provide shelter not only for religious observance but for various community functions, including instruction in the techniques of rubber culture.

Rubber will be the primary occupational concern of the settlers. At present they are still engaged in clearing and planting the rubber area and budding the trees with high-yield clones. By cooperative effort they are gradually extending the area under cultivation until there will be enough that each person can be alloted his promised six acres of rubber and two acres plus for other crops. By the time the rubber comes into production, approximately six years after planting, the settlers will know the techniques of tapping, coagulating, and processing. When each settler has his own six acres of mature rubber trees, he will be able, according to the original project estimate, to earn approximately M$7,000 per year from rubber alone—well above the present average family income for Malaya, which is already the highest in Asia. By that time too, allowing for the subsidy of M$400 per acre of rubber from the replanting fund, allowing also for accumulated indebtedness for family maintenance and administrative overhead while the project is getting under way, he will be several thousand dollars in debt to the government. Forecasts of earnings from rubber are based upon the conservative estimate of M$0.80 per pound, whereas rubber at present fetches about M$1.25-1.30 per pound and shows no imminent tendency toward sharp decline. The surviving Bukit Tembaga squatters of 1955 and the new settlers of 1959 stand a very good chance of being debt-free and self-sufficient by 1970. They should become, in fact, prosperous rubber smallholders enjoying a dramatically improved standard of living.

Bukit Tembaga, in other words, now gives clear indication of being a highly successful project, barring, of course, such contingencies as collapse of the rubber market, natural disaster such as blight or drought, or the international disaster of war. The original manager has recently been promoted and transferred to take charge of much larger projects now being undertaken. The new manager and his two assistants are young men of energy and dedication. They work seven days a week providing such miscellaneous community services as organization of a cooperative store and operation of an emergency ambulance, for which they make use of the settlement's one motor vehicle, a new Landrover. The settlers themselves are obviously proud of their achievement and eager to show visitors the extent of their planting, the tidiness of their homes, and the proliferation of their crops and families. They are not, however, without their outspoken complaints, as became apparent when the Mentri Besar of Kedah showed up on a visit of inspection last year. The Mentri Besar was politely but emphatically informed that the settlers did not wish to wait much longer for such amenities as a school—which they have since acquired—or for more frequent visits by a mobile clinic, or a better access road, or even for electricity and piped water.

The very success of the project, as a matter of fact, is itself a cause of anxiety both to the settlers and to the government. Within a couple of miles of the Bukit Tembaga project is a Malay kampong occupied by people originally displaced by the Communist terror. The kampong homes are makeshift, tumble-down, and overcrowded. The occupants have neither lands nor possessions nor steady employment. They are still classed as squatters and are under standing order to move out. The question is when, where, and to what.

The spectacle just over the hill of the onetime squatters, now resettlers, who are obviously going to be people of property and prosperity in a few years, creates at least as much jealousy as hope. The Bukit

Tembaga settlers are now living on government bounty but will soon be living, if not upon the cream, certainly upon the latex of the land. Why not us, too, ask the nearby kampong people. The same question will soon occur to thousands if not tens of thousands of poor Malays, poor Indians, and poor Chinese. It will occur to all those 250,000 persons throughout the Federation who have applied for but have not yet received the eight to ten acres of land which the government has repeatedly promised but seldom as yet delivered.

19

Island Incident

June 15, 1960

THE SMALL island of Pangkor, located one mile off the coast about 400 miles north of Singapore and 150 miles south of Penang, has several times in its history commanded attention far out of proportion to its size (about six square miles), its population (about 8,000), or its natural resources (the fish of the surrounding seas). Pangkor was the scene in May 1950 of the first and only serious racial disorders which have occurred in Malaya since achievement of independence. It thus served to focus attention both upon the highly inflammable racial sentiments of the nation and the manner in which they can get out of hand and then, fortunately, be brought under control again. Pangkor has more recently (June 1959) served as an example of the dangerous overspecialization of the national economy. Since almost any given area of Malaya is dependent upon one or at most two industries—fishing in the case of Pangkor—temporary dislocation can be a very serious matter.

Pangkor has also provided over the years an idyllic retreat for vacationists to whom the appeal of bustling Singapore and Penang is outmatched by that of Pangkor's rocky promontories and sandy beaches, its 1,200-foot hills and dense jungle, its busy if dilapidated fishing villages, its poor but by no means depressed fishing people, also its schools of brilliant tropical fish for the skin divers and its flights of noisy hornbills for the bird watchers. Pangkor is of historical note besides, having been one of the points of early European penetration into Malaya. The persevering hiker can still discover the ruins of a Dutch fort abandoned in 1743. The persevering reader can still rediscover that Pangkor was once ceded outright to Britain (1826) by the Sultan of Perak along with the

Dindings area and other off-lying islands. It featured in various episodes of nineteenth-century piracy, violence, and diplomacy. In 1874, for instance, it was the site for the signing of the British treaty with Perak which introduced British order into the troubled Malay states. In 1878, just four years later, it was the scene of the murder of the British superintendent of the Dindings. Pangkor Island and the Dindings, incidentally, were unobtrusively and gratefully returned to Perak in 1935, after it had been conclusively demonstrated that they did not pay for their keep. Pangkor Island, therefore, warrants at least a footnote in any account of the development of Malaya, and some of the material for a fairly elaborate footnote is herewith accumulated for the benefit of the historian, the traveler, or anyone interested in examining a minute but significant segment of the new Malayan nation.

In the Federation of Malaya the name Pangkor is now almost automatically associated with racial tension and disorder. The island's inhabitants, some 6,000 Chinese, 1,500 Malays, and 200 Indians, make their living directly or indirectly and more or less cooperatively from the fishing industry. The Chinese are the latecomers, the prosperous middle class, the big operators. The Malays in particular, and to a lesser extent the Indians, have felt their own position jeopardized by Chinese organization, initiative, and competition. Pangkor was the perfect setup, therefore, for the racial conflict which practically everyone has expected to break out at some time or other in the new Malaya. Disorders came to Pangkor during four frightening days, May 2–6, 1959. The story is still subject to variorum report, depending upon whose version— Chinese, Malay, Indian, or British—one listens to. Even participants and on-the-spot observers are none too sure exactly what struck the spark or how and by whom the flames were fanned. The account, as condensed below, is based upon inquiries made to persons who were present during or immediately after the disorders and upon the various reports carried by the local press.

Episode One was the accosting of two pretty Chinese sisters by two merry Malay youths. It is futile to attempt to determine how much encouragement the youths received or how much progress they made. Episode Two was the chastisement of the two youths by the girls' father. It is futile to speculate exactly how severe the chastisement was. Episode Three was the report by the two Malay youths to the male Malay community, just then, as ill luck would have it, assembling for Friday noon prayers, that the Chinese had threatened or mistreated them and that the Chinese community was deploying itself to put the Malays in their place. Episode Four was delayed for twenty-four hours, excitement meanwhile having been rising in the Malay community and apprehension in the Chinese. At noon on Saturday, May 2, a gang of Malay men, armed with parangs, sharpened bamboo poles, and sharpened coconut fronds, marched from the Malay kampong into the Chinese area of Pangkor town. The Chinese resisted their advance. Rioting started, and a series of Chinese shops and Chinese fishing piers were set on fire.

The Mentri Besar (Chief Minister) of Perak, as it happened, was paying a visit to the island at the time. He found himself marooned in the police station, unable to locate any of the three policemen presumably on duty. He managed, however, to put through a distress call to the mainland for dispatch of security forces. Episode Five was the arrival by stages of some two hundred policemen (including units of the Federal Riot Squad), their dispersal throughout the island, their frustration of the Chinese community plan to take reprisal upon the Malays, and their enforcement of special security measures which included a curfew and numerous arrests. Episode Six was the evacuation from the island of two thousand Chinese, tensions continuing high and sporadic attempts being made on the part of a few troublemakers to provoke new disturbances. Episode Seven was the arrival on the island of prominent representatives of the Malay and the Chinese groups, among them the acting Prime Minister, Tun Abdul Razak, who reasoned with the island's Malays and Chinese in order to achieve an end to disorder and an effort toward *rapprochement*. Episode Eight was the return to the island of the *évacués* and the resumption of business-almost-as-usual, with fishing boats putting out to sea again on May 6 and Chinese schools reopening on May 8.

The Federation Government had acted fast—not fast enough to prevent the initial riots, as it might quite possibly have done, but fast enough at least to keep them from spreading and to bring the situation back under control without much further violence or destruction. The final tally of death, injury, and damage was: one Malay killed; eight Malays and three Chinese injured and hospitalized; several big Chinese fishing establishments and numerous shop properties burned out or partially destroyed. Total property loss was officially estimated at only M$150,000, but gainful activity on the island had been paralyzed for about four days and did not for weeks return to normal level. The Pangkor disorders thus resulted in serious losses, but not half as serious as might easily have been the case. They served to alert the nation, however, to the continuing danger not only on Pangkor but elsewhere, and to the need for swift, decisive, constructive steps to avert it.

The constructive measures taken by the government subsequent to the riots still leave a great deal to be desired. Certain of the measures are mere precautionary routine. The island police force has been increased from five to fifteen and supplemented by a minute fire brigade of three men and two hand-drawn pumps. Longer-range measures relate to island development to promote improved living conditions and hence, it is hoped, improved psychological attitudes. The island has been provided with a new electric transformer station; electric cables have been laid to carry current from the mainland, and electrical service is being gradually extended to the population of the largest of the island's three villages. A new shore road is being built between the villages so that traffic will no longer be limited to footpaths and ferry service. The new road, about a mile and a half in length, will almost exactly double the existing roadways of the island and will no doubt increase motor-vehicle traffic proportionately. Prior to the riots, automobiles on the island totaled two decrepit unregistered taxis, both of which were destroyed. Automobile service is now limited to one recently imported taxi of vintage and condition appropriate to the distance it travels.

The government has also promised a new ferry landing to expedite service to the mainland. It is giving consideration to the problem of providing piped water and either improving or eliminating the shallow, brackish wells on which most of the islanders now depend for all except their drinking water, which is hand-carried from the hills. It is giving thought also to various schemes of community and economic development such as are mooted for other areas as well. As a quick ad hoc device to bring the various racial communities into closer and friendlier contact with each other, it has sponsored new sports events. A tug-of-war between a Malay and a Chinese team, however, ended in a not very friendly draw. It was called off after half an hour of huffing and puffing in which neither side was able to pull the other across the line, neither team being willing to yield although tuggers on both sides were experiencing severe cramps and spectators were growing bored. A football match between teams on which Malay and Chinese players were mixed yielded even less satisfactory results, for the game broke up in near physical violence between a Malay and a Chinese player. Still the efforts continue to be made and the hope is that they will catch on.

The basic problem, not just of an isolated multiracial fishing community, but of the nation as a whole, is that of reconciling many conflicting communal interests. The Chinese of Pangkor own the big power-driven fishing boats (about sixty of them of ten to fifty tons each) and the fishing piers where the catch is landed, processed, and shipped. They own the nets which the Indian fishermen use for inshore fishing, and they buy the Indian catch at prices reduced accordingly. They also buy the catch of the independent Malay fishermen, who paddle their own small boats a few miles out to sea and return to sell their fish to a Chinese middleman waiting on the shore or in a shop. The Chinese naturally own the most valuable properties on the island, including beach-front suitable for resort development, well-drained land planted in coconut and rubber, and also, of course, the retail shops, the money-lending establishments—even the island's single taxi, although it is licensed to a Malay and piloted by a Malay driver. Most of the Indians, by far the most depressed of the island's inhabitants, own little more than the shacks they live in, the clothes they work in, and a few head of cattle. The Malays are better off, some of them owning a little property which is indifferently planted with a miscellaneous assortment of fruit, coconut, and rubber. A good many of them occupy very tidy little stilted houses, some of which have been quite recently built. Nevertheless, the Malays have watched the Chinese swiftly move in and expand operations in the postwar years, and they feel that they themselves have become a depressed and exploited minority. Furthermore, the fishing industry, which is basic to their well-being, suffers from recurrent increase of costs and depression of prices. While the Chinese suffer too—the biggest Chinese operator on the island having almost gone broke a couple of years ago, although his son has now taken over and more than recouped the losses—the Chinese are better equipped either to tide themselves over during the lean periods or to make the most of a boom.

The last lean period occurred in June of 1959. Pangkor Island fish, of which there was a record catch, could find no adequate market and piled up on the fishing piers until the Chinese owners begged anyone and everyone to help himself, hoping merely to get rid of the catch before it putrified. One major reason for the difficulty was the closure of the Indonesian market for dried fish—a notoriously unreliable market which, depending upon the political and economic whim of the Indonesian authorities, flaps open and shut to the Malayan shipper. The Federation Government negotiated with the Indonesian Government, also the

Ceylonese, to purchase Pangkor fish, but even though agreement was reached, purchases failed to follow. The Federation Government then put on a campaign to get its own citizens to buy and eat more fish, but the Pangkor fishermen did not really experience relief until the onset of the monsoon season brought a decline in catch on the East Coast and an improvement, therefore, in the market for the Pangkor supply.

The long-range solution to the Pangkor fishermen's economic problem involves a combination of improved fishing, processing, shipping, and marketing facilities, none of which is quick or easy to achieve. Part of the catch is now shipped fresh on ice; part is boiled and shipped for immediate sale in nearby urban markets; a large part is dried and salted; the remainder is converted into fertilizer, or poultry or stock feed. As yet, none is deep frozen or canned. The differential in price as between what the fish brings to the fisherman, what it sells for among the middlemen, and what it costs the housewife is still unreasonably great. A pound of *ikan kembong*, the most common Pangkor fish and one of low quality, for which the independent Malay fisherman receives at most about ten cents, sells generally on the Kuala Lumpur market a day or two later for about 40–50 cents.

The government is attempting on Pangkor and elsewhere to encourage fishing cooperatives. So far it has achieved no particular success on Pangkor, even though the basic economics of the industry make the plan seem most inviting. A seagoing fishing boat, complete with nets and pier facilities, constitutes an investment of about M$100,000—a sum which the Chinese can raise but the Malays cannot unless they organize themselves to qualify for government assistance. One good night's catch during a period of good prices is worth M$10,000 on Pangkor Island and much more in Kuala Lumpur. The M$10,000 catch, to be sure, is infrequent, but M$1,000 catches are common. According to present employment practices, the members of the crew—about twenty-five men, mainly Chinese, but some Malays—get a 10 per cent cut in the profits. On a cooperative venture the individual share would rise dramatically. The ordinary Malay fisherman, who is self-employed and probably works a little land in addition to fishing, earns at the present time about M$100 to M$200 per month in cash income. The figure might readily be doubled and redoubled if the cooperative idea should catch on.

Fish and the sea and the spectacle of an industrious fishing community working against an extremely beautiful tropical island backdrop make Pangkor Island, regardless of its unsound economics and its touchy tempers, a spot of special appeal for the vacationer. Stilted Malay towns built under coconut palms stretch along clean, sandy beaches. The nearby Chinese villages, to be sure, are rather squalid even though the population is much more prosperous, but the long fishing piers, with huge festoons of dark maroon nets drying in the sun, the fishing boats silhouetted against a brilliant sky, the combination of mountain, jungle, palm, sand, and sea add up to a resort spot of the travel advertisement genre. On the seaward of the island, away from the villages, the Indian fishermen put out their long nets from the shore, then draw them in to the accompaniment of chanting that rises to a crescendo as the catch comes closer. Malay fishermen paddling fragile boats bring in catches that display all the variety and brilliance of the tropical fish aquarium. If anyone wishes to view the fish in their native habitat, then a couple of miles offshore, in Emerald Bay on Little Pangkor Island, the fish obligingly display themselves swimming through coral beds in crystal-clear water.

Little Pangkor Island itself, once a leper settlement, is now abandoned to forest reserve, inhabited only by birds and monkeys which forage in the fruit gardens the lepers once planted or prospect the coastal rocks for shellfish. It is just one stage further removed than Pangkor itself from the urban rush. It might one day, if a few million dollars were put into its development, provide part of the answer to Pangkor's problem. It could afford a little more land suitable for cultivation, a little more sea-coast suitable for fishing establishments, and little resort coves which would attract the tourist dollar and thus, of course, irretrievably ruin a truly idyllic retreat.

20

Legacy of the White Rajahs

August 5, 1957

EVERY SUNDAY supplement reader a generation ago knew quite a good deal, if not about the Borneo rajahdom of Sarawak itself, at least about its ruler, the White Rajah, Sir Charles Vyner Brooke, his vivacious wife, the Ranee Sylvia, and his three beautiful daughters, one of whom married a prize fighter, another a dance-band leader, and the third an earl. But current readers of Sunday supplements or even of more deathless literature probably have heard little about the new state of Sarawak. Since July 1, 1946, a Crown Colony within the British Empire, Sarawak is the scene of what seems to date a successful effort at guided transition from colonialism to eventual independence.

The signs of change were conspicuously evident about two months ago (May 19–25) when there was convened for the first time, in the capital city of Kuching, the new Sarawak Council Negri (State Council). On it, side by side with British colonial officials, sit Chinese bankers, Malay nobles, and Dayak tribal chieftains. The council is soon to organize itself to assume legislative responsibility under the British governor for a state with a population of 625,000 people (including 2,000 Europeans) and an area of 47,500 square miles.

The signs of change are every day apparent to any visitor to Kuching. Once a remote and sleepy Borneo river settlement under the benign but Victorian paternalism of a British rajah, Kuching is now briskly converting itself into a progressive modern city. Recently acquired landmarks, counterbalancing the rajahs' nineteenth-century palace, fort and government buildings, include a splendid Anglican cathedral of advanced modern design, an excellent hotel, government housing developments of

241

bungalows and apartments, spacious hospitals and schools, the complete broadcasting facilities of Radio Sarawak, and a new museum building that doubles the already extensive space of the old and serves as head-quarters for significant anthropological and archaeological research. The city is populated by 56,000 Chinese, Malays, Dayaks, Indians, and Europeans who seem genuinely at ease with one another and do not seem to worry much about the possibility of interracial conflict and tension. In this modern Sarawak you hear quite a good deal of sober discussion about the need for joint British-Chinese-Malay-Dayak effort to build up Sarawak gradually to the stage at which Crown Colony status may safely give way to—what? Independence? Alliance with the nearby Federation of Malaya? Federation with the other states of British Borneo?

Discussion about the future status of Sarawak tends to be both objective and tolerant, whether the discussion occurs in British, Chinese, Malay, Dayak, or mixed circles. There is as yet in Sarawak no political party formulating irreducible demands; in fact, there is no political party. There are no slogans—"Sarawak for the Sarawakians," "Merdeka Now," "Go Home, Limeys," or, for that matter, "The British Must Stay." Sarawak, it may be worth adding, has no public debt, no unemployment, no significant labor problems, virtually no pauperism, no personal income tax, little crime, and no traffic jams.

To be sure, all is not perfect in Kuching. There are troubles in the Chinese schools reminiscent of the beginnings of trouble in Singapore's Chinese schools several years ago. There are jockeyings for position among Chinese groups more or less favorably disposed toward British subject status or rapport with Peking. (This latter faction is still small and quiet.) There are suspicions that the British favor and pamper the Malays, that the Chinese exploit everyone else, that the Malays want to enlist nationalistic support from the Malays of the Federation, that the Dayaks may gradually awaken to the nationalistic theory that the whole state was originally theirs and everyone else is an unauthorized interloper. Despite these undercurrents, and despite the ever-present possibility that other and more dangerous overcurrents may develop momentarily, the present political and social condition of the state of Sarawak, like its economy, is distinctly healthy. The credit goes historically to the white rajahs who ruled in such a manner that British prestige was firmly established in the area. The immediate credit goes jointly to a tolerant population and to an intelligent British officialdom. The latter, as many local informants point out, has kept quite a few steps ahead of public demand in conferring political and economic opportunity. In Sarawak the British have managed most adroitly to obviate public indignation over the slowness of change and to create, instead, a healthy public trepidation as to its speed.

Sarawak, now in the first stage of development toward eventual self-government, has a new constitution, granted on August 3, 1956, by the British Crown. Under the terms of the constitution there have been created new municipal, district, divisional, and state councils. The lower councils are basically elective, with representatives chosen by traditional group selection process rather than by ballot. The Council Negri is semi-elective, with twenty-one members elected from the divisional councils, three elected from the municipal councils, and twenty-one either appointed by the governor or automatically designated by reason of official position. Legislative measures adopted by the Council Negri will be subject to the veto of the British governor, but indications are that a practical working agreement will be reached as regards the Council's succession to a gradually expanding area of legislative competence.

The day-to-day administration of the state remains in the hands of a civil service headed by the governor and his staff of Colonial Office officials. It is staffed at lower levels by Chinese, Malays, and Dayaks, with due regard for equitable distribution of jobs among qualified candidates of the different racial groups. One sign of British alertness to keep constantly ahead of the trend is the introduction by the British governor at the first meeting of the Council Negri of a resolution calling for the early replacement of British by local officials. The subject will no doubt come up in the forthcoming legislative sessions. It will lead, in all probability, as in Singapore and Malaya, to a definite schedule of replacements—also to a schedule of compensation of British officials whose careers are thus interrupted.

The new system, obviously, is not without its blemishes. Members of the Council Negri, for instance, must serve on three or four other councils, down to the local level at which they were originally selected. They are already beginning to discover that the practice of self-government requires sacrifice of personal and business affairs if they are to attend the frequent meetings and to head the numerous committees. Dayak members of various councils unfortunately speak no English—the language of the sessions. They have contributed more in decorativeness than in discussion and may soon tire of their role of window dressing. Younger Sarawak groups complain that the indirect and complicated elective system, combined with the system of official appointments, causes the councils to be heavily loaded with the aged and the conservative. Reformers complain that even prior to the adoption of the new system the government afforded such opportunity for spoils and squeeze that there had to be created a Commission for Investigation of Corruption. Many fear the activities of the Commission will increase, not diminish, as the new system comes more fully into effect. Still, in present-day Sarawakian terms, corruption is measured not in peanuts—as compared with corruption, say, in nearby Indonesia—but in units of the most famous local crop, i.e., peppercorns. Other political evils, to date at least, seem of comparable dimensions.

Sarawak does not yet have even the first symptoms of the political troubles that have recently developed in its northern neighbor. In the sultanate of Brunei there has emerged a new Partai Rakjat (People's Party) with rather contradictory demands for "independence" and "federation." One reason, perhaps, that Sarawak does not have Brunei's political troubles is that it does not have Brunei's wealth—which leaders of the Partai Rakjat seem eager to get their hands on. Even without Brunei's oil, however, Sarawak's finances are in good shape.

Sarawak's total state revenue in 1956 came to M$51,443,347; its ordinary expenditures came to M$43,170,607. It thus had a surplus of M$8,272,740 for transfer to a special fund for implementation of its M$100 million five-year Development Plan. Sarawak's annual surplus—a reliable item for the last few years—is likely now to decrease, just as Development Plan expenditures are rapidly increasing. The difference between Sarawak's revenues and its total expenditure is now being made up—and will probably continue to be made up—from the Commonwealth Development Fund. At any rate, the Sarawak Development Plan should be completed by 1960, with perhaps as much as 50 per cent of it paid for from local funds. The development projects, which appear to be going well, will some of them soon begin to feed money back into the national treasury.

In the meanwhile, of course, Sarawak may manage to strike it rich in oil, as has its neighbor, Brunei. Sarawak has hopefully developed its own small oil field in Miri, close to Brunei's Seria fields; it has poured a good deal of Development Plan money into explorations for oil elsewhere; it managed in 1956 to pump out 70,616 tons of oil valued at M$3,758,040—but nothing to compare with Brunei's M$313,739,509 oil yield which Sarawak refined or transshipped.

Until such time as Sarawak strikes oil in quantity—which all loyal Sarawakians trust may be soon and some believe may be expected momentarily—the state is dependent for economic development largely upon rubber, pepper, and timber. Pepper, Sarawak's number-two product, deserves primary mention. It is a commodity peculiarly suited to Sarawak's soil and climate and to its Chinese and Dayak farmers. These pepper farmers tend their small holdings of an acre or two of vines with such devotion that their production per vine, per acre, or per man far exceeds that of the competing areas of Malaya, India, and Indonesia. Sarawak since the war has captured the world—meaning, the American—pepper market. Black and white peppercorns, in quantities which would appear sufficient for any conceivable human consumption, make pungent the Kuching bazaars. (But Kuching eating establishments, "progressive" sometimes to a disappointing degree, dispense the imported—hence more elegant—Western processed variety.) For the sake of the statistical shock, it is worth reporting that Sarawak exported in 1956 some 19,818 *tons* of peppercorns to the value of M$24,610,131.

Sarawak's number-three export item is timber, cut from the limitless stretches of Borneo jungle. In 1956 exports came to 197,089 tons, valued at M$19,064,435. The limiting factors on the growth of the industry and on the growth of permanent settlements on the land cleared by the industry are the near inaccessibility of the swampy and mountainous jungle land, the prohibitive cost of maintaining even the rudimentary roadways built to bring the timber out, and the lack of any great population pressure to provide laborers and settlers. This latter deficiency, of course, could be remedied in conjunction with the overpopulated nations of Southeast Asia, but few expect that it will be.

Sarawak's number-one industry is rubber. All local production is in the hands of smallholders—no alienation of land for foreign estates having been permitted either by the white rajahs or by their successors. Quality and quantity are far below normal expectation, exports in 1956 having come only to 41,234 tons, valued at M$68,635,041. The government is busily pushing a program of subsidized replanting and improved production methods. It will require some little time, however, before the Chinese or the Malay farmer, let alone the Dayak tribesman, adopts precision methods to replace the present system of haphazard tapping of wild-looking rubber growths.

As part of its Development Plan, the government is also making energetic efforts to introduce diversified farming, to improve methods of rice culture, and to introduce better strains of livestock. It is likewise encouraging improvements in the fishing industry, still largely unmechanized and confined to coastal waters. In these and other efforts it is having to overcome public lethargy. Even though Sarawak is a boom country as compared with much of the area, it is still Southeast Asian and leisurely. Overseas Chinese capitalists, for instance, seeking new, safe, and profitable areas of investment, find Sarawak attractive but strangely limited in opportunity.

Regardless of such limitations, and as a result largely of the government's program, Sarawak in general and the city of Kuching in particular are showing the evidences of progress and prosperity. Kuching is provided now with adequate piped drinking water, electric power, and telephones—facilities which in less remote and presumably better-developed countries of Southeast Asia seem to be in chronically short supply. It has plentiful buses and taxis. It has few, if any, squatters. It has big new public housing developments which, if not yet adequate to meet demand, do supply quite a lot of modern bungalows and apartments at rentals that come, say, to M$52 per month for a two-bedroom flat. Its shops are well stocked with local and foreign merchandise, including such items as pens, watches, cameras, typewriters, cosmetics, and outboard motors. These sell not as highly taxed luxury items, as in the case in various neighboring areas, but at reasonable prices within the means of the local public. The principal bookstore offers a wide range of new and older publications; the British Council and the Museum libraries give excellent service to general and specialized readers. Kuching is a clean, well-shaded, cool, spacious, and attractively gardened town, and it gives every appearance of being well administered.

The efficiency of civic administration extends, naturally, to social welfare and improvement projects. Hospitals, including a mental hospital and a leprosarium, are handsomely built and efficiently run. Schools are receiving priority attention, government expenditures on education increasing from M$1.5 million in 1955 to M$5.5 million in 1956—a period in which enrollments increased by 10,000.

Sarawak's educational system, historically, has been based upon government-operated elementary schools for Malays and Dayaks, privately-operated elementary and secondary schools for Chinese students, and elementary and secondary interracial schools operated by foreign missions (principally Catholic and Anglican). The government has now greatly increased its allocations for government schools and has established new government secondary schools (English language) in the urban centers. It has also established a Malay teacher-training college in Kuching—operating, incidentally, in the reconstructed POW camp that was the setting for *Three Came Home*, Agnes Newton Keith's account of the Japanese occupation. It is sending Sarawak students abroad for further training—including teacher training—in Malaya, Australia, and the United Kingdom. Until the time that its own supply of teachers is adequate to its needs, it is recruiting teachers in Malaya.

Thus by various devices the government of Sarawak is seeking to bring the level of Malay and Dayak education up to the level which the Chinese had managed privately to achieve for themselves. By making grants to the Chinese schools and insisting upon greatly increased government supervision in return, it is attempting to adapt the Chinese curriculum to the new educational needs. The government is making grants also to mission schools—these grants also introducing problems of control. The development of a coherent educational system is far from easy and has led to charges of discrimination and favoritism; but educational facilities are expanding rapidly in present-day Sarawak and even higher education is no longer unknown. A few Chinese students have now returned from abroad with professional degrees; a few Malay students have left for extended study abroad; and the first several Dayak students have qualified—at least two having already experienced short periods of advanced study in the United Kingdom.

The differences and the rivalries among the various racial groups in Sarawak may well pose the most urgent problem of the near future. The distribution of population is: Sea Dayaks (Iban), 34.8 per cent; Chinese, 26.6 per cent; Malays, 17.9 per cent; and local tribes other than Sea Dayaks, 20 per cent. The Chinese control most of the business of the area. The Malays—the "pampered" group under the Rajahs Brooke and, some say, under the present administration as well—are in a position of social and political ascendancy over the local peoples. The Dayaks retain claim to the huge stretches of relatively underdeveloped land, although Chinese, Malays, and Dayaks share the small farms of the developed areas. The British, of course, control the administration.

Insofar as the various groups are considering the eventual status of Sarawak, there seems at the present time to be a considerable area of agreement, with realization that in a state racially so divided and in a section of the globe politically so troubled, most groups may have to settle for second rather than first choice of alternatives. Complete independence, separate Commonwealth status, and alliance with the new Federation of Malaya are all proposed, but none is very seriously pushed. Many more people talk in terms of the federation of Sarawak with Brunei and North Borneo into a new alliance on the model of the Federation of Malaya, presumably with Commonwealth status.

The British, in general, are the most single-minded advocates of this solution and are working quietly to achieve it. The Chinese, most of whom would probably prefer separate Commonwealth status for Sarawak and British subject status for themselves, seem to realize that they are not in a position to dominate or to decide. They seem to feel that the best they can hope for is treatment such as the Chinese receive in the Federation of Malaya, and few of them seem inclined, as yet at least, to complicate the situation by maneuvering with Communist China. The Malays, many if not most of whom would probably prefer affiliation with the Federation of Malaya, recognize that in British Borneo they are considerably outnumbered by the Borneo tribes. They seem indisposed, by rash agitation for affiliation with Malaya, to call down upon themselves the discrimination which Southeast Asian nationalism deals out to immigrant minority groups. The Dayaks and the other native tribes, as noted, are not yet politically articulate, but they may eventually become so. The British, to repeat, seem very shrewdly to have calculated the various checks and balances, and the proposal of federation which they are cautiously advancing makes a very great deal of sense from many points of view.

The concept of federation does, however, raise certain serious problems. First is the problem of Brunei, by far the wealthiest of the states of British Borneo and quite unwilling to share its wealth with the others. The Sultan of Brunei, additionally, has historic claims to sovereignty over both Sarawak and British North Borneo. When and if federation is definitely scheduled, the question of paramount authority will arise. The course of legalistic logic indicates the return of sovereignty to the rightful heir of the sultans from whom it was wrested. But Brunei has for the last century or more been the most backward of the states. It is still held in low esteem by large numbers of Sarawakians who remember the oppressive rule of Brunei in past centuries and the piratical expeditions of Brunei in recent generations. Few Sarawakians would even now gladly acknowledge Brunei or Brunei's Sultan as the paramount power in British Borneo.

But despite the difficulties, sooner or later, the three states of Sarawak,

Brunei, and British North Borneo will probably achieve federation if for no other reason than proximity to a large and troubled neighbor—the Republic of Indonesia. Indonesian Kalimantan—the southern two-thirds of the island of Borneo—is at present no less disturbed than are Sumatra, Java, and Sulawesi, and the leaders of the British Borneo states are becoming more and more aware that the troubles might spread.

Communications between British and Indonesia Borneo are infrequent and irregular—save, of course, for the small but steady traffic of Indonesian smugglers and laborers and of Dayak tribesmen, traveling between certain ports and along the jungle rivers and trails. The cities of Kuching and Pontianak, less than one hour's distance from each other by air and a few hours' distance by sea, are widely separated by communications and immigration obstacles. The extraordinary traveler who makes the journey by conventional means takes three days by air or several weeks by sea, proceeding via Singapore and Djakarta. Current information crosses the communications barriers more readily than do legitimate travelers, and the leading citizens of Kuching, for instance, are fairly well informed about conditions in Indonesia. They know that their neighbors in Indonesian Kalimantan are undergoing upheavals and hardships such as they hope they themselves may be spared, perhaps by slowing down the pace of *merdeka*.

The lesson of Indonesia is brought home to Kuching daily by the spectacle of Indonesian smugglers landing cargoes of rubber. In Indonesia they would have to sell this rubber through government agencies at virtually confiscatory prices. In Kuching they can sell at world market prices for good hard currency. These Indonesian smugglers take back with them to Indonesia the fountain pens, watches, radios, even the outboard motors which in Kuching they can buy freely, without tremendous markup, and without complicated application and screening of requests. They report that in smuggling their cargoes out of Indonesia they have only to pay a bribe in order to hitch a tow on an Indonesian government patrol craft. On their return they have only to pay off with gifts of cigarettes and pens and watches. They are still far better off than they would be if they abided by the cumbersome Indonesian production, import, and export controls.

The situation in Kuching, through which, after all, the flow of smuggled goods is merely a trickle, is reproduced and magnified in Tawao. This small seaport of British North Borneo, as every well-informed person in Borneo knows, flourishes on the smuggling of copra and other produce from Sulawesi and the Moluccas. Not only the smugglers, but the few thousand Indonesian workers who are more or less permanently domiciled in British Borneo, make it quite clear that they prefer the standards of living, pay, and government in colonial British Borneo to those of independent Indonesia.

Should conditions greatly improve in Indonesia, or should conditions greatly deteriorate in British Borneo, the political affiliations which grow out of historic, racial, and cultural ties might greatly increase in strength. For the present, however, except for an Indonesian-educated Brunei Malay named Azahari who has formed the Partai Rakjat demanding "Merdeka for Brunei," the affiliations are still weak. In Sarawak, in particular, local bodies are disposed to judge by their own recent experiences. They have failed completely, for instance, to elicit any Indonesian response whatsoever to proposals for joint effort in malaria control in border areas. They have had experience with Indonesian armed gangs causing disturbances in Sarawak territory. After one such episode a Sarawak official party—including high-ranking Malays—traveled by boat to Pontianak to consult with the Indonesian authorities. Even though they had laboriously secured all advance clearances, they were placed under arrest the moment they entered Pontianak harbor. They found Indonesian administrative channels so labyrinthine that it was only with great difficulty that they could establish their bona fides.

On the whole, the leading citizens of the new state of Sarawak, as they contemplate their own political future, tend to take an unhappy lesson from the example of nearby Indonesia. They watch with some apprehensiveness the emergence of the independent Federation of Malaya. They regard the nearby state of Brunei as a special problem which they must somehow take the initiative in resolving if they are to achieve federation. They do not commit themselves as to their future status within or without the British Empire. But the feeling among the local people of all groups and the feeling between them and the British seems at present quite good. A visitor to Sarawak today comes away with the impression that in Sarawak British Commonwealth is likely to succeed British Empire, and, on the whole, smoothly.

21

Shellfare Sultanate

July 1, 1957

VISUALIZE a tropical Southeast Asian state without poverty, disease, over-population, undernourishment, budgetary deficit, political agitation, armed insurrection, maladministration, or any of the other concomitants of mid-twentieth century nationalist evolution, such as strikes, riots, and demonstrations. You will not be visualizing precisely the tiny British Borneo sultanate of Brunei, but you'll be close. Brunei is wealthy, healthy, and to all appearances happy and well-administered. To be sure, it is also tiny, comprising only about 60,000 people on 2,226 square miles of northern Borneo delta, jungle, swamp, clearing, and—what is more to the point—oil land.

Brunei's happy circumstances are of recent origin and uncertain expectations. Prewar Borneo was a runner-up for rating as the most poverty-stricken scrap of the British Empire; its oil resources may not last the next two decades or even, say its jealous neighbors, the next one. Brunei in 1957 is that ultimate anachronism of the mid-twentieth century. a traditional sultanate with protectorate status within the British Empire and without either clear-cut demands or plans (save for an exception to be noted later) for "independence." The spectacle of present-day Brunei is one that may prove revealing in many and in contradictory respects to the observer seeking the signs of progress and of retrogression among the highly nationalistic, highly independence-minded Southeast Asian countries.

The contemporary sultanate of Brunei is two bulbous enclaves extending into the surrounding state of Sarawak. It is the remnants of the ancient and powerful Brunei sultanate which the British Rajah James Brooke, about one hundred years ago, reduced to impotence, inertia, and, he assumed, indigence, when he created his own adjacent and more enlightened rajadom. "Filthy rich" is the way the Sarawakians describe Brunei today. "Jealous" is the adjective applied in Brunei to Sarawak, and the problems of the potential new Federation of British Borneo are complicated accordingly.

In recent years Brunei has been the scene of a guided economic and social experiment under conditions which I.C.A. planners dream of. It is an experiment in converting a feudal, tropical, underdeveloped sultanate into a new sort of state that will be viable in the mid-twentieth century world. To date at least the experiment looks remarkably good—and this despite reports (readily forthcoming in Sarawak, for instance) of muddle, waste, and fiasco. The visitor to the capital, Brunei Town (population 15,000), is confronted with the spectacle of change and contrast on every side. He arrives at a spotless new airport (cost: M$2.5 million), handsomer and better run than the airports in cities of one million or more in nearby countries. He drives into Brunei Town over a fine new highway, one of a network of highways now being driven through the jungles by British and Australian engineers using the most up-to-date construction equipment. He drives past scores of neat government bungalows, looking like giant prefabs set on piles, and if he visits them later he finds them furnished with good Singapore rattan, equipped with American-style kitchens, sometimes provided—at the occupant's expense —with air conditioning and automatic washing machines. Everywhere he sees new government building—a complex of secondary schools of the very newest design, a government headquarters in traditional bureaucratese, a customs house looking like an advertisement for all the latest in baffles, louvers, cantilevers, pastel concrete mixes, structural steel, aluminum, and glass devices. He drives through a bustling business district—a sort of planned Oriental shopping center, government-built to replace the prewar business district blasted both by the Japanese and the Allies. There are private projects too—a handsome new hotel, modern apartments (at least one of these complexes built by the Sultan as a private investment), and private homes, many of them built on 3 per cent government loans, repaid in monthly installments which, in the case of government employees, come to just about what they draw in rental allowance.

The historic Brunei Town, however, is not this modern town of shops and government buildings and living quarters for the Europeans, the

Chinese, the civil servants of many nationalities, and the few Brunei Malays who have so far taken to such a life. The real Brunei Town is still the *kampong ayer* where some ten thousand Brunei Malays live in small houses built on stilts over the tidal river bed. The *kampong ayer* is idyllically situated along the inlets of a broad, winding jungle river. It is set against a backdrop of low, green hills, along which, by contrast, are located the Western-style palace of the Sultan and the porticoed prewar bungalows of the top British officials. The houses of the *kampong ayer* are interconnected by swaying footbridges. Communication with land is via innumerable small boats, some large enough to support an outboard motor, others mere splinters, just large enough to support exactly one small passenger and one small bundle. Almost all of the houses now sport battery radio sets. Almost every male citizen now seems to own a Swiss wrist watch, an American fountain pen, a jeweled ring, some gay sport shirts, a wide-brimmed hat, not to mention one or more outboard motors. The women own gold and silver jewelry, bright sarongs (manufactured in Indonesia, Japan, and Germany), Max Factor cosmetics, and tea sets of Chinese or Japanese make. The children, who still like to play naked in the cool muck of the river bed at low tide, are being enticed ashore by free room-and-board scholarships in bright modern schools. The Brunei Malays, whose sultan took up permanent residence ashore only in 1909, are now beginning to mingle more and more with the other half of the Brunei population (19 per cent Chinese, 27 per cent Borneo "native" peoples), and the government program of creating a new society is gathering impetus.

The Brunei government's program is one of rapid modernization, with emphasis upon provision of all the physical facilities necessary to a modern state and upon simultaneous education of the Brunei Malays and the Borneo tribes to appreciate and profit from them. There can be and there is a great deal of dispute whether such a program is calculated to make the people more or less happy, in the future, than they have been in the past and whether welfare statism in Brunei has not already passed into a mollycoddle phase. The Brunei Malays seem rather more at their ease in the innumerable coffee shops than economic dynamism would dictate. There can also be dispute whether the Chinese minority is getting its fair share of the advantages. The Chinese shopkeepers, however, still almost monopolize the business of the area and come sooner or later into possession of most of the money that passes through the hands of the Malays. There can be dispute whether the British administration is going too fast or too slow in creating the state of affairs in which a British administration will no longer be necessary or possible. On the whole, however, the mixed population of Brunei Malays, Chinese, "native" peoples, and British civil servants seem genuinely friendly with each other and even, despite the pace of progress, fairly relaxed about the serious conflicts it may ultimately induce.

Any serious consideration of Brunei must start with some consideration of its recent oil wealth. Oil exploitation is in the hands of the British Malayan Petroleum Company which pays copious royalties and taxes to the government. By conservative calculation, Brunei state revenue from oil is expected to come to about M$120 million in 1957. The figure in 1950 was M$17,302,869, and since both state planners and oil geologists are wary of prediction, it is anybody's guess what it may be in 1960. These oil revenues, it should be emphasized, accrue not to the Sultan and not to the British, but to the state, meaning, in the end, to the Brunei people. At the 1957 rate, therefore, Brunei's income from oil alone comes to M$2,000 per capita, thus in theory assuring the happy Brunei citizen, even if he does not do a stroke of work, of the highest per capita income in Southeast Asia. (Wealthy Singapore's per capita income is M$1,200.) For a state whose total revenue never rose above M$500,000 until the mid-thirties, then skyrocketed to M$4,389,974 in 1947, the rate of enrichment has been breath-taking.

It became apparent a few years after the war that Brunei state revenues were piling up much faster than they could be spent. The British administrators sat down and made what is, for Southeast Asia at least, a stunningly simple and logical series of assumptions. The oil revenues, it seemed, would continue for a few more years if not for a few more decades. They would obviously be in excess of all normal government requirements. They might clearly be depended upon not only to meet all normal expenses of administration but to allow for great surpluses. A large sum could safely be earmarked as a special fund for economic development. The balance could be set aside as a reserve fund constituting, in effect, a massive endowment from which the state could cover its operating expenses for the foreseeable future. The British administrators, with the full concurrence of the Sultan and the Sultan's Council of State, have acted accordingly. The result is that the sultanate of Brunei is probably the most unshakably solvent small state in the world today. It has already banked M$300,000,000; it has meanwhile embarked upon a M$100,000,000 development plan; as its annual expenditures rise, its oil revenues rise even faster, a happy disequilibrium that is likely to persist. One of the minor items on the budget, incidentally, is M$381,790 for maintenance of H. H. the Sultan. Of this amount, M$150,000 is personal stipend for the Sultan himself; M$12,000 for his wife; M$13,855 for a tutor (British) for his children; other sums for a secretary, an aide-de-camp, a valet, a ladies' maid, houseboys, amahs, gardeners, cooks, four "Royal Nobat," one "Ghillie,"—a total payroll of forty-five which also includes grooms, drivers, and mechanics for the fast horses, cars, and boats which the Sultan fancies.

The effects of the M$100 million Development Plan are still far more readily apparent upon the towns than upon most of the townspeople. The government has not yet had much success in persuading the Brunei Malays to move ashore from the *kampong ayer*, to take up the new land which the government is clearing for them, to build new homes ashore (with government subsidy), to plant rubber and fruit trees, rice, and vegetables, to develop small industries, and otherwise to build a new and modern economy. The Brunei Malays still prefer the *kampong ayer*, with its built-in fishing, boating, bathing, and refuse-disposal systems, and its opportunity for casual employment by hauling building stone and gravel from upriver to the Brunei Town collection points of Chinese contractors. The government is making concessions now by starting to run electricity lines and drinking-water pipes right out into the *kampong ayer* itself. It is counting upon the inducements of education, medicine, and social services in the long run to persuade the *kampong ayer* dwellers to move ashore, as did their sultan only about fifty years ago.

First priority on the development program, therefore, is assigned to education. In prewar days Brunei had a total of twenty-two small vernacular primary schools. It had no secondary schools at all, although a few Brunei students did manage to get to Labuan, in North Borneo, and to Malaya for secondary training. The new M$100 million Development Plan allocated M$10,650,000 for education (an estimate since revised to M$13,150,000), this sum to provide for school buildings, staff salaries, scholarships, teacher training, and other expenses. Brunei is now building or has recently completed twenty-three new primary schools, all of them spacious modern buildings far more than adequate to care for the present crop of students, all of them provided with bungalows for the teaching staff. Higher primary schools are being built in the urban centers. English-language secondary schools, one for boys and another for girls, are now being completed in Brunei Town. This complex of fine modern buildings includes dormitories, a gymnasium, fully equipped science laboratories, libraries, teachers' lounges, plus the usual classrooms. A trade school is being operated at Seria in conjunction with the oil company. Teacher training is being accomplished by sending students to Malaya, to England, and to Australia. At the present time about 90 per cent of the children of primary school age are actually enrolled—a total of about 10,000 students. Of the non-school-going 10 per cent, some are children who live beyond the range of the school buses and school ferries; most of them, however, are the girl children of Malay parents who do not yet accept the modern principle of equal education for both sexes. Virtually all Brunei students who can qualify for secondary education now receive it—often with free board and lodging provided. Those who complete secondary education with any degree of distinction can count upon being sent abroad for further study.

Medical and public health services have kept pace with educational development. Brunei's population centers are now provided with modern hospitals and clinics. Civil servants receive medical attention in accordance with a medical insurance scheme requiring small payments from their salaries. Private citizens receive services either free or for very small fees. What is even more distinctive of Brunei—indeed, unique for Southeast Asia—is a government scheme whereby at the age of sixty any Brunei citizen, irrespective of racial background, becomes eligible without means test for receipt of a state pension of M$20 per month. The physically disabled and the blind are also eligible for pension, the blind receiving M$20 per month from the age of fifteen and allowances up to an additional M$80 per month for their dependents.

In addition to educational and social advancement, Brunei is now going through a period of religious revival. The Sultan, who is deeply devout, is to a great extent responsible. He has brought in religious teachers from Malaya and is promoting the establishment of a Muslim theological seminary. He has actively supported one special Development Plan project —the building of a huge new mosque which the Brunei residents enthusiastically compare in size with the Hagia Sophia and in beauty with the Taj Mahal. The mosque, originally estimated to cost M$4 million, has already cost M$5 million, and estimates are still rising. It will boast such unique mosque features as a four-passenger electric lift in the main minaret; Italian marble facing and flooring, laid by Italian experts; and Venetian gold tile for the dome and turrets—more durable and more expensive than mere gold leaf. The building was designed by a British firm of architects, using a Malayan mosque as a model; it is being put up by a Chinese contractor using Chinese labor imported from Hong Kong. To its dedication, a year or so from now, will be invited top dignitaries from all over the Muslim world. Facing on the river and the *kampong ayer*, set off by a vast artificial lagoon for which parts of the *kampong ayer* itself will be razed, set against low hills and green jungle, the mosque even now, with scaffolding still in large part concealing it, appears to be exactly what its sponsors declare: the largest mosque east of Suez. For a state of 60,000 and a town of 15,000, in which only about half the population is Muslim, the Brunei Town mosque strikes the visitor as unexpected, to say the least.

All this change and progress in Brunei inevitably intensifies some old problems and introduces some new ones. In briefest summary, some of the emerging difficulties are these:

1. Relations among the various racial groups. The Brunei Malays constitute slightly less than one half of the population, the half with historic claim to political control, although, to be sure, the Borneo tribes may yet claim historic rights to the land. The Borneo tribesmen make up 28 per cent of the population (Kedayans, 17 per cent; Dusuns, 7 per cent; Dayaks, 3:5 per cent; and Muruts, 0.5 per cent); Chinese, 19 per cent; Indians and Europeans, 1.5 per cent each; others, 1.0 per cent. The Sultan, being a Brunei Malay (of Arab descent), naturally favors the Malays, as have the British. The Chinese, who constitute the tradesmen of the area and have traditionally handled its wealth, are now finding themselves excluded more and more from official position and special privilege and are becoming increasingly apprehensive about the future. The Chinese, for instance, get only 50 per cent government support for their schools; in Brunei Town, near the splendid new secondary schools meant primarily for Brunei Malays, the Chinese secondary students are now housed in an antiquated, dilapidated shambles of a building. The Chinese make no secret of the fact that they feel they are subject to increasing discrimination. The Borneo tribesmen are not yet politically or economically self-conscious enough to feel that they have a cause, but that day, too, may come.

2. Effects of welfare statism upon a naturally easygoing population. The Brunei Malays, the special beneficiaries of the wealth and planning of the government, are not as yet taking very full advantage of their new opportunities. They are not moving ashore in any significant numbers to become industrious tillers of the soil or, for that matter, to cash

in on the government's offers of easy loans to set up small private businesses. Although they are taking to modern education and to modern
medicine, it is sometimes still a struggle to persuade parents to educate
their daughters. It is also a struggle to persuade the boys to study very
diligently or to take up technical trades and crafts rather than white-
collar employment.

3. The crosscurrents between the politics of the sultanate and of the
foreign bureaucracy. The Brunei sultanate, a one-thousand-year-old
Oriental oligarchy, is riddled with cliques and animosities. The modern
administration—in the hands of a British Resident with a staff of some 500
civil servants recruited largely from the British Colonial Service, from
Australia, and from among the Indian, Malay, and Chinese civil servants
of Malaya—has its own intrigues and its inevitable differences with the
sultanate. In theory, according to the agreement of 1906, the Sultan has
absolute powers only with reference to religious and *adat* (customary)
matters; he is required to accept the advice of the British Resident in all
other matters. In actuality he remains a key figure in all Brunei affairs,
the British policy being not to dictate or to bypass but to accommodate.

The present ruler is His Highness the Sultan Sir Omar Ali Saifuddin
Wasa'dul Khairi Waddin ibni Almerhom Sultan Sir Mohamed Jemal-ul
Alam, D.K., S.P.M.G., K.C.M.G. He is an enlightened young man, educated in Malaya, happily married to only one wife despite his religion's
provision for more, deeply conscious of his responsibility for the welfare of his people. He is tradition-minded enough to favor elaborate
court costume and etiquette, modern enough to be fond of racing his
speedboats at seventy miles per hour on the Brunei River. He is aware
that times are changing fast, but like everybody else, he is frequently
baffled what to do about it.

Both the Sultan and the British have to reckon with the Council of
State, primarily a body of feudal dignitaries appointed by the Sultan,
plus a few British official members. The British administrators, intent
upon pushing the Development Plan expeditiously and efficiently forward, encounter on the part of both the Sultan and the State Council
(and of the Brunei Malays in general) a frequent disinclination to do
things in quite the manner or at quite the speed or with quite the personnel which the British recommend.

The matter of foreign personnel is one of peculiar delicacy. There are
very, very few Brunei citizens with the necessary training or experience
for the new government jobs. There are plenty of good openings else-

where for the highly qualified foreign personnel which the British would like to engage. Delays and misunderstandings in recruitment and in authorization for entry of new personnel into the country and shortages of qualified personnel at all levels have seriously slowed down the whole Development Plan. Differences between the sultanate and the British administration on these and other matters, while not critical, are nevertheless real and significant. Superimposed upon them is a good deal of feuding within the royal court and a good deal of bureaucratic inertia within the modern administration itself—the sort of feuding that leads to unexpected official removals and appointments, and the sort of inertia which holds up building operations by blocking delivery of contractors' supplies.

4. The inevitable question of the future status of Brunei. The Federation of Malaya is becoming independent on August 31, 1957. The contiguous state of Sarawak has recently taken the first step toward self-government. The realization is spreading that the various states of British Borneo are certain to grow restless under colonial status, although they are too small and weak to stand alone. The question naturally arises, in Brunei as elsewhere: what of the political future? The Sultan, working with his British advisers, has attempted to catch up with the times. He has recently announced that in the near future half the members of the State Council and of the local councils will be elected and that members of councils will be assigned more direct responsibility for government. The government has also announced that allocation of development funds will be made to the local councils so that they, too, as well as the central administration, can initiate and carry out projects.

One reason for the recent series of announcements has been the emergence in the last year of one Azahari as a Brunei Malay political leader. Azahari is the head of the autonomous Brunei branch of the Partai Rakjat (People's Party), with headquarters in Kuala Lumpur, a new Malayan party of no very clear platform founded by a well-known leftish leader whom the British have several times jailed. Azahari himself, a young man in his early thirties, began his political career years ago in Indonesia where he had been sent by the Japanese as a student of veterinary medicine. There he remained during the early years of the revolution as an associate of Indonesian revolutionary leaders and a member of a revolutionary youth band. After his return to Brunei, he became active in politics and for a few months he was jailed by the British authorities. About a year ago he began busily organizing the Brunei Partai Rakjat. By early 1957

he claimed 16,000 members—or 75 per cent of the total adult male population of Brunei. He organized a big political rally which was held in
April of this year. At it he won acceptance by acclaim for a group of
resolutions demanding immediate elections in Brunei; the right of Brunei
laborers to strike; the creation of a Federation of Sarawak, Brunei, and
North Borneo, with safeguard for the position of the Sultan of Brunei
(presumably as Paramount Ruler); and preparation for *Merdeka*. He has
proposed also to form a mission to London to discuss the Partai Rakjat
claims with the British Colonial Office. He intends first, however, to visit
the Philippines, Indonesia, and India to enlist Asian support. Lately he
has taken to giving newspaper interviews and putting out releases on such
matters as the Suez crisis—with exhortation to Brunei to "nationalize"
its oil. Some of his party members have been heard to make remarks
about dividing up Brunei's oil revenues among the Brunei Malays and
about "highly paid, highly privileged" foreign civil servants being "an
undue drain upon the state's finances." They still take the public position
that they do not wish to drive the British out of Brunei, only to demand
"equality of treatment."

Azahari and his followers may signify new but not necessarily better
times and ideas for Brunei. There are many, including Brunei Malays,
who point out that the Partai Rakjat's demands seem inconsistent. A federation, a Paramount Sultanate, and *Merdeka* are thorny matters in which
not only the Brunei Malays but also the indigenous people (who constitute the over-all majority among the three states of British Borneo), and
indeed the Chinese, Indians, Malays, and British of the area, have something important to say. The combination of federation, Paramount Ruler,
and independence may prove a bit difficult to reconcile. Azahari and his
Partai Rakjat are indicative, however, that modern politics, along with
modern education, medicine, and economic development, have come to
Brunei to stay and must be lived with. If Azahari's formula for the future
is vague and inconsistent, so, too, is any other yet proposed.

Even the pessimistic, however, commonly give Brunei another five
years or so of relatively calm and swift development before political
problems become really acute. In this part of the world five years of
respite from political crisis seems a major miracle—one allowing perhaps
for evolution of the strength whereby future crises may be met.

22

Model Capital

June 20, 1959

KUALA LUMPUR, the Overseas Chinese city that is the capital of the newly independent Federation of Malaya, has seemed until the recent past almost as dependent upon tin and rubber as was the Model T, and, in comparison with cosmopolitan Singapore 250 miles away, just about as up to date. Today things are changing fast. As Kuala Lumpur's 350,000 people this week celebrate the city's 100th anniversary, tin, rubber, and provincialism are giving way to politics, diplomacy, and cosmopolitanism. Both in business and in government, furthermore, Kuala Lumpur is exhibiting the symptoms of a bullish market.

In Kuala Lumpur at least one of the city's new office buildings is tacking on a couple of additional floors as it nears completion; real-estate values have gone up 40 per cent or more in less than two years; both local and foreign firms are finding favorable climate of investment, and political observers are confidently predicting an easy August election victory for the present progressive government. Life in Kuala Lumpur is still geared to tin, rubber, and good living, but the symbol is no longer the Model T or its British equivalent. It is that prestige vehicle, as much favored by Kuala Lumpur's businessmen and officials as by those of Paris, Rio, and Cape Town: the Mercedes-Benz.

Kuala Lumpur's leading citizens have just gone on record (June 13) with their Centenary Day remarks. They departed drastically from the regional predilection for viewing the recent past as an iniquitous period of Western imperialist and capitalist exploitation and the future as an invitation to some sort of manipulated mass movement. To those accustomed to the kaleidoscopic alarms of Manila, Saigon, Rangoon, Singapore, and Djakarta, this centenary celebration in Kuala Lumpur, with Chinese and British more conspicuous than the Malays and practically no one challenging their right to be here, may have seemed an exercise in complacency rather than vigilance. It may be of advantage, therefore, in explaining the amity which marked the Centenary Day program, to compress history, politics, economics, and tourism into one quick panoramic survey of present-day Kuala Lumpur.

The logical starting point for any future Gray Line Service through the nation's capital is the Embankment along the Klang River, just opposite the confluence with the Gombok, at the point where one corner of Old Market Square meets the river front. From this spot the visitor can sight simultaneously the various racial and temporal divisions of the town. This is where eighty-seven Chinese tin prospectors—Kuala Lumpur's founding fathers—waded ashore in 1857. In the 1880's the first of the British settlers found extraordinarily good snipe hunting here in the high grass of the riverbank; but that was before they built the Hong Kong and Shanghai Bank which now dominates this section of the Embankment and discourages such frivolous downtown activities. Close to the spot where the Hong Kong and Shanghai Bank now stands, Yap Ah Loy, the Capitan China from 1868 to 1885, had his rather primitive installations for the processing, storage, and shipment of tin. Here there tied up the barges which carried tin ingots downstream and discharged incoming provisions. Old Market Square itself was Yap Ah Loy's private property, rented out for booths of the dealers in foodstuffs and supplies. All about it were Yap Ah Loy's buildings, rickety wood and thatch sheds or at best adobe-type godowns, which rented for $5 to $10 per month. At the far end of the square, approximately on the site of the present Mercantile Bank (itself about to be demolished and replaced by a more modern building), was Yap Ah Loy's home and garden—the finest property of any Chinese in Malaya at the time. Nearby were such Yap Ah Loy supported or supporting institutions as a gambling house fronting the river, open twenty-four hours a day for fan-tan; a temple dedicated to Sen Ta, the patron god of Chinese immigrants; and a "sick house" toward the support of which the butchers paid $1.00 on every pig slaughtered for the pork-fancying Chinese miners, not to mention opium dens and brothels, the latter provided as early as the 1890's with kimono-clad Japanese girls.

Just across the Klang River from the Embankment, on a triangle of land where the Gombok meets the Klang, was located the Muslim cemetery; today this piece of land is occupied by the big Suleiman mosque, soon to be surpassed, if government plans go through, by a new multi million-dollar structure. Beyond the cemetery was located a part of the early Malay quarter, but the main center of Malay life was on the Embankment side in the area of Malacca Street. Here Malay houses of bamboo and thatch were built on stilts over the marshy riverbank and above the main channel of the river itself. Such structures were intensely vulnerable to the double hazards of flood and fire but advantageously placed for intercepting any cool breeze, for supplementing a meager diet with freshly caught fish, and for disposal of all manner of refuse. In this same area survive some of the last of Kuala Lumpur's typically old-style Malay homes, squatter homes today, soon to be cleared away when the occupants are provided with new land on which to build and materials to build with.

The sections in the neighborhood of Old Market Square remain as typical of the business section of Kuala Lumpur today as in the days of Yap Ah Loy. Ever since the 1880's and the 1890's Old Market Square has been an area of three- to four-story buildings of brick and plaster, constructed originally in conformity with British regulations and Chinese predilections, but since then several times renovated or rebuilt. The streets present a solid front of pastel-colored shop-houses, the ground floors given over to standard-sized Chinese stores wide open to the public, the stores fronting a covered "five-foot way" above which the upper office and residential stories project to the line of the street. Old Market Square having previously been subjected to disastrous fires and serious floods, the British required that the new buildings be made of brick and tile and that the streets in front of the shops be widened, paved, and provided with deep open drainage ditches to carry off the heavy rains.

Through these streets in the 1890's passed a leisurely traffic of bullock carts, loaded with merchandise, of pony traps driven often by British gentlemen and ladies rather than by the drivers whom they all employed, and of ornate carriages favored by the wealthy Chinese, drawn sometimes by as many as six horses. Presently the traffic was complicated by the introduction of the rickshaw, one of the very first of which attracted particular attention by reason of the bulk of its proprietor, Justice Sercombe Smith, and the necessity for one coolie to push and one to pull. It was complicated also by the introduction of the bicycle, the first specimen of which, appropriately enough, was owned by a son of Yap Ah Loy but pedalled by one of his servants. Through these streets today

passes a dense traffic of lorries, cars, trishas, and bicycles, all so circui-
tously routed by one-way traffic rules that newcomers feel the need of
celestial navigation to determine in which direction they are really headed
at any given moment. Into the "five-foot ways" are packed pedes-
trians, hawker stands, parked bicycles and motorcycles, packing cases
full of merchandise, not to mention clerks and workmen who overflow
from the shops into the main stream of pedestrian and even vehicular
traffic. The prevailing congestion, together with the necessity for staying under cover as protection from sun or rain, make a trip afoot through
Old Market Square and the adjacent areas no more relaxing today than
it was in Yap Ah Loy's time, when all the rubbish of the town was swept
into the streets and the stenches were such that queasy British visitors
thought Kuala Lumpur achieved a malodorous high even for the Orient.

Very early in the history of Kuala Lumpur, both Malays and Chinese
began to push out from the center of town; in order to acquire air and
space they began clearing and developing great stretches of jungle, a
task in which the British enthusiastically cooperated. The Malay section
in particular, still more or less traditionally Malay in large part rather than
nondescript "modern," is best typified today in the section called Kampong Bahru, located on the other side of the Klang River between the
riverbank and the newer Chinese-Indian business district. In Kampong
Bahru are to be found pleasant little Malay houses of wood and lattice,
frequently on stilts, often modernized by the substitution of red roofing
tile for thatch or tin and gay floor tiles for wood or packed earth. These
houses are generally built under shade and fruit trees and are surrounded
by hibiscus and oleander and other flowering bushes.

Kuala Lumpur's newest extension is the satellite town of Petaling Jaya,
built seven miles out on lands that were once mined for tin or planted in
rubber. In Petaling Jaya, Kuala Lumpur's middle-class citizens, assisted
often by government loans and committing themselves to ten- to fifteen-
year hire-purchase plans at rates beginning at M$30 monthly, become
owners of homes that are valued at about M$10,000–30,000, or, if they
increase their payments to M$300 per month or more, much more im-
pressive figures. The ordinary houses resemble the more modest but
still substantial California beach developments, with pastel-painted concrete, louvered windows, and tiled terraces—plus modern kitchen, bath-
room, car port, and public utilities.

In the main parts of Kuala Lumpur itself the Chinese and European
residential areas have always been far more extensive than the Malay,

and generally more pretentious. Working-class Chinese, however, have packed themselves into tenementlike lodgings in the upper floors or back alleys of the business buildings of central Kuala Lumpur, generally in the vicinity of busy, noisy street markets, the immediate proximity of bright street lights and blaring radios being accepted not as disadvantages but as added, free attractions. The well-to-do or wealthy Chinese have imitated and outdone the British in their dedication to vast frame or stucco bungalows, frequently elevated on piles to allow for air circulation. Such homes are provided with wide verandas whose wooden shutters can be thrown open to catch the morning and evening breeze. They are commonly set in spacious grounds planted with rain trees, flame of the forest, jacaranda, and whole hedges of ground orchids, gardened to allow for stretches of smooth green lawn and rotation in season of potted plants.

The most elegant of the old Chinese and European residential areas of Kuala Lumpur, now being rapidly redeveloped in modern style, can be seen on a five-mile drive down Ampang Road to Ampang village. The road itself, which led originally from the river landings to the tin mines, now winds beneath giant rain trees past the mansions of the Chinese *towkays* and the British taipans. Some of these properties have now been converted or rebuilt into schools or diplomatic residences; many of them remain much in their original form, and some of them are quite well maintained. To run an establishment of this sort in the old days required a household staff of a dozen at the very least, including cooks, houseboys, gardeners, grooms, and drivers. When occupied by a patriarchal Chinese family of parents, married sons, and numerous grandchildren, with servants and their families living in the wings, each compound became in effect a small village.

Of the late examples of the Chinese *towkay* architecture, the biggest and the handsomest is Bok House, now the fashionable Coq d'Or restaurant. In this tremendous old mansion—which in Cleveland or Toledo would almost inevitably have been converted into a funeral parlor—embellished by columned portico and porte-cochere, amidst mother-of-pearl inlaid redwood furniture, gilt mirrors, French paintings, Italian statuary, and Victorian plush, there lived until a few years ago a Chinese multimillionaire, whose widow still lives in the slightly less pretentious quarters in the rear. This particular *towkay* was unusual for not having made his fortune in tin or rubber. He started life as an illiterate bicycle repairman and ended it as proprietor of the Cycle and Carriage Company—now agents for Mercedes-Benz—and as owner of whole blocks of the most valuable real estate in Kuala Lumpur, Singapore, and Hong Kong.

Not far out Ampang Road beyond Bok House, one begins to see the tin mines and rubber estates which symbolize Kuala Lumpur's wealth. They symbolize also Kuala Lumpur's economic dilemma—whether to concentrate upon tin and rubber or to diversify. In this one particular area the dilemma has been reduced to even simpler form—whether to concentrate upon tin *or* rubber. By mining tin one ruins the land for decades to come for any agricultural purpose and becomes dependent upon a fickle market. By planting rubber one becomes dependent upon an even more capricious market and subject to temptation, when rubber prices fall, to cut down full-grown rubber trees and mine for tin, if, of course, tin can be found. The best answer, of course, one which some owners have happily discovered, is to cut the rubber, mine the tin, and then lay out real estate developments.

For the most striking evidence of British, as contrasted with Chinese influences, upon Kuala Lumpur, one must visit the administrative center of the town. Just across the river from Yap Ah Loy's Kuala Lumpur is to be found a complex of buildings dating from 1894 onward which represent, physically and psychologically, the peculiar impact of British institutions upon an indigenous Southeast Asian system. These buildings, which are frequently misidentified as Malay-Islamic, are in actuality British-Indian rather than Malay both in conception and execution. They perpetuate in solid masonry that peculiar British colonial combination of sensitivity and obtuseness in giving the indigenous people what is judged right for them and what in the end, even though it may be neither authentic nor appropriate, is frequently accepted as though it were both and to the advantage, sometimes, of most concerned. Kuala Lumpur's public architecture is an Arabesque pastiche of cream plaster, red brick, and gray limestone, referred to in architectural studies as Mogul, in officialese as "Modern Saracenic," but more vulgarly and accurately described as "Victorian Moorish." This collection of public buildings covers more acres of city property than anyone except the courageous and "spendthrift" Sir Frank Swettenham thought would ever prove necessary. They are at least arresting, if not always inspiring, to the visitor today. Moorish arches, spiral outside staircases, crenelated towers, onion domes, columned porticoes, and soaring pinnacles, all these adorn even the Railway Administration Building and the railway depot-cum-hotel, from whose illuminated minarets seems to come not the call to prayer but the call to trains.

The railway depot itself warrants special contemplation, if not for its artistic, then for its historic interest. On this site, but not in this building (which was erected twenty years later), occurred in 1886 the ceremonies marking the opening of Malaya's first railway. The event touched off one of the biggest civic celebrations in the city's history prior to Queen Victoria's Diamond Jubilee in 1897 and Independence Day in 1957. There foregathered for the occasion an impressive line-up of the city's great of that day, minus, unfortunately, Yap Ah Loy, who had died the previous year, and Sir Frank Swettenham, temporarily absent from his post as Resident. Yap Ah Loy had been replaced as Capitan China by Yap Ah Shak, almost equally rich and influential, physically more impressive by reason of his unusual height and his resplendent Chinese dress. Yap Ah Shak tried to maintain his composure as the "Lady Clarke," the first locomotive on the line, gathered steam and then roared along at a full thirty miles per hour, but he could not for long disguise his immense interest and admiration. Sir Frank Swettenham was represented by Mr. John Rodger, the Acting Resident, who yielded precedence to Sir Frederick Weld, Governor of the Straits Settlement, a gentleman of the most impressive age, whiskers, and deportment, who presided regally at the various state occasions. Sultan Abdul Samad, then aged about eighty, made the first visit of his life to Kuala Lumpur, riding in from his capital town of Klang on the inaugural run of the new train. He had been assigned a seat of honor in the plush-upholstered and swelteringly hot first-class carriage and declared at the end of the trip that it had been by all odds "the best bullock cart he had ever traveled in." He gave every evidence of enjoying the prolonged festivities, perhaps because his brilliantly colorful Malay costume festooned with diamonds was attracting much envious attention, perhaps also because he was singled out to be invested by Sir Frederick Weld with the insignia of a Knight Commander of the Order of Saint Michael and Saint George. Raja Laut, then the most influential and prosperous Malay resident of the city, a gentleman who had not previously rated very high with the British, took the occasion to ingratiate himself with the administration and to enhance his own prestige by delivering, whenever occasion offered, rather fulsome declarations of loyalty to both the British and the Malay thrones, more particularly the former. The Malays of Kuala Lumpur, he declared, had formerly "felt like one wandering in the jungle, our way beset by thickets and thorns," but "since the arrival of the British Resident, we have felt as one lifted up and placed between earth and sky, so great has been the change from our previous to our present condition."

The railroad had been built at the insistence of Sir Frank Swettenham, who deemed the projected $600,000 and actual $750,000 investment no deterrent even though total state revenues at the time were a mere $300,-000 per year. Swettenham's confidence was swiftly vindicated, for the railroad returned a 28 per cent profit in the year 1889 alone and opened up great stretches of new land for agricultural enterprise. Much of the land was used for the planting of coffee, also of a shade tree for coffee which soon turned out to be far more profitable than the original crop. It was the rubber tree, newly introduced into Malaya in 1877 and the basis for a tremendous boom about 1910. New railroads, for which the Klang-Kuala Lumpur line had been the pioneering venture, served to open up the whole peninsula. The city of Kuala Lumpur, as the railway headquarters and the main stop on the north-south trunk line, became the logical and convenient choice as capital of the Federated Malay States, now of the independent Federation.

To sample the special flavor of the new Kuala Lumpur, one needs to visit an institution which a mellowed Somerset Maugham might select if he were to return after forty years to capture with modern updating the local psychology of both Westerner and Asian. It is the Selangor Club, built in the British colonial manner as a rambling, wide-open bungalow set along the Padang (playing field and parade ground), in the old days the center of British society and sport. Today the Selangor Club, with bright new murals spoofing the Victorian ladies and gentlemen of a vanished era, is the center of Kuala Lumpur's international set, which includes not only Westerners and Westernized Eastern diplomatic personnel but local Chinese, Indians, and an increasing number of Malays as well. On the playing field below the long veranda cricket and soccer lure not only the Englishmen but many more Chinese, Indian, and Malay players into the midday or at least the late-afternoon sun. "Going to The Dog"—with reference to the name "Spotted Dog" which the club acquired from the frequent presence of Dalmatian dogs belonging to a British lady patron of the 1890's—attracts little unfavorable attention even from the more outspoken anticolonialists and anticapitalists. Only a few politicians have been heard occasionally to suggest that "privileged clubs" such as this be nationalized and that their properties be opened to "the people"—as, indeed, the Padang is opened up for frequent parades and rallies and sporting events but not for political purposes.

For really big events today, whether sporting or ceremonial, one goes not to "The Dog" but to the Merdeka Stadium, which was rushed to completion in ten months at a cost of US$830,000 in order to seat some 30,000 people for the 1957 Independence Day celebrations. The stadium occupies a whole hilltop in downtown Kuala Lumpur and provides, in conjunction with a Chinese community project adjacent to it, not only a sports complex and a site for speeches and parades but a meeting hall, a variety of good restaurants, a swimming pool, and spacious surrounding grounds. It is the scene of domestic and international sporting events in which the various Malayan teams are made up of Malays, Chinese, and Indians selected and applauded with reference to athletic skill, not racial origin. The Merdeka Stadium is of as great significance for what it does not feature as for what it does. It does not feature any monster political demonstrations; it is not the home base, therefore, of any mass movement or of any political-action cadres. Furthermore, even though it was built on a crash-program basis at a time when official responsibilities were being shifted rapidly from British to local officials, it has given rise to no scandal over maladministration of the project or misappropriation of funds.

This politically and financially aseptic Merdeka Stadium is an evidence of the good government which has characterized Kuala Lumpur both before and after achievement of independence. It is a government which has achieved such rarities in Southeast Asia as financial solvency and relatively adequate government salaries—US$1,000 per month for a minister of state, US$300 for a medium-grade official. Kuala Lumpur has achieved such other regional anomalies as plentiful electric current, a reliable water and sewage system, adequate public transportation, regular collection of rubbish, even systematic extermination of mangy dogs, stray cats, and—less successfully—market-place rats.

Kuala Lumpur, it should quickly be appended, is no Southeast Asian utopia and its relatively serene *status quo* could be subject to swift and disastrous change. The city is troubled by Chinese secret societies, teen-age "low-waist" sets, "blue film" parties, vice rings, prostitution (reportedly 1,200 girls from a nationwide syndicate), gangster and kidnapper rackets, unemployment, and other problems including a Muslim divorce rate which is almost half the number of Muslim marriages. Kuala Lumpur has its quota of potential subversives and near or actual Communists, about 225 of whom have been rounded up in recent months by the police. The city is not without official corruption, although as yet there seems to be more talk than substantial evidence of it. In nearby countries of Southeast Asia it requires the embezzlement of a million or so to attract much attention. In Kuala Lumpur, however, the standard of official morality is sufficiently high that the shortage of a mere US$270,000 worth of equipment and supplies from the police depot is occasion for a full-scale investigation. Functionaries accepting bribes of M$1 to M$5—virtually a perquisite of office elsewhere—have been sentenced recently to fines of up to M$400 and prison terms of up to six months. The bribe-givers themselves have drawn M$25 to M$500 fines. Corruption, subversion, and social maladjustment do not now threaten to reach critical proportions. The one problem which could prove truly critical and in a very short time is that of racial conflict.

The maintenance of harmony among Malays, Chinese, Indians, and other elements of Kuala Lumpur's population requires a nice sense of balance on the part both of the leaders and of the public. The delicate equilibrium achieved so far could be upset at any moment. Had the public temper been a little more readily inflammable or the communal leaders a little less alert to the danger, one recent episode could have caused very serious trouble. A young Malay, the son of an aristocratic family, was murdered in cold blood a few months ago by a gang of Chinese teddy-boys, as he was escorting the daughters of another prominent Malay family from a public restaurant. A few experienced rabble rousers could have used this incident to provoke riots, but none did. Nevertheless, the memory of race riots in Penang a couple of years ago, shortly before independence, and the more immediate example of race disorders last month on little Pangkor Island, serve to keep people aware of the danger. The frictions of Malays, Chinese, Indians, British, and others attempting to adjust to each other's widely disparate customs and status are always close enough to the surface to cause ripples and may one day, if any great number of people falter in their determination to prevent it, churn up great and destructive waves of violence.

As of mid-1959, two years after independence and a hundred years after its founding, the city of Kuala Lumpur is a small oasis of progress and near placidity in a very troubled sector of the globe. For this very reason, perhaps, it does not yet rate as a five-star attraction for the increasing thousands of travelers—tourists, businessmen, and international agency personnel—who keep the air lines in business. BOAC, QANTAS, SAS, KLM, and GARUDA have added Kuala Lumpur to their schedules in anticipation of rapidly growing traffic, but the city lacks two features to recommend it to the special attention of the travel agents, the boards of directors, and foreign offices. It lacks any really spectacular ancient ruins, such as Angkor-Wat. It lacks also any really spectacular evidence that it is about to convert itself into modern ruins, such as Djakarta threatens intermittently to become.

The tourist can do Kuala Lumpur rather thoroughly, including visits to a tin mine or a rubber plantation, also the Hindu shrines of the nearby Batu Caves, in less than a full day of tolerably vigorous sight-seeing. Unless he decides to go off to enjoy the cool breezes of Frasers Hill (seventy miles away and 4,300 feet up), he is likely, if he stops off in Kuala Lumpur at all, to hustle on to Singapore or Bangkok by the first connecting flight in order to savor their far more colorful and lively attractions. The international businessman is likely to find his Kuala Lumpur office generating so little in the way of problems that he takes the next plane out in order to have more time to cope with the all-too-copious dilemmas of Djakarta, say, or Rangoon. The foreign office or international agency official finds Kuala Lumpur already so well assisted by the British, so well staffed by trained civil servants, and so thoroughly analyzed by his local informants for political and economic trends—which don't reverse themselves overnight—that it seems to offer little challenge for really fresh and positive thinking and almost none for aid. As they enter their second century of urban existence, the people of Kuala Lumpur like to think of their city as the model capital of a model Southeast Asian nation, a civic conceit with which it is difficult to quarrel.

23

Conclusion:
Contours of Confrontation

August 25, 1964

AUGUST 31, 1964—the pre-confrontation target date rather than September 16, the actual date—was picked by the Federation of Malaysia for celebration of its first anniversary. Of the Federation's four components, Malaya itself on that day would be seven years old, Singapore would have passed its fifth anniversary (June 3) of near autonomy, and only the Borneo states of Sabah (formerly North Borneo) and Sarawak would be in fact yearling newcomers to the troubled world of national independence. Still, for both Malaya and Singapore, as well as for Sabah and Sarawak, into the Year One of Malaysia there had been compressed as much excitement as all of them had experienced in the whole of the past decade. The turmoil had been far less their doing than Indonesia's. There, on August 17, in celebrating Indonesia's own nineteenth year of independence, a year in which he had steadily escalated his campaign of anti-Malaysian political, economic, and military confrontation, President Sukarno had exhibited even more than his usual flair for felicity of language and provocation of politics by dubbing his last twelvemonths' harassment of Malaysia as Indonesia's "Year of Living Dangerously."

Indonesia's reckless crusade to "Smash Malaysia" precipitated the new nation from the very day and hour of its birth into a crisis which induced a reflex flexing of national sinews even before they had yet had a chance to grow firm. On being suddenly exposed to the violent animosity of its neighbor, Malaysia encountered a national hazard such as only South Vietnam among the other new states of Southeast Asia had previously been exposed to. The nation reacted vigorously to Indonesia's belligerency without compromising its own principles of democratic gov-

272

ernment and economic free enterprise and without prejudice to its policy of cooperation with the Western world. This set of circumstances bespeaks both the degree of Malaysia's commitment to what the Western world regards as enlightened self-interest and the degree of its vulnerability to Indonesia's accusation that it violates the most basic principles of Afro-Asian revolutionary nationalism.

The component parts of the new Federation of Malaysia, as becomes apparent in the foregoing chapters, had already managed between 1957 and 1960 to establish a record unique in Southeast Asia for constructive resolution of the problems inherent in transition from colonial to independent status. The original Federation of Malaya achieved not only a functioning parliamentary democracy on the British model but also a rapidly developing economy in which international aid was an extra, not a crucial, factor and both local and foreign enterprise enjoyed active encouragement. Malays, Chinese, Indians, and other racial groups succeeded in living peacefully with each other while cooperating both in government and in economic and social development. The excitable and insecure little island city-state of Singapore, preponderantly Overseas Chinese in population, enjoyed efficient government and prosperous business conditions such as are almost unknown in Southeast Asia outside of the Malaysia region. Sabah and Sarawak experienced national development programs which, if reproduced to scale for bigger states, would seem marvels of high return on small investment; and minute, oil-rich Brunei—where the 1962 sequel, unhappily, was insurrection—telescoped into less than half a decade more project expenditure per capita than developmental economists ordinarily even dream of.

In what is now Malaysia, the 1957–1960 period was one which students of the troubled history of postwar Southeast Asia might well investigate for reassurance that transition to independence need not necessarily signal a dangerous degree of deterioration. The 1961–1963 period,[1] correspondingly, provides evidence that actual or impending independence need not induce nationalistic manifestations such as make for friction with neighboring states. All of the Malaysian states, to be sure, were beginning to run into serious trouble with Indonesia, a circumstance for which they themselves can scarcely be held accountable, since virtually every nation, Eastern, Western, or Afro-Asian, experiences recurrent

[1] For a detailed account of the years 1961–1963, see Willard A. Hanna, *The Formation of Malaysia: New Factor in World Politics*. New York: American Universities Field Staff, 1964.

difficulty in maintaining amity with the Sukarno regime. Among themselves, however, and vis-à-vis the Commonwealth nations to which they are most closely tied, the Malaysian states experienced not jeopardization but enhancement of friendly relations. Notwithstanding certain minor disputes between Singapore and Malaya, for instance, and notwithstanding the special circumstances in Brunei which resulted in insurrection and withdrawal from the Malaysia scheme, on the really critical issues the Malaysian states arrived at a consensus, most significantly of all, the proposal for merger. The process of liquidating almost the last remains of colonial empire in Southeast Asia resulted, therefore, despite the continuing anomaly of the British-protected sultanate of Brunei, not in the creation of weak, isolated, and possibly inimical little independent political entities, as nationalistic pressures might have dictated, but in the emergence of three new member states of a new federation in which the big senior partner, Malaya, had already set the precedent for orderly national development.

The story of Malaya, Singapore, Sarawak, and Sabah from 1961 to 1963 thus is one of continuation of steady, healthful development, such as was already apparent from 1957 to 1960, and of swift progress toward realization of a proposal for federation. On May 27, 1961, Malayan Prime Minister Tengku Abdul Rahman made a tentative suggestion, hinting but not actually proposing a five-state merger as a formula for resolving the long-threatened conflict between the right-wing Malay-dominated Malaya and the left-wing Chinese-dominated Singapore, with the Borneo states to participate in order both to counterbalance Singapore's influence and to resolve their own problems regarding postcolonial status. The Tengku's original proposal of "cooperation" presently transformed itself into a specific agenda and timetable for outright federation, meanwhile stirring up both vigorous support and vigorous opposition throughout the region.

Singapore's Prime Minister, Lee Kuan Yew, whose People's Action Party had staked its political future on achieving merger with Malaya, immediately became the staunchest proponent of the Tengku's proposal. Lee Kuan Yew's political enemies—onetime associates who had broken away from the P.A.P. in early 1961 to form the extreme left-wing Barisan Sosialis—became the strongest domestic opponents. The Barisan, like virtually every other Singapore faction, publicly endorsed the Malaysia concept, but like all anti-Malaysia factions throughout the area, it attacked the specific details, its obvious strategy being to sabotage while seeming to support a generally popular project. Lee Kuan Yew and the P.A.P. responded by mounting an all-out "Battle for Merger." At every turn they out-thought, out-talked, and out-smarted the opposition, never hesitating, when dealing with the Communists, to resort to Communist devices. Without offering the alternative to vote No, the P.A.P. persuaded 71 per cent of the active electorate to vote Yes to the one feasible formula for merger and thus to reject two other alternatives, one of them the Barisan's own, which it was itself maneuvered into repudiating.

By its referendum victory the P.A.P. firmly re-established itself as the paramount power in Singapore politics. In its subsequent negotiations with Malaya on the specific details of merger, it was able, therefore, to gain important concessions—favorable financial conditions, for instance, which allow the Singapore Government to retain a high percentage of its own revenue for its own purposes. When new elections were held in Singapore shortly after merger, the P.A.P. so resoundingly redemonstrated its popularity as to give rise to a dangerous new factor in Malaysian politics—rivalry between the P.A.P. and the M.C.A., and hence the Malayan Alliance, for political influence throughout the new Federation.

In the Borneo states the original reaction to the Malaysia proposal was a surge of resentment on the part of the local leaders that they themselves had not been consulted. The Tengku thereupon consulted them and acceded to many of their requests, thus gaining widespread acceptance, ultimately even enthusiasm, for the project, although an important minority still remained either recalcitrant or obstructive. In Sabah, under the leadership of Mr. Donald Stephens, who eventually became the state's first Chief Minister, a good 90 per cent of the heretofore apolitical population rallied behind the Malaysia plan, Chinese leaders swinging from resistance to support as they began clearly to perceive the alternatives—annexation, for instance, to the Philippines or to Indonesia. In Sarawak the politicians fell into bitter disagreement among themselves, but better than a clear majority of the voters endorsed the proposal. The actual percentage of the Sarawak majority was obscured by a complicated multiple-tier election system and by a rearrangement, in the course of the elections, of party line-ups. The strength of the minority was underscored by reason of the articulate adherence on the part of the activists to a propaganda line emanating from Communist China and from Indonesia. In Brunei the Sultan and the court wavered and procrastinated and rather belatedly threw in with the Malaysia plan. A great part of the Malay population, however, under an Indonesian-trained revolutionary leader, one Azahari, on December 8, 1962, staged a week-long insurrection which had to be put down by British troops from Singapore. Azahari's professed purpose was to restore the Sultan as paramount ruler of all of British Borneo, but the real motivations in Brunei—Azahari's, his followers', the Sultan's—are exceedingly difficult to disentangle, and the state remains today outside of the Malaysia framework.

The Brunei insurrection was a violently dramatic illustration of a highly significant fact which might have escaped notice in the aura of optimism attending the otherwise orderly progress toward realization of the Malaysia plan. Throughout the Malaysia area there were many people who were opposed, privately if not publicly, to the creation of the new federation, and whatever their reasons, no matter how conflicting, a great many of them looked to Indonesia for support.

In Singapore the Barisan Sosialis obstructed the formation of Malaysia because a successful new state would mean greater regional stability and hence less prospect of a Communist take-over. In Malaya the P.M.I.P. opposed it because of racial and religious prejudice against the Singapore Chinese and all other non-Malay or, even more specifically, non-P.M.I.P. influence. In Malaya the Socialist Front campaigned against Malaysia on the basis, it seemed, of preference for association with "progressive forces," among them the Indonesian. Many Borneo people feared that their own interests would be sacrificed to those of Malaya and Singapore, which, as relatively advanced states, would dominate the other members. Everywhere there were those, some of them Communist sympathizers, who regarded the Malaysia plan as a British "plot" for perpetuation of Western control over a strategic area of Southeast Asia.

International opposition to the Malaysia plan was spearheaded by the Indonesian Communist Party, which, in December 1961, officially branded Malaysia as "an unacceptable colonial intrigue." "The Indonesian people," said the P.K.I., "will certainly support the righteous, patriotic, and just resistance of the people of Malaya, Singapore, Sarawak, Brunei, and North Borneo against the efforts for the establishment of this Federation of Malaysia." In late 1962 and early 1963 Indonesia's President Sukarno made the P.K.I. thesis his own and called upon the adherents of "guided democracy" to "volunteer" for a campaign of "confrontation in all spheres" to "Smash Malaysia."

Domestic and international anti-Malaysia campaigns, which thus converged on the basis of "anti-neocolonialist" sentiments, occasioned some of the most unlikely and unstable alliances yet to emerge in Southeast Asia. Within Malaysia itself, extreme left-wing Chinese, many of them Communists, made common cause with extreme right-wing Malays, some of them feudalists, and both of them looked for encouragement to the anti-Chinese, anti-feudal, anti-Malaya, and anti-Malaysia P.K.I. There occurred such incidental aberrations as the defection from Sarawak to Indonesian Borneo of disaffected Chinese youth, revolutionary activists who sought military training in a country and from an army notorious for discrimination against the Overseas Chinese. Brunei's Azahari, while ostensibly proposing to restore Sabah to the Brunei Sultanate, sought and found support in the Philippines, which claimed North Borneo as its own, then skipped to Indonesia, where he mysteriously vanished to the accompaniment of loud praise. The Philippines, which had for years regarded Indonesia as a dangerously Communist-prone neighbor, suddenly found itself lining up alongside Indonesia against strongly anti-Communist Malaysia. Both Sukarno and Macapagal began to develop for each other's benefit and for that of the United States the thesis that Malaysia was a push-over for Communist Chinese subversion and a threat, therefore, to the security of the Philippines, Indonesia, and even the Western world. Peking, to the dismay of Manila, strongly supported Sukarno. Moscow also announced its endorsement, but only faintly and distantly until Peking's sway over the P.K.I. and Sukarno threatened to exceed the Soviet's own recently and expensively purchased influence, which had cost over U.S.$1 billion worth of arms and other aid. Great Britain strongly supported Malaysia—at a loss of some hundreds of millions of dollars in investments in Indonesia and at risk of endlessly protracted jungle warfare. The United States assumed an unequivocal posture in favor of peace and then, taking its cue from Sukarno and Macapagal, boldly endorsed the principle of amicable Southeast Asian handling of Southeast Asian problems; meanwhile, however, unobtrusively suspending most of its aid projects in Indonesia.

The record, obviously, is difficult either to clarify or to condense. Now that Malaysia has become the center of an explosive new Southeast Asian crisis which Southeast Asians demand the right to resolve in their own way without Western interference, the Philippines and the Indonesian cases at least require some further elaboration. The Philippines claims that the Sulu Sultanate (to which it is the legal heir) retained unimpaired sovereign rights to the territory when it signed an 1878 agreement by which some Borneo real estate passed to the British. The

Philippines demanded, therefore, that its residual rights be acknowledged by the British and that the plan for transfer of the territory from Great Britain to Malaysia be suspended, in fact that it be made contingent upon Philippines concurrence. The British, tactlessly, no doubt, ridiculed the Philippines claim. They argued that the Sulu Sultanate had ceded North Borneo outright and that in any event legitimate Philippines interest in the area had long since lapsed. The Philippines press, politicians, and public became incensed, and President Macapagal, who had himself been responsible back in 1948 for dredging up the North Borneo case out of the almost forgotten files, became a prime mover in the campaign to assert Philippines rights. When Indonesia, at the time of the Brunei insurrection, suddenly denounced the British for conspiring, contrary to "genuine" Southeast Asian national interests, for the creation of Malaysia, Macapagal found himself unexpectedly and uneasily aligned with Sukarno.

Indonesia's case against Malaysia is far more complicated and combustible than that of the Philippines and therefore far less susceptible to rational adjustment. Indonesians would be "traitors to their own souls," said President Sukarno, if they did not oppose the British "neocolonial conspiracy" to "encircle" Indonesia by creating a "sham state" under a "Malay puppet." When Sukarno and his colleagues put their case in its most moderate terms for the benefit of Western auditors, they explain that even though they risk national and international disaster, they have in fact no honorable alternative but must "struggle for the realization" of all of the "many facets" of the "unfinished revolution" in which Indonesia leads the "new emerging forces" in challenging the "old established order." "Historic necessity," they say, now dictates the conflict, just as it will dictate victory for the "progressive peoples." Indonesia's own desperate need to devote its energies and its resources to domestic development, they say, must be no deterrent to Indonesian support to "freedom fighters everywhere." Indonesia's Number One Priority, they say, is to "Smash Malaysia," and when Sukarno and his followers begin shouting slogans and deploying volunteers, the conclusion is inescapable: they really mean it.

The Sukarno apologia, on being translated out of Sukarnoese, means that Indonesia is a self-consciously revolutionary nation which seeks to perpetuate revolution at home and to export it abroad and that it regards Malaysia as deplorably, indeed intolerably, reactionary. Behind the apologia lie the facts: Malaysia is prosperous and progressive, and Indonesia, nineteen years after its declaration of independence, is a political, economic, and social shambles. Indonesians, other than the corrupt and privileged elite, are hungry, ragged, restive, and conditioned to expect demagogic diversion. The ruinous Sukarno regime retains its hold on power only by the familiar totalitarian device of mobilizing the nation to combat an alien enemy. For years Sukarno worked up national hysteria over Irian Barat; the Western world on August 15, 1962, gave him Irian Barat; in December 1962 he began working up new hysteria over Malaysia.

The real Malaysia crisis, then, began in December 1962, with Sukarno's propagandistic support for the Brunei insurrection. In early 1963 Sukarno began staging guerrilla attacks in Borneo and piratical raids in the Straits of Malacca. After that he intensified his hit-and-run tactics while repeatedly threatening full-scale military action. Philippines President Macapagal, while reiterating the validity of the Philippines claim, assumed the role of mediator between Sukarno and the Tengku, but attempts at peaceful negotiation resulted merely in further inflammation of Sukarno's wrath. Macapagal's great contribution was a compromise formula carefully calculated to bypass the clear-cut issue over Sabah, to obscure most of the undefined issues, and to concentrate attention upon creation of a new super- or supra-state, a "loose confederation" of Malaysia, the Philippines, and Indonesia, to be known as "Maphilindo."

The Macapagal revelation of Maphilindo proved momentarily euphoric. Sukarno's repeatedly and publicly expressed intent, even in joining Maphilindo, was to wreck Malaysia, one of its three presumed pillars. Every concession to which Tengku Abdul Rahman agreed became the basis for a new and more arrogant Sukarno demand. The concept of Maphilindo soon evaporated and along with it what had been briefly but widely applauded as the "Maphilindo Spirit" of amicable Southeast Asian resolution of Southeast Asian problems. Tengku Abdul Rahman had yielded, for instance, to Philippines and Indonesian demands for a United Nations "ascertainment" of public opinion in British Borneo, prudently committing Sukarno and Macapagal in advance, however, to accept the findings. Secretary General U Thant thereupon appointed an investigative commission, which succeeded in carrying out its mission, notwithstanding diligent Indonesian attempts at obstruction. When the investigators reported what was already quite obvious—that the majority of the people of British Borneo favored Malaysia—Sukarno was so outraged that he repudiated the report, as, in fact, did Macapagal. Sukarno, it was clear, would tolerate no contradiction, but Macapagal became increasingly wary of being trapped into a Sukarno-style rejection of reason.

On September 16, 1963, two weeks behind schedule, to allow for the United Nations "ascertainment," Malaysia became an accomplished fact, thus triggering even more violent renewal of Indonesian outbursts. Sukarno refused to recognize Malaysia and declared an embargo on his own trade with Penang and Singapore. Mobs of youths sacked and burned the British Embassy in Djakarta, then moved on to sack and burn British official and private residences. Labor unions, meanwhile, seized British estates and British offices. Soon Sukarno stepped up both the scale and the frequency of armed actions, ordering the Indonesian military to participate openly in raids which were no longer disguised as "spontaneous" actions by "volunteers." The United States Government took alarm and in early 1964 President Johnson dispatched Attorney General Robert F. Kennedy on a "mission of peace." Sukarno consented to a partial suspension of military operations while he tried—and failed—to gain new concessions through negotiations.

In mid-1964 Sukarno once again stepped up the tempo of confrontation, while adding a new element of suspense and speculation as to how far he was in fact prepared to go in risking full-scale war. On returning empty-handed from a Tokyo "summit" with the Tengku, Sukarno played host to Soviet Deputy Premier Mikoyan and, as a climax to the celebrations, staged big new Borneo raids and induced Mikoyan to join him in announcing a Russian promise to supply Indonesia with arms superior to anything the British possessed in Singapore. But Sukarno's apparent triumph turned out to be part illusion. The Soviet Union, it soon became apparent, was using an ambiguous promise of armaments to win at the very least an ambiguous promise of support in its quarrel with Communist China. Both Russian promises of armaments and Indonesian promises of cooperation proved considerably more ambiguous, however, than either party could very happily condone in the other. Massive new Russian shipments of munitions seemed contingent upon sonorous new Indonesian professions of solidarity, and neither seemed imminent. The Sukarno Government wanted Soviet arms and money, to be sure, but it was either unwilling or unable to resist the Indonesian Communist Party, which had chosen to side with Peking rather than with Moscow and had recently signalled its decision by permitting some of the Indonesian comrades to boo Russian Ambassador Mikhailov when he addressed the

Djakarta May Day rally. From Peking, Sukarno can acquire neither arms nor money, but Chairman Mao might, of course, be happy to supply volunteers—whether or not Sukarno actually wants them.

Regardless of his new dilemma, Sukarno celebrated Indonesia's Independence Day (August 17, 1964) by launching his first little expeditionary force against the Malayan mainland. It was a 90-man party, most of which was quickly rounded up by the Malaysians, and it may, in fact, have been merely a mad adventure on the part of some unit which had misread Sukarno's mind. In the light, however, of Sukarno's obsession with symbols, it would be rash to assume that the Independence Day excursion was not a portent of worse to follow.

Indonesia's new motto, as Sukarno framed it on August 17, 1964, for his Independence Day audience, is *"Vivere Pericoloso."* The Malaysian states, by way of contrast, lived very happily when they lived also for the most part safely. From 1961 to 1963 the pace of life quickened and the element of hazard mounted. In 1964, as Sukarno deliberately accelerated Indonesia's drive toward disaster, he implicated many bystanders, the nearest of them the people of the previously placid little Federation of Malaya and its new Malaysian partners.

Index

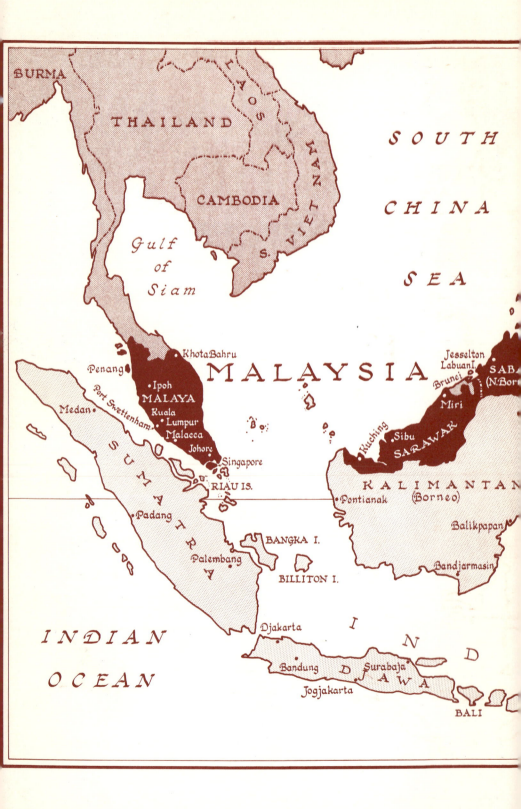